Globalisation of
Higher Education
political, institutional, cultural,
and personal perspectives

Globalisation of Higher Education
political, institutional, cultural, and personal perspectives

John Branch, Anne Hørsted
and Claus Nygaard

THE LEARNING IN HIGHER EDUCATION SERIES

LIBRI
PUBLISHING

First published in 2017 by Libri Publishing

ISBN 978-1-911450-09-2

Cover design by Helen Taylor

Design by Carnegie Publishing

Printed by Edwards Brothers Malloy

Libri Publishing
Brunel House
Volunteer Way
Faringdon
Oxfordshire
SN7 7YR

Tel: +44 (0)845 873 3837

www.libripublishing.co.uk

Contents

Foreword

If you seek to truly understand both how we got to the current state of affairs regarding the globalization of higher education as-well-as where we are headed next, this anthology is must reading.

You'll come to understand through this insightful and rigorously researched publication, that globalization of higher education isn't simply a natural byproduct of a more "global world," but a unique and ever-evolving phenomenon growing from a complex interplay of political, institutional, social, economic, technological, cultural and individual factors, on a global scale.

As the president of Eduvantis, a higher education consulting firm that works with a large group of leading colleges and universities to help them achieve competitive success and growth in today's complex higher education environment, I've had the pleasure of presenting my views on issues related to the globalization of higher education to audiences ranging from university presidents in China, senior academic leaders and faculty in Europe and business school deans in India to Executive MBA program directors in the United States. All of these groups had at least one thing in common, differing views on the subject of how the globalization of higher education should evolve.

My perspectives have predominantly been formed based on a phenomenon comprehensively addressed in this book known as transnational education. Many of the colleges and universities we've worked with seek not only to globalize and internationalize their faculties, student bodies, classroom experiences and world views, they also seek to "market and sell" their particular institutional culture, values, knowledge capital, brand and credibility internationally. Theirs is a model based on the pursuit of an effective global competitive strategy, as they seek visibility, distinctiveness and "market share" for their enterprise, on a global scale.

I've seen first-hand the many fits and starts that have accompanied these efforts. It's been my experience that many times the challenges, disappointments and failures that have sometimes accompanied such initiatives grows directly from a lack of understanding of the factors, issues and complicated interrelationships detailed in this book.

But beyond the growing set of academic enterprises that are pursuing a transnational strategy as their means to global engagement and growth, a larger set of primarily place-bound institutions are wrestling at a basic level to identify their best "way to play" in the rapidly evolving and challenging world of creating and distributing knowledge capital and educating the next generation of globally informed and aware leaders and citizens within their own country or region.

Many such institutions, particularly in the United States, today rely heavily on enrollments of students from countries other than their own as a means of maintaining growth and financial stability. It is well understood that most such institutions are questioning the long-term sustainability of such a model, given the massive and important shifts that are occurring in the global higher education landscape. How the globalization of higher education will unfold in the coming years is of critical, if not existential, importance to many institutions.

Higher education as an enterprise has been jolted from its long-enjoyed comfort zone in the past few years by technology and the associated release from its historically place and space based delivery constraints. For most institutions, this has been both liberating and frightening, for it has upended definitions of mission and most of the basic rules of competition, resource allocation, owned internal competencies, even the very nature of the class-room experience and teaching methodologies. It has also – theoretically and operationally – for the first time in history made the entire world the market of every institution.

Whether it is the extensive treatment this book offers on Europe's Bologna Process, or of the critical process China is undertaking to evolve its histori-cally centrally controlled education system into a more open, competitive and globally engaged system representative of a global leader, the reader of this book will learn through extensive historical analysis and insightful visions of what is next, how to better process the profound impact of politics, cultural differences, technology and institutional agendas – as well as the changing roles, expectations and motivations of individuals – on the globalization of higher education.

This book is a must read for anyone who seeks to understand the profound impact higher education will have on the future of the global economy, on our emerging "global culture," and as the increasingly interdependent steward of our world's most valuable asset, global human capital.

Tim Westerbeck, President
Eduvantis
tim@eduvantis.com

Chapter 1
An Introduction to Globalisation of Higher Education

John Branch & Anne Hørsted

Bill Backer, Margaret Thatcher, and Howard Schultz

On 13 May 2016, William (Bill) Backer passed away at the age of 89. You can be forgiven if his name is unfamiliar. But most people of a certain age will remember his greatest achievement. In 1971, as advertising agent who was in charge of the Coca-Cola account, Bill launched the now famous *Buy the World a Coke* television advertisement, which featured a happy shiny multicultural group of teenagers on a hill singing harmoniously "I'd Like to Teach the World to Sing". The advertisement stood in stark contrast to the dominant us-versus-them narrative of the Cold War period, but somehow captured the latent zeitgeist of the masses. It also foreshadowed the age of globalisation which was ushered in by the 1980s.

Ahh, the 1980s! Pacman, E.T.: The Extraterrestrial, MTV. But less visible (although equally if not more impactful) to the average person were the surge in foreign direct investment and the increase in international trade, both of which were triggered by economic liberalisation: freer flow of capital and a reduction of trade tariffs on goods and services. Indeed, the 1980s marked an inflection point in globalisation—an acceleration of the globalising process which had arguably begun the moment at which humans began walking upright. No single person epitomises this period more than Margaret Thatcher...and her boyfriend Ronald Reagan.

Of course, globalisation did not stop at the end of the 1980s. Indeed, with each passing day, the nations of the world become more and more entwined, economically, politically, and culturally. Using the imagery of

Thomas Friedman (author of the bestseller *The World is Flat: A Brief History of the Twenty-First Century*), the forces of globalisation—the 'flatteners' as Friedman called them—have resulted in a world which is increasingly borderless, or 'flat'. En route to the symposium at which the authors of this anthology met to revise their chapters and assemble the anthology, John was struck by the seething crowd at the Starbucks near Piraeus Port, the jumping off point for the ferry to the Greek Island of Aegina. Imagine that. Despite (perhaps even because of) Greece's economic woes, the global expansion of Howard's Schultz's little Seattle coffee shop marches on.

Globalisation

So what is globalisation anyway? According to globalisationguide.org, globalisation is *"primarily an economic phenomenon, involving the increasing interaction, or integration, of national economic systems through the growth of international trade, investment, and capital flows"*. Consider that t-shirt which you wear every morning, for example. The cotton might be grown in Uzbekistan, Egypt, or the United States. After harvesting it would be shipped to Pakistan, say, where it is processed and woven into cotton fabric, on weaving equipment which is most likely manufactured in Austria or Germany. From there, the fabric would be sent to China to be cut and sewn into a t-shirt, probably on sewing machines from Japan. After that, the t-shirt would be bundled in cardboard boxes which are produced in Ireland, stuffed into a Danish-owned container, which in turn would be loaded on a South Korean boat, and so on and so on, until that t-shirt which you wear every morning finally lands on the shelf of your favorite Spanish or Swedish retail shop. Globalisation indeed!

But surely globalisation is more than just economics—more than simply the de-centralisation/de-nationalisation of the factors of production. To many, globalisation also intimates the increasing sharing of cultural artefacts, social ideas, and technological developments. John remembers taking a group of students to Russia for a study tour a few years back. The group was comprised of some Americans, a few Chinese students, an Indian, an Argentine, and two Brazilians...plus, John is Canadian. That group itself reflects globalisation. But while in Russia, the group ended up going to O'Malley's Irish Pub for drinks and a bite to eat. In the background was playing Shakira (one of Colombia's greatest exports). On the menu was a full page of Sushi. And for 'dessert' was a full hookah bar. Globalisation indeed!

Sociologists also have an interesting take on globalisation. According to Anthony Giddens, for example, globalisation signifies a decoupling of space and time. It embodies *"a transformation in the spatial organization of social relations and transactions, expressed in transcontinental or interregional flows and networks of activity, interaction, and power"* (Andrew McGrew). In simple terms, globalisation means that spatial and temporal boundaries are disappearing. Think about your (social) network of friends who are now scattered around the world, and with whom you can chat at any time of day. And how seemingly commonplace it now seems to 'jump on a plane to _____' for a long weekend. Globalisation indeed!

Globalisation, however, is certainly not without its critics. Indeed, globalisation might be defined as "a worldwide drive toward a globalised economic system dominated by supranational corporate trade and banking institutions that are not accountable to democratic processes or national governments" (globalisationguide.com). Globalisation also smacks of imperialism, a modern take on colonisation, which reveals the the hegemony of American values (Simon Reich).

Whatever your particular perspective on globalisation, it can scarcely be denied that it has had (and continues to have) an impact on higher education. The number of foreigners studying on exchange or as full fee-paying students, for example, grows year on year. Instructors are no longer limited by their national boundaries. And institutions increasingly look internationally for new opportunities.

The 2016 Aegina Anthology and Symposium

For this anthology, therefore, we the editors sought chapters which explored globalisation...in the context of higher education, and with an emphasis on learning, as per the focus of LiHE. We welcomed chapters from all scientific disciplines and which followed any methodological tradition. We were guided by the two broad but interrelated perspectives of theory and practice:

Theory: What are the effects of globalisation on learning, for example? How does learning differ with culture? When can learning be standardised, and when must it be customised, based on cultural differences? How does globalisation change demand for education? Why do students want to study internationally? How does international education change human resource capabilities? What are the effects of international education on economic development? Answering these types of questions, it was hoped, would help to increase our understanding of the *nature* of the globalisation of higher education.

Practice: What are the different modes of globalisation in higher education? How can a college or university globalise its programmes? What are the best practices of globalising higher education? Which activities facilitate the learning of globalisation? What are the requirements for a global classroom? Which novel pedagogical tools have been introduced in response to globalisation? Answering these types of questions, it was hoped, would increase our understanding of the *implementation* of the globalisation of higher education.

Any chapter, however, irrespective of the guiding perspective, ought to address *globalisation*, *learning*, and *higher education* explicitly. The call for chapter proposals, plus the subsequent review and re-submission process resulted in the 11 chapters which follow in this anthology.

The LiHE symposium at which the chapters were revised and the anthology was assembled was held in June 2016 on the Greek Island of Aegina, about 30 km off the coast of Athens. In addition to the academic symposium activities, authors explored the ruins of the 5th century B.C.E. Temple of Aphaea, visited the monastery of Saint Nektarios, and sampled the culinary delights of the Mediterranean.

LiHE

This anthology is the product of *Learning in Higher Education* (LiHE), an academic association which, as intimated by its name, focuses entirely on learning at the post-secondary level. The focus of the association reflects the shift from a transmission-based philosophy to a student-centred, learning-based approach. And its scope is limited to colleges, universities, and others institutions of higher education.

The main activity of the association is a symposium. About 10 years ago, Claus noted that professors attend conferences at which they present their scientific research in a 10–20 minute session, receive a few comments, then very often 'head to the bar for a drink'. He proposed an alternative, therefore, which *au contraire* returns to that ancient Greek format— the symposium— at which co-creation is key.

So, about 6 months prior to a symposium, a call for chapter proposals which has a relatively tightly focused theme is announced on the association's website and on various electronic mailing lists. The June 2015 symposium, for example, had the theme *Assessing Learning in Higher Education*; previous themes have revolved around games and simulations, classroom innovations, and learning spaces (in higher education).

Authors submit chapter proposals accordingly, which are then double-blind reviewed. If a proposal is accepted, its author is given 4 months to complete it. The whole chapter is then double-blind reviewed, and if it is accepted, the author is invited to attend the symposium. There, all authors revise their own chapters, work together to revise each other's chapters, and collaborate to assemble an anthology which, about a month later, goes off to the publisher.

The Editors and the Globalisation of Higher Education

As editors, of course, we bring our own perspectives to the role, which are based on our own experiences with and in globalisation. We have our own disciplinary backgrounds, which come with their own specific approaches to globalisation. And we have our own philosophical assumptions about globalisation which, in turn, influence our views about its appropriateness in higher education.

John

I have lived in or traveled to more than 70 countries around the world. I have now spent almost half my life living as an expatriate, with lengthy stints in France, England, and the United States. This is remarkable, considering that I grew up as a uni-lingual, narrow-minded, culturally-clumsy kid from small-town Canada. So why the change? Indeed, what exactly triggered that 180 degree turn in my life?

I suppose that I can trace it to early January of 1992, when I was in my second semester of a two-year Master of Business Administration programme. My Strategic Management professor, who originated from Poland, came to class one day, beginning the session with the question, "Would anyone like to do an internship in Poland this summer?". I looked around for signs of life from my classmates, and after a few moments, raised my hand cautiously with a shrug of my shoulders. "Sure, nothin' else to do," I said to myself. Not exactly an enthusiastic launch of my international career, but…

That summer, 15 of us flew off to Warsaw, spending the first two weeks studying economic re-organisation and re-structuring at the Warsaw School of Economics. We enjoyed cultural activities in the evenings and on the weekends. We ate traditional Polish food, and visited some beautiful and historic cities which had been spared in World War II. It is difficult for me to to pinpoint any single thing, but it was the most incredible two weeks of my life. And I simply 'knew in my bones' that international would be my thing.

The next ten weeks in Poland solidified my newfound destiny. I was paired with another engineer in a medium-sized city in the north of Poland. The company to which we were assigned was part of the state rubber-manufacturing behemoth, responsible for truck and tractor tires specifically. Our posting was in the marketing department. Two days into the job, however, revealed that it was not really a marketing department. Remember that this was 1992, less than two years after the political changes in Poland and elsewhere in Eastern and Central Europe. The company managers knew nothing about marketing, having operated for many decades under a centrally-planned system. But they did know that all foreign companies had marketing departments…so it would also have a marketing department!

There were five employees in the new department. Jerzy, the chief was an engineer by training, but had most recently spent some time in the commercial (sales) division. Another man, whose name I cannot remember, spent the summer essentially trying to figure out how Microsoft EXCEL worked. Two Polish interns just sat around and played video games all day. The only employee who did anything remotely marketing-like was Alicja, a recent graduate of the Faculty of Foreign Languages of Torun University. She was our host, and spoke English beautifully. Her job was to purchase company knick-knacks, such as pens, cigarette lighters, and little sewing kits—all with the company logo and address—which were used for promoting the compnay at trade fairs and other sales events.

So our summer actually consisted of teaching marketing to the marketing department manager and Alicja. Garry realised early on that he was not a teacher. He understood the material, but could not teach. He could not find examples in the Polish streets around him, or take the very foreign (and I mean foreign) concepts and make them understandable to these students. I, on the other hand, 'found my calling'. Indeed, Garry looked at me one day when we were laying on our single beds in the tiny room of the Hotel Robotniczy (Worker's Hostel) and said matter-of-factly, "You ought to be a teacher. You are really good." And here I am many years later, still passionate about teaching.

I also learned that summer of 1992 that it is not international travel which energises me. No, absolutely not. It is being there. That is to say, it is the cultural differences, and to a large degree the discomfort of being out of my own element, which drives me. Alicja, our host, took us everywhere that summer. The first weekend, for example, we drove to the Polish lake district where the company had a lakeside resort for its employees, complete with fishing and boating equipment, sports facilities, and hiking and leisure trails...a hangover from the socialist period during which the company was also responsible for worker vacations. We took one of the small sailboats and went yachting for the weekend. So there we were, under the stars on some tiny island in the middle of Lake Mikołaiki around a fire, cooking Polish kiełbasas, drinking vodka, and singing camp songs, they in Polish and we in English. And you know, I have spent my life since then seeking out other cultural adventures like this.

Another personal formative experience with respect to the globalisation of higher education occurred in the second year of my Master of Business Administration programme, after returning from Poland. The Faculty of Administration had a pot of money from the Indonesian government which was meant to be used in support of its three employees which it had sponsored to go to Canada to study. I was awarded a teaching assistant position; my role was essentially to re-teach the lessons from the day's lectures to Erwin, Tri, and Surek. It confirmed my decision to become a professor. But it also made me keenly aware of the challenges which students can face when studying in a foreign language, in a strange place, away from the supportive network of family and friends. To this day, I believe that I am better teacher because I began my teaching career to non-native English speakers. As an aside, I also remember very vividly the university's insensitivity to its growing international population. All the documents which Erwin received—including his diploma—were always addressed Erwin Erwin…you see, the university computer information system did not allow for people with only one name.

And one final important early-career experience which shaped my international life and my approach to the globalisation of higher education… Shortly after returning to the second year of my Master of Business Administration programme, I approached my Polish professor who had organised the previous summer internship, inquiring about another international opportunity. I was hooked, and I had to have my next fix. Coincidentally he had just been speaking with a colleague at York University in Toronto about a new project in Kyrghyzstan which was to be funded by the Ontario government. The money was to support the development of a new business school in Bishkek, the capital. It would be the first of its type in Kyrghyzstan and would follow a North American approach to business education. I offered my services without hesitation…then ran to the university library to find out where this place (of which I had never heard) was located.

It was an unforgettable experience in every way. But from a teaching perspective, I learned very quickly that to teach effectively, lessons must be grounded in the local culture. Case in point: a common idea when teaching marketing is the concept of consumer choice. This is something which is taken for granted in North America, where the cereal aisle at the grocery store might have one hundred or more different brands and types of cereal. Imagine me standing there in front of 50 post-soviet students saying, "So, you know when you go the store and are deciding which of the many types of bread to buy…" Blank stares. I asked my translator to repeat. Again no response from the students. You see, there were only two types of bread in Bishkek, Russian-style loaf bread or *хлев* and Kyrghyz flatbread or *нон*. And in fact, in essence there was only one type of bread, *хлев*, because *нон* is not considered bread, but *нон*. Being a successful teacher in Kyrghyzstan or anywhere else—despite globalisation—requires a conscious reflection on one's own assumptions, an *autocritique* which will lead to culturally relevant examples which will resonate with students.

Anne

I have experienced three different national approaches to education during my own years of schooling. I have attended pre-school in Greenland; primary school, gymnasium (college), and university in Denmark; and professional vocational courses in Norway. Reflecting on the natural and cultural settings, as I remember them, it appears to me that they shape three different approaches to education. Three cultural dimensions especially stand out to me: power distance; individualism/collectivism, and uncertainty avoidance (see also Hofstede, 2016).

Although I have only vague memories of my early childhood years in Greenland, I have sustained discussions of our time there with my family, and I have continued to read about the schooling system of Greenland. The culture of Greenland originates from the Greenlandic Inuit tradition. It is a country where some people to this day live as sealers and hunters in small communities, and in which the family plays an important role in the upbringing of children. In reality, woman and men participate equally in this. This has led to the development of a culture driven by collectivism. The extreme natural conditions under which the population has lived also form part of the culture. Being so geographically isolated, there is an inherent tradition to develop things from the materials at hand. And people have had to go into nature at high risk to catch fish and seals. This has led to a low uncertainty avoidance, as much focus has been on acquiring natural resources. People have been forced to live as part of nature's elements, and they have culturally adjusted to that. Much more than we experience in industrialised societies today. The power distance is low in Greenland. Greenlanders do not have a management philosophy, but have trained their children and youngsters according to family and community traditions. Even centuries after schooling was first established by the Danish colonists in the 18th century, the education of children had resemblances to communities of practice. If the weather changes and opportunities appear to have a good catch, children may leave school to help in their families. These cultural traits seem to have made their impact on the Greenlandic education system, and I remember my pre-schooling in Greenland as a family-oriented, community-based practice where days would be governed by community activities, weather conditions, and cultural spontaneity.

Moving to Denmark the experiences from the schooling system were different. It was more structured. It was well-planned. It was professional in a different way. Still embraced by family values, but more individual. And with a very low power distance, and a very low uncertainty avoidance. The recent national Danish culture has been influenced much by the reverend N. F. S. Grundtvig, who in the 19th century became a prominent figure and thinker. His main educational focus was to bring enlightenment to people from the lower classes of society and it became a reality through the establishment of a network of folk high schools throughout the country, which still flourishes today. It was the aim of Grundtvig to elevate the country through personal development of its people. He argued for an education system with two pillars, the School for Life (folk high school) and the School for Passion (university). And his pedagogical approach was governed by the dream of promoting a spirit of freedom and creativity within education. For example, Grundtvig was against exams, he was in opposition to compulsion, and he would argue that such would kill the soul. With Danish school reforms owing much to the thoughts of Grundtvig, Denmark developed as a country with an egalitarian mind-set and a belief in independence, and equal rights for educated people. It made me grow up in an education system where my own development as a human being would be seen as my individual right, although the curriculum and activities in school were governed by ministerial dispositions and legalities. Individual learning goals, self-responsibility for learning, individualised curricula, etc., are governing principles of the Danish school system under both left-wing and right-wing governments. This is how I remember my years in the Danish education system.

In between my gymnasium and university-years in Denmark, I lived in Norway for some years, teaching snow-boarding, parachuting and base-jumping. Compared to the power distance, individualism, and uncertainty avoidance of Greenland and Denmark, I found the Norwegian culture to be slightly different. Power distance seemed higher. Norwegians were self-directed, independent, and egalitarian too, like the Danes, but seemed to have more respect for authority than Danes and Greenlanders. In Greenland, we have experienced a freedom movement from Denmark in the late 1970s, which had shaped their culture. In Norway, there was a tendency to avoid formality on one hand, but also to be subordinate to power on the other hand. And to stick together in a tightly knitted family structure, much more so than in Denmark. But also, bearing a higher degree of uncertainty avoidance. It seemed to me that in Norway, people liked freedom and individuality, but at the same time did not want to take risks and go their own way to a large degree. As I have not been part of the formal schooling system in Norway, I have not lived the everyday life of a pupil in school. But from the stories I heard and the experiences I gained through vocational training, the education system in Norway differs from the Greenlandic and Danish education system as teachers there seem to remain more of their authority, work to the benefit of a more collectivistic society than the Danish, and focus on training their students within the predefined curriculum.

Summing up my personal experiences, I would compare the cultural traits of the educational systems in this way.

	Greenland	Denmark	Norway
Power distance	*	*	**
Individualism	*	***	**
Uncertainty avoidance	*	*	***

Figure 1: My personal comparison of three national educational cultures.

As I returned to Denmark and graduated from university with pedagogy and learning as my speciality, I caught an interest in the wider cultural changes of the European education system. That led me to do research on the way in which the Bologna-process played a role on quality enhancement of university education in Europe. In this book, I am co-authoring a chapter with Jens Smed Rasmussen and Claus Nygaard, in which we explain the role of Bologna for globalisation of Higher Eduation. To me there is no doubt that Bologna plays an important role for the development of Higher Education in Europe. But as my initial ramblings in this section suggest, the national cultures of the individual member countries of the EU, which go back centuries, have a much stronger impact on the formation of higher education in Europe. And may continue to have so for many centuries to come. This, however, does not mean that we should forget the idea of changing higher education or globalising higher education. It just means that we should do so with a larger focus on the cultural dimensions of our educational contexts.

A Framework for the Anthology

A significant challenge when editing an anthology is developing a device for structuring its chapters, even when they all share a common theme. During the symposium, therefore, together with the authors we identified the common features of the chapters. We have settled on a categorisation which classifies the chapters according to their focus of research on globalisation: 1. chapters with political focus, 2. chapters with an institutional focus, 3. chapters with a cultural focus, and 4. chapters with an individual focus. The grouping of the chapters is shown in Figure 2.

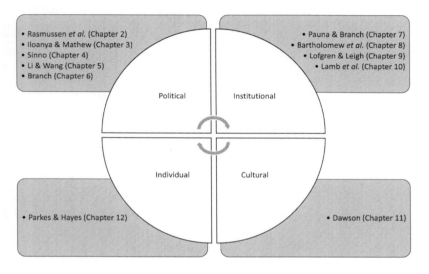

Figure 2: The grouping of the chapters in the book.

Political focus on globalisation

In chapter 2, Jens Smed Rasmussen, Anne Hørsted & Claus Nygaard focus on the Bologna Process of harmonising and globalising European higher education. They examine the role of the Bologna Process for the globalisation of Higher Education (HE). Based on their research they develop a central model for quality enhancement based on the themes of the Bologna Accord, at the same time trying to answer the central question: *"Does Bologna help HEIs to globalise or is it merely an institutional construction at the macro-political level?"* The key lesson from their chapter is that there is a discrepancy between institutional policy making and developing a globalised mindset at the university level.

In chapter 3, Jane Iloanya & Ivy Rose Mathew examine the development and practice of globalisation of higher education in Botswana. They discuss the relationship between globalisation and internationalisation of higher education and their overarching influence on higher education in Botswana. They show how the international and global dimensions in Botswana's higher education are manifested in international research collaborations, recruitment of international students and academics, curriculum development and instruction, international strategies and engagements, the role of technology in teaching and learning processes, which culminates in the establishment of branch campuses.

In chapter 4, Zane Siraj Sinno examines globalisation relative to the role of Global English in higher education. She concentrates on globalisation, the role the English language played in globalisation, the role and employability trends of NNEST (non-native English-speaking teachers) and the NEST (native English-speaking teachers), as well as the spread of a globalised form of education through MOOCs (Massive Open Online Courses) and offshore universities. Throughout her chapter she seamlessly draws in political aspects for both institutional, cultural and individual aspects of globalisation, making this an integrated reflected view on the use of English language as both dominator and diminisher for globalisation.

In chapter 5, Xiaobin Li & Xiaoyang Wang take a Chinese perspective on globalisation of higher education. With 37 million students, the Chinese higher education system is the largest in the world, and it continues to grow. And in the light of globalisation, more than 500,000 Chinese students go abroad to study. China today is such an important political player in higher education that the findings of their chapter will contribute to helping us have a better understanding of the globalisation of higher education in the world.

In chapter 6, John Branch explores a new, and relatively unknown, phenomenon—transnational higher education, which is a deviation from the broader and long-running internationalisation of higher education.

Politically it follows a different logic than internationalisation, and is, the author argues, an issue of importance (and concern) for a number of stakeholders within higher education.

Institutional focus on globalisation

In chapter 7, Diana Pauna & John Branch explore the internationalisation of the Stockholm School of Economics in Riga, with a view to identifying whether or not it follows a specific model of institutional internationalisation as per Chan & Dimmock (2008). Through their institutional focus they argue that different institutions internationalise differently in response to globalisation, and as a result of different contextual circumstances. They show how SSERiga has followed three models of institutional internationalisation at various stages of its evolution.

In chapter 8, Nicola Bartholomew, Geraldine Nevin, Hannah Abbott, Deborah Pittaway, and Robyn Nash explore their experience of designing and delivering an international virtual exchange programme for students on healthcare courses as a collaboration between Birmingham City University (BCU) in England and Queensland University of Technology (QUT) in Australia. The initiative they describe was a response to the globalisation of both healthcare and higher education. They show how this is reflected locally by the strategic aim for internationalisation at both universities through a range of activities including overseas student placements and increased globalisation of the curricula.

In Chapter 9, Joan Lofgren & Elyssebeth Leigh present lessons learned from the experiences of an international 3-year, 180 ECTS undergraduate programme conducted on the Mikkeli campus of Aalto University in Finland. The international nature of the approach, enshrined in the original design, has created opportunities and challenges on the programme's path to becoming a flagship response to globalisation. Now in its 28th year, the Mikkeli BScBA has much to share about its well-earned global reputation. The lessons learned are discussed in relation to the literature on globalisation in higher education, drawing on the strengths and experiences of students and staff involved in creating its unique approach to international education.

In chapter 10, Julian Lamb, Paul Bartholomew & Sarah Hayes address the practice-facing challenge of supporting collaborative partners across diverse geographical, cultural, and economic settings. By "collaborative partners" they mean universities (and occasionally commercial higher education providers) which have entered into formal contractual arrangements with their university to co-deliver credit-bearing programmes of study. In their chapter, they explore the challenge of requiring overseas partners to embrace UK quality values for teaching in HE but using a methodology for support that encourages emancipation, critical reflection, and choice. They focus on three cases of globalising higher education from the UK to Italy, Vietnam, and India.

Cultural focus on globalisation

In chapter 11, Chris Dawson looks into the notion of a global culture, which has been mooted and disputed. He argues that something new is beginning to emerge which may be more deserving of that name and that a new global intellectual tradition may be founded on it and in it. His conclusion is based partly on findings in the literature from psychology, sociology, political theory, theory of education, and philosophy, and partly on survey-based research into student attitudes conducted in Switzerland.

Individual focus of research on globalisation

In chapter 12, Geoff Parkes & Sarah Hayes focus on the challenges facing universities engaged in transnational education (TNE). TNE refers to the provision of educational qualifications from institutions in one country to students in another. They focus, in particular, on the aspect of developing people and building relationships for the many challenges that global TNE partnerships present in a digital age. Central to their discussion is the individual academic and their involvement in new programme introduction. The authors emphasise the importance of sensitive and critical cultural exchanges, at home and abroad, as central in their response to the TNE agenda in Higher Education.

References

Earle, L. (n.d.). Online Resource: http://www.education.vic.gov.au/Documents/about/research/rilornaearl.pdfp.1 [Accessed 10 November 2016].

Hofstede, G. (2016). Online Resource: https://geert-hofstede.com/national-culture.html [Accessed 10 November 2016].

About the Authors

John Branch is Academic Director of the part-time MBA programmes and Assistant Clinical Professor of Business Administration at the Stephen M. Ross School of Business, and Faculty Associate at the Center for Russian, East European, & European Studies, both of the University of Michigan in Ann Arbor, U.S.A. He can be contacted at this e-mail: jdbranch@umich.edu

Anne Hørsted is Adjunct Professor at the University of Southern Denmark, Senior consultant at cph:learning in Denmark, and Adjunct Professor at the Institute for Learning in Higher Education (LiHE). She can be contacted at this e-mail: anne@lihe.info

Chapter 2

The Bologna Process as a possible driver for the globalisation of HE?

Jens Smed Rasmussen, Anne Hørsted & Claus Nygaard

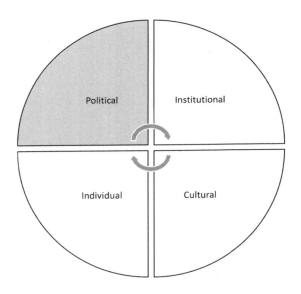

Introduction

This chapter is an important contribution to the book on globalisation of higher education as it focuses on the Bologna Process of harmonising and globalising European higher education. In this chapter we examine the role of the Bologna Process for the globalisation of Higher Education (HE). The chapter begins by introducing the Bologna Accord and its Ten Action Lines (see figure 1) governing the Bologna Process. It then develops a central model for quality enhancement based on the themes of the Bologna Accord. Finally, it reflects on the globalisation aspects of

Bologna and tries to answer the central question: *"Does Bologna help HEIs to globalise or is it merely an institutional construction at the macro-political level?"* The key lesson from our chapter is that there is a discrepancy between institutional policy making and developing a globalised mindset at the university level. We see our chapter as an important contribution to this book on Globalisation of Higher Education as it discusses the Bologna Process as a possible driver for the globalisation of HE and shows the requirements it places on Higher Education Institutions (HEIs). The Bologna Process has as its aim to create a European Higher Education Area (EHEA) and may be seen as the world's largest coordinated international programme for the globalisation of HE. In that respect, the main question is, of course, if and how the Bologna Process helps HEIs in their efforts to globalise. In the chapter we briefly describe the historical development of the Bologna Process and its Ten Action Lines. We also make a brief analysis of the content of the Ten Action Lines of the Bologna Accord. We find that the Ten Action Lines places requirements on HEIs in five central dimensions: curriculum, research, administration, students, and staff (CRASS). We argue that Bologna may be a prosperous driver for Quality Enhancement at the institutional level, as HEIs aim to accommodate the Ten Action Lines. Reading this chapter, you will gain the following insights:

1. you will learn about the Ten Action Lines of the Bologna Accord and the requirements they place on HEIs;

2. you will understand the consequences of the Bologna Process for Quality Enhancement at institutional level;

3. you will gain insight into the role of the Bologna Process as a possible driver for the globalisation of HE.

The chapter is divided into three sections. In section one we introduce the Bologna Process. In section two we analyse the quality themes under Bologna and integrate those in a central model for Quality Enhancement at the university level. In section three we reflect on the globalisation aspects of Bologna and try to answer the central question: *"Does Bologna help HEIs to globalise or is it merely an institutional construction at the macro-political level?"*

Section one: The Bologna Process

The Bologna Process is a very extensive educational development initiative. Today 50 signatory countries strive to gain a harmonisation within their systems of higher education. The Bologna Process is driven by ten so-called "action lines". The process includes way over eight hundred (this is where we stopped counting) national and international political institutions ranging from governments, ministries, government agencies, national accreditation and evaluation bodies, regulative institutions, interest organisations, sector institutions, to lobby groups and interest groups. These political institutions, organisations, and groups are collectively driving the process of formulation, reformulation, adaptation, and implementation of the Bologna Process in the national educational contexts. Add to that the more than 2,000 universities of the 50 signatory countries.

An overall vision of creating one European Higher Education Area (EHEA) guides the Bologna Process: *"Building on our rich and diverse European cultural heritage, we are developing an EHEA based on institutional autonomy, academic freedom, equal opportunities and democratic principles that will facilitate mobility, increase employability and strengthen Europe's attractiveness and competitiveness. As we look ahead, we recognise that, in a changing world, there will be a continuing need to adapt our higher education systems, to ensure that the EHEA remains competitive and can respond effectively to the challenges of globalisation"* (The London Communique, 2007). With EHEA the ambition is to enable both students and graduates to move freely between the European education institutions and the national labour markets. This is considered the best vehicle for the globalisation of higher education. The vision of EHEA is in line with the Presidency Conclusions of the European Council in Lisbon in 2000 where the following strategic goal for the next decade was set for the European Union: *"...to become the most competitive and dynamic knowledge-based economy in the world, capable of sustainable economic growth with more and better jobs and greater social cohesion"* (European Council, 2000). The deadline for creating EHEA and enabling this vision was set for 2010, and The European Higher Education Area (EHEA) was launched along with the Bologna Process' decade anniversary, in March 2010, during the Budapest-Vienna Ministerial Conference. New goals for further integration and globalisation were set for 2020. This process has required intense harmonisation and coordination between the signatory countries. At the same time, it has required substantial quality enhancement and coordination between HEIs to fulfil—as providers of education—such goals.

Over the years, the Bologna Process led to a stepwise development of the "Ten Action Lines", which set the vision and governed the implementation of the aims of the process. In 1998 France, Italy, Germany, and the United Kingdom signed the Sorbonne Declaration in which three of the Action Lines were present. In 1999, 29 countries signed the Bologna Declaration now with six Action Lines. In 2001, 33 countries signed the Prague communiqué with nine Action Lines. In 2003, 40 countries signed the Berlin communiqué now with Ten Action Lines. The remaining countries have joined Bologna subsequently after the forming of the Ten Action Lines. It is important to state that joining the Bologna Process and working to implement the action lines in their national HE-context is a free choice of the member states.

Introduced in the Sorbonne Declaration 1998	1. Adoption of a system of easily readable and comparable degrees 2. Adoption of a system essentially based on two cycles 3. Establishment of a system of credits
Introduced in the Bologna Declaration 1999	4. Promotion of mobility 5. Promotion of European co-operation in quality assurance 6. Promotion of the European dimension in higher education
Introduced in the Prague Communiqué 2001	7. Lifelong learning 8. Higher education institutions and students 9. Promoting the attractiveness of the European Higher Education Area
Introduced in the Berlin Communiqué 2003	10. Doctoral studies and the synergy between the EHEA and ERA (European Research Area)

Table 1: The Ten Action Lines of the Bologna Accord.

Naturally, these Ten Action Lines place a significant pressure on the signatory countries to harmonise their higher educational systems to live up to the vision of the EHEA. Bi-annual Bologna summits are held between the signatory countries, and between summits each country has to publish a follow-up report explaining how far they have got with the implementation of the Ten Action Lines. As such the action lines have national consequences for governments and political institutions, and as the implementation takes place in the national HE-sectors, they have institutional consequences for the individual HEIs as well. Figure 1 shows the national and institutional requirements following from the Ten Action Lines. We shall not slavishly go through all action lines here, but rather exemplify what is meant by requirements by looking at action line 1 (AL1): *"Recognition of degrees: Adoption of a system of easily readable and comparable degrees".*

At the Prague summit in 2001 it was agreed that in order to develop EHEA, a qualification framework ought to be developed that makes transparent the qualifications achieved at the different levels of the higher education system in all member countries. It had immediate consequences for the signatory countries, as it was now required that they—as national authorities—together with their key stakeholders (such as Rectors Conferences) formulated qualification frameworks. To do so they needed to analyse their degree structure for higher educational programmes in order to describe in much detail the qualifications given at each educational level. In many instances, this would require much more explicit and systematic work than was already required by current national educational legislation. This work on the national level would affect the individual HEIs as they were now to formulate qualification profiles for their study programmes in line with the national/international qualification frameworks. Such should describe qualifications in terms of workload, level, learning outcomes, competences, and profile. As these qualification frameworks on the national level have consequences for the curriculum planning at the institutional level, such transparency and alignment of qualifications benefit both students and HEIs within EHEA. It simplifies credit transfer and helps improve national and international mobility. When graduates move abroad to work in other member countries, the value of their formal education can be more easily determined and recognised. Furthermore, the qualification frameworks may function as evaluation criteria when judging the quality of a certain degree or study programme.

At the Berlin summit in 2003, it was further agreed that all members of the Bologna Process should ratify the Lisbon Recognition Convention, which was originally formulated and signed by 24 member states of the Council of Europe on April 11, 1997. The convention concerns *"the Recognition of Qualifications concerning Higher Education in the European Region"*. It deals with:

1. basic principles related to the assessment of qualifications;

2. recognition of qualifications giving access to higher education;

3. recognition of periods of study;

4. recognition of higher education qualifications;

5. recognition of qualifications held by refugees, displaced persons, and persons in a refugee-like situation;

6. information on the assessment of higher education institutions and programmes;

7. information on recognition matters.

As such it is required of the national member states that they establish basic sets of qualification principles, that they work to secure recognition of the qualification principles (of all member states) within their national contexts, and that they provide information to national and international students about their possibilities for international mobility and recognition. Regarding recognition, it was particularly required of member states that they *"promote, through the national information centres or otherwise, the use of the Unesco/Council of Europe Diploma Supplement or any other comparable document by the higher education institutions of the Parties."* (Lisbon Convention, 1997). Hereby the Berlin summit put the requirement on HEIs to formulate Diploma Supplements (typically in English) in order to make possible the international recognition and mobility.

In a study examining how the Bologna Process impacts the academic management discipline in US, Inamete (2015) found that the European harmonisation of academic degrees into three cycles, which in consequence lowered the level of the first degree from masters to bachelor level in most European countries, actually has positive impacts on those who want to transfer between the US and Europe for study. One issue was the broader Bachelor education in the US with more components of the liberal arts while the European Bachelor education is narrowly focused on the discipline and the professional skills. But the specialised European HE curriculum is based on students receiving a broader general secondary education of very high quality before intuition at HE (Inamete, 2015). The harmonisation of degrees into three main cycles has thus contributed to curriculum transparency between systems of HE and produced globalisation of education between the US and Europe by making transfers possible.

At the Bergen summit in 2005, it was agreed that higher education should not be seen as activity isolated in time, but should be recognised as the stepping stone for lifelong learning. On the national level the signatory countries should help create opportunities for flexible learning paths, also recognising prior learning, and the individual HEIs should further build on the transparency and flexibility of the educational system (following the implementation of the qualification profiles and the Diploma Supplement) to foster employability and facilitate recognition for further studies, thereby also recognising prior learning.

As can be seen from this brief exemplification of action line 1, the Bologna Process is driven with a significant push-strategy that imposes requirements on national member states and their HEIs. The same is the case with the other action lines. It is beyond the scope of this chapter to go into detail with these individual requirements. Our aim here is to show the requirements of the Bologna Process and discuss how HEIs needs to deal with the requirements of Bologna.

Section two: Quality themes under Bologna

In this section, we provide a thematic analysis across the ten action lines and point out what needs to be included in the quality system of HEIs if they wish to follow the Ten Action Lines of Bologna. When one looks at the requirements put on HEIs, it seems like a very diverse picture ranging from qualification frameworks for study programmes over the establishment of internal quality systems to increased international cooperation between students and staff. Bologna is all over the place as an external pressure for harmonisation and transparency. For management groups of HEIs, the Bologna Process and its Ten Action Lines may well be seen as "a monster" that is rather difficult to deal with and one that requires a lot of resources (be it time, information, or money). However, if one makes a thematic analysis of the requirements put on HEIs across the Ten Action Lines and link that analysis to the ambitions of HEIs to work with quality enhancement on a more general level, the Bologna Process offers a range of interesting themes and issues that can be picked up and implemented in the internal quality work of HEIs.

Based on a thematic analysis, we will argue that the requirements of the Ten Action Lines can be grouped into five quality dimensions as shown in figure 2. We entitle these dimensions CRASS, and we further argue that HEIs can work proactively with quality enhancement according to the requirements of the Bologna Process if they establish an internal quality system that systematically addresses these quality dimensions. Below we look at the five quality dimensions (CRASS) that HEIs are required to systematically address if they wish to enhance quality while living up to the requirements of Bologna. Following each dimension, we exemplify the possible normative implications it has for quality enhancement.

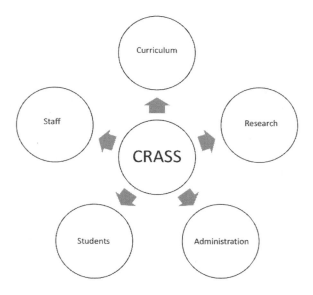

Figure 2: The CRASS model: Five quality dimensions of Bologna.

Curriculum

[C] Requirements regarding curriculum:

The main requirement regarding curriculum is the converging of qualification profiles into a harmonised process (AL1) that allows a comparison of countries and institutions, simplifying the demands for continuity among the three different degree cycles (AL2). Qualification profiles need to be aligned with the three-degree cycles (AL2) and with national and international qualification frameworks (such as the Dublin descriptors). The curriculum has to prepare graduates as multi-skilled knowledge workers in alignment with the ambitions of the Lisbon Convention and the objectives of a knowledge-based society (AL10). It is required that curriculum is based on a transferable and accumulative common system to define knowledge and learning outcomes, which enables mobility for students. ECTS is chosen as such a system and each curriculum must be based on ECTS (AL4). Another requirement is flexibility, so curriculum can be adapted to different contexts and be applicable to a wide range of circumstances, such as different learning sources and paths, languages, and methods (AL1). It is also a requirement that curricula focus on European history and society, as the ambition is to develop a shared social discourse about European identity and culture (AL6). Furthermore, it is also required that curriculum is seen as relevant by the students and that it empowers students and include them in the decision processes about their own learning (AL8). It is also required that curriculum has a high focus on investigation and research (AL2, 10), which is argued to benefit the creation of a knowledge-based society.

Normative implications for quality enhancement of requirements regarding curriculum:

These requirements have some normative implications for HEIs. First, they have to professionalise curriculum development in the sense that the requirements of Bologna are to be seen as a part of a wider processual and structural debate and practice within the institution. Second, curriculum development cannot be a matter of a group of teachers formulating a syllabus for their students; it needs to be coordinated and aligned across different study programmes, departments, faculty groups, and research groups. Third, HEIs have to professionalise administration of curriculum development and study programmes in order to facilitate the necessary legal support for faculty groups, enabling them to develop and teach within the regulations surrounding Bologna. It cannot be left to the teachers and faculty alone to align their procedures and practices with the action lines. Fourth, HEIs have to provide a centralised administrative and financial support for international coordination, development, and alignment of curricula. It may not be left to teachers and faculty alone to find administrative and financial support for network creation, knowledge sharing, and mobility. Such technostructure (Mintzberg, 1981) has to be established within the HEI.

Research

[R] Requirements regarding research:

Research is seen as a fundamental part of knowledge creation, and as a pillar in the development of competitiveness and attractiveness of HEIs. The aim is to also create a European Research Area (AL10), where researchers can move freely between HEIs (AL4). It is required of HEIs that they develop new frameworks for the development of research and that they develop appropriate career paths and opportunities for young researchers and doctoral candidates (AL2). It is also required that they increase mobility at the PhD and post-doctoral level (AL4), and increase their cooperation in doctoral studies and training of young researchers (AL4). HEIs are also required to particularly address the technological, social, and cultural evolution and needs of the European society in their research (AL10) in order to create EHEA and ERA as important elements of the knowledge-based society.

Normative implications for quality enhancement of requirements regarding research:

The normative implications of these requirements are multiple. First, funding, management, and evaluation of research need to be carried out in regard to the needs of contemporary European society. Second,

HEIs need to develop research strategies in which PhD programmes are an integrated part. Third HEIs have to take coordinative actions to increase mobility of PhDs and young researchers. This can be through the formulation of joint PhD programmes, joint research applications, etc. In practice, this could be reached by establishing an international office for researchers where exchange agreements, research applications, research programmes and PhD programmes were coordinated. Much like the function of the international offices for student exchange already present at most HEIs.

Administration

[A] Requirements regarding administration:

Institutions are required to make full use of the Diploma Supplement (AL1), formulate qualification profiles (AL1), and adopt ECTS (AL3), which is argued to increase the benefits of mobility and reduce the disadvantages of bureaucracy. Flexibility and mobility are furthermore sought through the coordination and knowledge transfer that HEIs are expected to experience when developing joint study programmes (AL4), which are argued to positively affect the mobility rates. At the same time, institutions are required to diffuse European content in their curricula (AL 6). Cooperation is argued to offer HEIs an opportunity to create and maintain in the long term a network that allows them to exchange information and communicate best practices and recommendations. Institutions are also required to create flexible learning paths (AL7), which are argued to be easier when they are integrated in a network that shares information and best practices. HEIs are responsible in a part of the international diffusion (AL9) of the Bologna Process as well as the articulation of channels to share practices and information.

Normative implications for quality enhancement of requirements regarding administration:

Study boards (or equivalent governing bodies) must see to it that study programmes formulate qualification profiles and that the teaching and learning activities are aligned in relation hereto. Second, they must only approve study programmes that formulate their activities according to the ECTS. Third, HEIs must integrate into their administrative practices that all students automatically gets a Diploma Supplement when they pass an exam. Fourth, HEIs have to encourage cross-institutional programme development. Fifth, they have to work to establish exchange programmes for teachers and students. This may well be done through the establishment of an international office dealing with both teacher and student mobility.

Students

[S] Requirements regarding students:

In the dimension of students, the main requirement is to have students participate actively in the decision-making processes (AL8). Students represent a forum to exchange information, life experiences, and opinions that can be used positively in quality enhancement. Students are the main targets to increase the attractiveness of the EHEA (AL9), since they take an active part in the mobility programmes, together with the staff. The aim is to have students evolve from having a passive role as receivers of education to having an active role in the shaping of both study programmes and institutions. Students become both subjects and objects of quality, as they are contributing to the definition and shaping of the HEI.

Normative implications for quality enhancement of requirements regarding students:

First, HEIs can use bodies such as student associations to actively engage students in their quality enhancement. Second, they can establish governing bodies like study boards (responsible for study programmes) and have students as active members of these study boards. Third, they can improve student mobility through the establishment of international offices and the constitution of international exchange agreements. Fourth, HEIs can also advocate for and promote extracurricular activities where students are engaged in activities in relation to their studies. This could be international case competitions, university conferences, and coordination and knowledge exchange between international student organisations. All should be developed and managed by students. The role of HEIs is to give students freedom and responsibility to develop extracurricular activities that add to their learning experience and increase the international dimension of their study programme.

Staff

[S] Requirements regarding staff

The staff is to be an active part in curriculum development and in the creation of research results. The staff is also to be included in the mobility programmes so that they too will have an active role in creating EHEA. By engaging staff in activities beyond research, teaching, and administration, they will become future shapers of the HEIs (AL8), together with agents of mobility and promotion of the attractiveness of EHEA (AL9). The staff has a very important role in implementing a student-centred learning process that is considered to enhance the quality of the education and improve the learning outcome of students (AL5). The staff is also seen as a target of mobility (AL6) and an active part in the shaping of a network of communication and information across countries.

Normative implications for quality enhancement of requirements regarding staff

First, HEIs can normatively work with competence development of staff, both in relation to research, teaching, and administration. This is best done if it is written into the HR-policy of the HEIs. Second, the discrepancies between staff members that teach, staff members that do research, and staff members that administrate must be broken down, and the traditional career patterns of universities where research matters more than teaching must also be changed. Third, it is important that the developmental and integrative role of staff is enhanced as a feature of the HEIs, creating, in the long run, a culture where staff members see themselves as members of a network that works for increasing student-centred education with a strong international dimension. This requires an explicit HR strategy.

Section three: Reflections on the Globalisation Aspects of Bologna

It is our argument that quality enhancement of HEIs can be proactively developed and managed under the CRASS dimensions. Figure 2 summed up our thematic analysis of the ten action lines and showed the requirements put on HEIs when they work with the dimensions: curriculum, research, administration, students, and staff. To exemplify, AL1 requires of HEIs that they develop easily readable and comparable degrees, which is a requirement to work for the harmonisation of their curricula across institutions. They must formulate qualification profiles in line with international and national qualification framework, which is a requirement for harmonisation and recognition of their curricula. Administratively they must make full use of Diploma Supplements, which is a requirement for comparability. Students' employability must be fostered through improved flexibility and transparency in the curricula and qualification profiles, which is a requirement for flexibility and transparency in relation to students, employers, and the society at large.

HEIs need to integrate the requirements of Bologna in their internal quality system. However, they need to do this in a proactive way that enables them to gain valuable insights into the ongoing internal processes that lead to quality. In that way they can enhance their quality on selected dimensions and not only react to the requirements in an adaptive way.

One central question remains to be answered: *"Does Bologna help HEIs to globalise or is it merely an institutional construction at the macro-political level?"* At the ministers' meeting in 2010, it was decided that one could now speak of EHEA as a reality. As a macro-political construction, the European Higher Education Area (EHEA) is thus a reality. According to Ravinet (2008), that is a macro-political construction. This is in line with Ursin *et al.* (2008), who analysed the impact of the Bologna Process on quality assessment at Finnish and Italian universities. They concluded that, despite the harmonising aim of the Bologna Process, evaluation and quality assurance appeared to maintain their cultural and institutional features. According to Pettersens (2015) case study, while focused on hamonising learning outcome by standardisation, Swedish and Norwegian universities actually experienced dilemmas between academic and managerial logics while students' learning outcome was not addressed.

From the Dutch and English university sector Ter Bogt & Scapens (2012) reported in a case study how New Public Management drives increased use of quantitative measurement within universities, which posseses a threat to both creativity and innovation in teaching and research. Pérez-Montoro & Tammaro (2012) pretty much came to a similar conclusion in their study of two universities in Parma, Italy, and Barcelona, Spain. They found that despite the Bologna Process, research and education have developed in different directions at the universities.

If we look at the Ten Action Lines of the Bologna Accord, they bear the overarching theme of international harmonisation. The urge is that the HE-sector becomes global (at least within the European region), and students and faculty can move freely between signatory countries. In that respect the Bologna Process has helped increase a more global outlook at HEIs. When it comes to the focus points of the CRASS-dimensions, however, they focus much more on internal quality issues at the individual institution than on ways to bootstrap globalisation. It seems to be the perception that by putting macro-political requirements on signatory countries, HEIs will harmonise their offerings and that itself will lead to exchange and mobilisation across borders.

Conclusion

In this chapter we have described the history and the content of the Bologna Process. We have argued that the Bologna Process, driven by Ten Action Lines, is a political push strategy for the harmonisation and coordination of the HE-sector in Europe. Although the Bologna Process is focusing more on a macro-political level aiming to harmonise university education in the EHEA, it may well be used as a proactive tool by HEIs in their internal strive for quality enhancement. Doing so, we would suggest that the HEI perceive the Ten Action Lines as benchmarks to reach. As we see it, a prosperous strategy for HEIs is to perceive the Bologna Process as a guide for further internal development rather than as external demands. We have analysed the Ten Action Lines in terms of the requirements for the quality they put on HEIs, which led us to the formulation of five important dimensions: 1) Curriculum, 2) Research, 3) Administration, 4) Students, and 5) Staff. Based on these dimensions, we have formulated a possible model for quality work, the CRASS model, and discussed how it can be used as a guiding philosophy for institutional quality enhancement that may or may not lead to globalisation. We see the CRASS model as a way in which HEIs can proactively develop a quality system that positively addresses the challenges and requirements of the Bologna Process and at the same time engage in globalisation.

About the Authors

Jens Smed Rasmussen is Teaching Assistant Professor at the Faculty of Social Sciences, Department of Entrepreneurship and Relation-ship Management at the University of Southern Denmark. He can be contacted at this email: jsr@sam.sdu.dk

Anne Hørsted is Adjunct Professor at the University of Southern Denmark, Senior consultant at cph:learning in Denmark, and Adjunct Professor at the Institute for Learning in Higher Education (LiHE). She can be contacted at this e-mail: anne@lihe.info

Claus Nygaard, professor, PhD, is executive director at the Institute for Learning in Higher Education (LiHE) and executive director at cph:learning in Denmark. He can be contacted at this e-mail: info@lihe.info

Bibliography

Bergen Communiqué (2005). Communiqué of the Conference of European Ministers Responsible for Higher Education in Bergen. Online Resource: http://www.crue.org/espaeuro/lastdocs/Bergen%20Communique.pdf [Accessed 10 November 2016].

Berlin Communiqué (2003). Communiqué of the Conference of European Ministers Responsible for Higher Education in Berlin. Online Resource: http://www.crue.org/pdf/DeclaracionBerlin2003.pdf [Accessed 10 November 2016].

Billing, D. (2004). International comparisons and trends in external quality assurance of higher education: Commonality or diversity? *Higher Education*, Vol. 47, No. 2, pp. 113–137.

Coppieters, P. (2005). Turning schools into learning organizations. *European Journal of Teacher Education*, Vol. 28, No. 2, pp. 129–139.

Dill, D. D. (1999). Academic accountability and university adaptation: The architecture of an academic learning organization. *Higher Education*, Vol. 38, No. 1, pp. 127–154.

EUA - European University Association (2007). *Preparation of the Bologna Ministerial Meeting*. CRUE, EUA.

Garvin, D. (1993). Building a Learning organization. *Harvard Business Review*, Vol. 71, No. 4, pp. 78–84.

Inamete, U. B. (2015). The academic discipline of management and the Bologna Process: The impacts on the United States in a globalizing world. *Vision*, Vol. 19, No. 1, pp. 49–57.

Jeliazkova, M. & D. F. Westerheijden (2002). Systematic adaptation to a changing environment: Towards a next generation of quality assurance models. *Higher Education*, Vol. 44, No. 3, pp. 433–448.

Joint declaration of the European Ministers of Education (1998). *Harmonisation of the architecture or the European higher education system by the four Ministers in charge for France, Germany, Italy, and the United Kingdom, Paris, the Sorbonne, May 25 1998*. Online Resource: http://www.crue.org/sorbo-in. htm [Accessed 10 November 2016].

Joint declaration of the European Ministers of Education (1999). *Convened in Bologna on the 19th of June 1999*. Online Resource: http://www.crue.org/ decbolognaingles.htm [Accessed 10 November 2016].

Kanji, G. K. (2001). Forces of exellence in Kanji's Business Excellence Model. *Total Quality Management*, Vol. 12, No. 2, pp. 259–272.

Lisbon European Council (2000). Presidency conclusions from the Lisbon Meeting 23 and 24 March 2000. Online Resource: http://www.europarl. europa.eu/summits/lis1_en.htm [Accessed 10 November 2016].

London Communiqué (2007). *Towards the European Higher Education Area: Responding to challenges in a globalised world, Communiqué, in London on 18th May 2007*. Online Resource: http://www.cicic.ca/docs/ bologna/2007LondonCommunique.en.pdf [Accessed 10 November 2016].

Pérez-Montoro, M. & A. M. Tammaro (2012). Outcomes of the Bologna Process in LIS higher education: Comparing two programs in Europe. *International Information & Library Review*, Vol. 44., No. 4., pp. 233–242.

Pettersen, I. J. (2015). From Metrics to Knowledge? Quality Assessment in Higher Education. *Financial Accountability & Management*, Vol. 31, No. 1, pp. 23–40.

Prague Communiqué (2001). Towards the European Higher Education Area, Communiqué of the meeting of European Ministers in charge of Higher Education in Prague on May 19th 2001. Online Resource: http://www. crue.org/comcumbrepraga.htm [Accessed 10 November 2016].

Ravinet, P. (2008). From voluntary participation to monitored coordination: Why European countries feel increasingly bound by their commitment to the Bologna Process. *European Journal of Education*, Vol. 43, No. 3, pp. 353–367.

Sebkova, H. (2002). Accreditation and Quality Assurance in Europe. *Higher Education in Europe*, Vol. 27, No. 3, pp. 239–247.

Senge, Peter. (1990). *The Fifth Discipline. The Art & Practice of the Learning Organization*. New York, DoubleDay.

Ter Bogt, H. J. & R. W. Scapens (2012). Performance Management in Universities: Effects of the Transition to More Quantitative Measurement Systems. *European Accounting Review*, Vol. 21, No. 3, pp. 451–497.

Ursin, J.; M. Huusko; H. Aittola; U. Kiviniemi & R. Muhonen (2008). Evaluation and Quality Assurance in Finnish and Italian Universities in the Bologna Process. *Quality in Higher Education*, Vol. 14, No. 2, pp. 109–120.

Westerheijden, D. F. (2003). Accreditation in Western Europe: Adequate reactions to Bologna declaration and the general agreement on trade in services? *Journal of Studies in International Education*, Vol. 7, No. 3, pp. 277–286.

Chapter 3

Globalisation of Higher Education in Botswana

Jane Iloanya & Ivy Rose Mathew

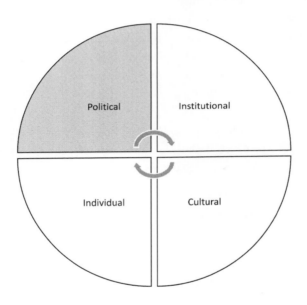

Introduction

This chapter is an important contribution to the book on globalisation of higher education, as it sets out to examine the development and practice of globalisation of higher education in Botswana. It discusses the relationship between globalisation and internationalisation of higher education and their overarching influence on higher education in Botswana. The international and global dimensions in Botswana's higher education is manifested in international research collaborations, recruitment of international students and academics, curriculum development and instruction, international strategies and engagements, and the role of technology in teaching and learning processes.

In this chapter, we examine the developments and practice of the globalisation of higher education in Botswana. The roots of this globalisation of higher education and the effects on the higher education system of Botswana are critically discussed. We further explore how Botswana is adapting to the global demands of higher education. The relationship between globalisation and internationalisation of higher education in Botswana and the underpinning theories of globalisation which informed our study are discussed. The chapter concludes by looking at the effects of globalisation of higher education on the Botswana education system. Two prominent institutions of higher education in Botswana were used as principal points of reference. One is the country's premier and state-owned university, while the other is the biggest private university in the country.

Reading the chapter, you will gain the following three insights:

1. an insight into the globalisation and internationalisation of higher education seen from a Setswana point of view;

2. a discussion of the differences between Modernisation theory and World-Systems theory in relation to globalisation of higher education;

3. a more detailed insight into the effects and challenges of Globalisation for the Botswana's higher education sector.

Introduction to Botswana

Botswana is a landlocked country in Southern Africa. With a population of slightly over two million people, the country has a land mass as big as France. At independence in 1966, Botswana's education system was modelled along the lines of those of the former colonial power Great Britain. In 1976, the first review of the country's education policy took place. This exercise culminated in the National Policy of Education, published as Government Whitepaper No. 1 of 1977, commonly referred to as Education for Kagisano (Republic of Botswana, 1997). Education for Kagisano stood for social harmony among the people of Botswana. In 1994, Botswana unveiled its revised National Education Policy with social justice as the main philosophy driving the policy. The emphasis was on Batswana meeting with the technological challenges of the 21st century through an education policy that would be championed by the spirit of social justice and greater access to modern education (Republic of Botswana, 1994). Education takes the lion's share of the national budget of Botswana. In 2008/2009, the Ministry of Education was allocated P5.51 billion or 26.8% of the recurrent budget and P1.058 billion or 12.2% of the development budget (Republic of Botswana, 2008). In 2015, the Ministry of Education and Skills Development received the biggest share at P10.31billion or 28.09% of the recurrent budget. Government's target of providing modern education to its citizens was further reinforced by the 1997 Vision 2016 document, which had as one of its pillars, *"the need to make Botswana a well informed and educated nation"* (Botswana, 1997). Vision 2016 represents a long-term vision of the kind of society Botswana would like to be by 2016, when it celebrates 50 years of independence from Great Britain. The transformation will require a lot of hard work coupled with continuous innovation, resilience, commitment and fortitude.

In pursuance of the above goal, one must not overlook the role of higher education in the provision of quality education that meets global standards in any country. Higher education plays a pivotal role in the creation of an innovative society and knowledge hub. Quality and accessibility of higher education must be improved and tailored to meet the needs of the international job market. This should be reflected in the teaching and learning processes through curriculum development and the implementation realities of the programmes offered at the higher education level. It is against this background that we have decided to examine the trends and developments in the globalisation of higher education in Botswana. This chapter will, in particular, discuss the roots of the globalisation of higher education in Botswana and the different ways globalisation of higher education has impacted on the operations of the institutions of higher learning in the country. The emphasis is on institutional practices and involvement in adopting and adapting to global trends in higher education.

Globalisation and Internationalisation of Higher Education

Globalisation of higher education is one of the new trends in higher education. As the world becomes more of a "global village", institutions of higher learning have a role to play, and a very big one at that, in ensuring that courses offered meet international and global demands and standards. According to Altbatch & Tiechler (2001), globalisation refers to the trends in higher education that have cross-national implications such as mass education, a global marketplace for students, faculty, highly educated personnel and a global reach of the new internet-based technologies. Globalisation of higher education should be understood in the context of economic and academic trends that are part of the reality of the 21st century. It is evident that institutions of higher learning, both public and private, are fast evolving into global actors, a trend found in many other industries (Altbatch & Knight, 2008; Naido, 2006). The character and behaviours of higher institutions worldwide are being influenced by globalisation (Enders, 2004). Scholars such as Carnoy & Rhotem (2002) argue that globalisation is a complicated phenomenon, with complexities to its interpretation and operations. Giddens (1990) describes globalisation as the intensification of worldwide social relations, which link distant localities in such a way that local happenings are shaped by events occurring many miles away. This, of course, entails a change in the way we perceive geography and experience localness. According to Mann (2013), globalisation involves the extension of distinct relations of ideological, economic and political power across the world. In the period after 1945, it meant the diffusion of ideologies, such as liberalism and socialism, the spread of the capitalist mode of production and the extension of nation states across the world. Nonetheless, globalisation permeates the spheres of economics, politics, culture and social interactions of the 21st century. In recent times, globalisation has become a worldwide phenomenon and higher education is a major engine propelling globalisation. Universities cannot divorce themselves from the profound influence of globalisation in the functioning of the education system.

Internationalisation of higher education, on the other hand, refers to the specific policies and initiatives of countries and individual academic institutions or systems aimed at dealing with global trends. These global trends include policies relating to recruitment of foreign students, the international content of the curriculum of homegrown institutions of higher learning, international staff and faculty composition, and international/foreign institutions established abroad. According to Sehoole (2006), the current debate on internationalisation is couched in relation to globalisation, giving the notion that internationalisation is something new and motivated by economic rationale. It further argues that internationalisation is not a new phenomenon and that it is in fact as old as the advent of colonialism. For the past decade, Botswana has witnessed some international and global dimensions in its institutions of higher learning. Apart from the higher education provided by the University of Botswana, which is the premier university, some private tertiary educational institutions have also been established, with international and global dimensions embedded in the system (Iloanya, 2013).

Trans-national higher education operations are finding their way in Botswana, as evidenced by the presence of some foreign institutions of higher learning in the country. According to Yang (2008), cited by Branch in this anthology, the emergence of transnational higher education signalled a dramatic shift in the higher education landscape. It has brought about a change that emphasised taking higher education to the community (transnational), in addition to making it international (Internationalisation). Transnational higher education involves all kinds of higher education study programmes and services where learners are located in a different country or countries, apart from where the awarding institution is situated. Globalisation of higher education has led to the emergence of different players in the field of higher education. These players could manifest in form of Internationalisation or Transnational higher education.

Globalisation Phenomenon and the Theoretical Underpinnings

There are many theories underpinning the globalisation phenomenon. Such theories include World-systems, Feminism, Marxism, and Modernisation. This chapter is based on World-systems and Modernisation theories.

World-systems theory

The World-systems theory sees globalisation as a phenomenon that emerged since the beginning of the world of Capitalism. In other words, globalisation is as old as the world of capitalism itself, dating far back to the 1500s (Arrighi, 2005). Developed by Immanuel Wallerstein, the world-systems theory is an approach to world history that shares the view that there is a world economic system in which some countries benefit, while others are exploited.

A key structure of the capitalist world system is a division of the world into great regions or geographically based hierarchical order. This division capitalises on the notion that the nations of the world are not on the same level in terms of economic and political development. Globalisation is not a new phenomenon. It is a process which was completed in the 20th century, through which the capitalist world system spread across the globe. Wallerstein (1998:32) states that the current *"ideological celebration of so-called globalisation is, in reality, the swan song of our historical system"*. Feudalism collapsed and gave way to technological innovation and the rise of the market economy. Increase in production and the urge for long distance trade gave way for the Europeans to spread to other parts of the globe. Therefore, the current wave of globalisation is not a new phenomenon. It is as old as capitalism itself and has taken different forms and directions. Critics of world-systems believe that globalisation makes some nations to be masters of other nations. In Botswana, globalisation of higher education has taken different forms. The wave of globalisation of higher education could be seen in the international dimensions of the research activities and the presence of cross-border institutions in the country.

Modernisation theory

Globalisation lends itself to the theory of modernisation, which entails a total transformation of the traditional society into a society of the new wave of technological advancement and economic prosperity. According to modernisation theory, a traditional society is characterised by irrationality, fatalistic attitudes and ascribed values, while a modern society is considered to be rational, forward-looking, competitive and achievement oriented (Romm, 1990; Webster, 1990). A key assumption of the modernisation theory hinges on the fact that Western countries are more developed than the third world countries. If given the right platform, the third world countries will follow suit in modern development. Globalisation is the driver that has radicalised the project of modernisation. It is, therefore, considered as the main instrument of the modernisation process, which would lead to the radical transformation of the third world countries. The world is a global village and institutions of higher learning, especially the universities, are the main agents of globalisation in knowledge accumulation and sharing. The theories of world-systems and modernisation are suitable for this chapter since the chapter discusses the developments and practices of the globalisation of higher education in Botswana. The developments take one through the origins of the globalisation of higher education as far as Botswana is concerned, and the practices, in particular, delve into the institutional practices and involvements in the global trends in education.

Perhaps, it is right to pause a bit and consider the causal determinants of globalisation. This will shed some light on our understanding of the philosophical and theoretical underpinnings of the theories of globalisation. Is the core of the process of globalisation economic, political or cultural? Does globalisation refer to a process or a condition, that is, a process of transformation or a global condition? What is the relationship between globalisation and the nation state, and is the nation state being undermined in the process of globalisation? How do modernity and postmodernity relate to globalisation? Is the nation being transformed in any way? (Robinson, 2004). There are different considerations on the issue of globalisation being perceived as a process or a condition. Globalisation should be seen as both a process and a condition. It is a global condition that has taken many years and periods to transform the events of the world. The transformation stems from a world system of economic condition championed by capitalism and the patterns of global economic activities and the transformation to the modern era of doing things. The effect of globalisation permeates all aspects of modern life and higher education is at the forefront of the current wave of globalisation. The advent of modern technology has widened the scope of globalisation and the effect cannot be overlooked.

The Developments and Practices of Globalisation of Higher Education in Botswana

The origin and the development of the international dimensions of Botswana's higher education date back to the arrival of the various European missionaries who introduced Western education to Botswana, alongside with the propagation of the Christian faith. Zeleza (2013) argues that the internationalisation and globalisation of higher education in Africa is not a new phenomenon. The ancient universities of Africa, Asia, and Europe were designed and served as regional communities of learning and scholarship. Universities such as Universities of Botswana, Lesotho, and Swaziland were staffed by foreign academics that were largely drawn from the former colonial power, and they attracted students from other countries in the region because of the shortage of universities after independence. In 2008, Botswana established the Education Hub (Botswana, 2008). It was an excellent strategy for the diversification and growth of the economy of the country. The Education Hub would contribute to the gross domestic product (GDP) through the revenue that would accrue from the enrolment of international students in the country.

According to Zeleza, the current trends in the internationalisation of higher education allow for perpetual global relationships. The current scenario is that students and academic staff flow from the north to the south. The borrowing of institutional and intellectual models from the north has dominated the historic patterns of internationalisation and globalisation of African higher institutions of learning. In Botswana, there are some current initiatives such as the American Fulbright Scholarship administered by the American Embassy. Fulbright has introduced several innovations to meet the changing needs of academics and professionals. Fulbright U.S. Scholar Program offers teaching, research, or a combination of teaching and research awards to various scholars in about 125 countries, including African countries such as Botswana, South Africa, and Nigeria. Opportunities are available for college and university faculty administrators as well as for professionals, artists, journalists, scientists, lawyers, independent scholars and many others. Other global initiatives in Botswana's higher education system include partnerships with various US universities for staff and student exchange programs. Botho University is a private higher institution of learning in Botswana. The University's strategic focus is to increase student diversity by attracting international students. In pursuance of this strategic focus, Botho University has a number of international partnerships with international institutions such as the University of Venda in South Africa, Teesside University in the UK, Ohio University, Black Hills State University and Wayne State University in the USA, Indian School of Mines, and Manipal University in India. Students are given the opportunity to take advantage of these international partnerships through student exchange programmes. While some students have embarked on internship projects in India, others have travelled to the USA and the UK, gaining international and academic exposure in a world experiencing globalisation of higher education at a very fast rate. All these moves are part of the university's immense focus on producing graduates for both local and international markets.

Contemporary higher education in Botswana has witnessed an increase in the recruitment of international students from different countries of the world. Botswana is one of the countries attracting the interest of international students and academic staff. The universities in Botswana attract academic staff from various countries across the globe such as Europe, America, Asia and other parts of Africa. The office of International Education and Partnerships (OIEP) at UB has two broad functions:

+ to facilitate the development of partnerships with international institutions for various kinds of collaborative projects including teaching, curriculum development, research, and staff exchanges;

+ to grow international student enrolment at UB and study abroad opportunities between UB and international institutions, as well as provide all necessary international student and staff services.

The Office of International Education and Partnerships (OIEP) was established in 2006 and is effectively coordinating a more focused approach to internationalisation. The recruitment of international students is currently above three percent and it was suggested that the target of 10% should be rolled forward into NDP10, with stronger efforts and improved structures to ensure that this target can be met. Similarly, Botho University established the Office of Internationalisation and Communication in 2012 with a mandate to attract international scholars and students from other parts of the world. Currently, Botho University has academic staff from more than 12 countries and students from countries in the region such as South Africa, Namibia, Nigeria, Liberia, Zimbabwe, Zambia, Democratic Republic of Congo, and Ethiopia amongst others. The pressure lies with the socialisation on the part of the international students and academic staff to be able to adapt to the culture of their new environment. The same scenario is applicable to students and academic staff of Botswana origin who go to other countries to study and teach.

Significant achievement has been made in the development of institutional academic partnerships and student and staff exchange. The University of Botswana's Policy on Internationalisation seeks the realisation of three major objectives such as, expanding international student and staff exchanges, expanding international research cooperation, and enhancing the internationalisation of all curricula. While the University has partnerships in Europe and North America, the University is also intending to expand its relationships, especially with Southern African Development Community (SADC) universities and institutions and those in other parts of Africa. It also wants to establish a limited number of partnerships with universities located in major countries within Asia, namely China, India, Japan and Korea (UB policy on Internationalisation, 2006).

International research collaborations

The University of Botswana (UB) which is the country's premier public university is involved in international research collaborations with universities in other parts of the world. There is a remarkable increase in international research collaborations as evidenced by the research grants awarded from the North to the South. International conferences, seminars, and research activities are published in well recognised peer reviewed journals around the world. Academics exchange ideas to enhance their teaching and learning methodologies. Networking is seen as very crucial to contemporary higher education students and academics. All these are made possible by the current wave of globalisation and internationalisation of higher education. There is no gainsaying the fact that collaborations in research activities between institutions of higher learning in different parts of the world have contributed in no small measures to the enhancement of the teaching and learning processes at the higher education level. Botswana as a country encourages the carrying out of research and dissemination of research outputs at all levels of education, especially at the higher education level. In Botswana, the institutions of higher learning organise various international conferences, which are well attended by participants from within and outside the continent of Africa.

The University of Botswana's further initiatives in research collaborations and enhancement include engaging in more collaborative and comparative international research, recruiting visiting research scholars to mentor or lead departmental and faculty research projects, establishing mechanisms for cooperative supervision of graduate students enrolled at UB and partner institutions by UB scholars and partner colleagues, encouraging students with research skills from outside of Botswana to participate in UB research projects, presenting more scholarly papers at international meetings, providing venues for UB staff to inform colleagues of papers and discussions at international meetings, developing partnerships that will expand international research cooperation. Similarly, Botho University has research collaborations with a number of other universities including Black Hills State University, University of Venda, and Great Zimbabwe University. Through the institution's research support grants, academic staff will get an opportunity to attend and make presentations in international conferences across the world as well as get published in journals and books. Botho University also takes the support of external examiners, visiting scholars, and professors with the intention of promoting research and academic activities among staff as well as students.

Internationalisation of curricula initiatives

The University of Botswana (UB) set up some initiatives towards internationalisation and globalisation of the curricula. Activities include augmenting international and comparative subject matter in both general education and disciplinary courses, developing curricula that make UB graduates more competitive in the international labour market, enhancing faculty and student appreciation of international diversity, encouraging foreign language studies, establishing joint or dual degree programmes with universities outside of Botswana when such programmes are not available or cannot be sustained at UB, providing internships for UB students outside of Botswana, participating in online courses offered outside of Botswana and offering such courses at UB for students in other countries, implementing flexible approaches to the transfer of credits from accredited universities outside of Botswana (UB Policy on internationalisation, 2006). Botho University towards its initiative on internationalisation of curriculum do activities such as benchmarking against international institutions, teaching modules on globalisation and internationalisation of higher education, and offering franchisee programs from recognised international universities in the UK. Some other universities in Botswana also offer franchisee programmes in partnerships with various international universities depicting the international nature of these institutions of higher learning in Botswana.

The government plays a major role in shaping campus' international strategies and engagement overseas. International expansion in the form of branch campuses highlights the current trend in the globalisation of higher education. In Botswana, globalisation and internationalisation of higher education have led to the establishment of international and foreign universities in the country. A number of private universities have sprung up in the country, some with campuses established in neighbouring countries, thus, reinforcing the globalisation trend in higher education. This has benefited the country in the areas of increased access to higher education and the creation of jobs for the citizens. Nonetheless, critics of globalisation challenge the unquestioning acceptance of globalisation as a driving and positive force for society in general and higher education in particular (Apple, 2010).

Role of technology in globalisation of higher education

The role of technology in disseminating knowledge through online courses, distance learning, blended learning and flipped classrooms reinforces the globalisation and internationalisation of higher education in Botswana. The University of South Africa (UNISA), one of the leading and oldest institutions in distance learning in Southern Africa, has benefited immensely from globalisation as a result of increased enrolment of students from different parts of the world. This is made possible through the use of information technology (Machingambi, 2014). Botswana's education policy of 1994 laid emphasis on the need for the citizens to embrace the technological advancement and challenges of the 21st century. The use of technology in teaching and learning is highly encouraged at all levels of education, especially at the higher education level. This trend further facilitates the globalisation of higher education. As a result, people engage in online courses and can earn their degrees from foreign countries without necessarily moving out of their countries. The use of technology in higher education has swept across institutions of higher learning in Botswana as they run classes in distance learning mode. The University of Botswana, Botho University, and Botswana College of Open and Distance Learning (BOCODOL) have all benefited from the use of technology in instruction, through the distance learning mode. All these give credence to the globalisation of higher education and the positive effects thereof. The use of technology has benefited both students and academic staff, albeit with some challenges. For instance, the cost of acquiring good quality technological equipment for teaching and learning and the availability of Internet connectivity in this part of the globe is still a teething problem.

Effects of Globalisation of Higher Education in Botswana

Globalisation of higher education comes with a lot of benefits for the institutions of higher learning as well as for the nation as a whole. In Botswana, the effect of globalisation remains noticeable. The universities strive to produce graduates who are well rounded with a global outlook. It is expected that these graduates should be able to exhibit certain traits. They should be knowledgeable, hardworking, articulate, innovative, entrepreneurial, ethical, scholarly, confident and socially responsible. The shift towards globalisation has encouraged academic institutions to work extremely hard to meet the needs of national and international markets. There is stiff competition in the field of higher education as everyone tries to go global (Mishra, 2013).

The competitiveness in quality of education and training is enhanced through academic collaborations with universities from the developed countries. This also helps to attract both students and scholars of high calibre. As indicated earlier in the chapter, University of Botswana, the oldest university, and Botho University, the biggest private university in

Botswana, are actively involved in the process of globalising their teaching and learning. Both universities have international collaborations with universities in Europe, Asia, America, and Africa. They have visiting scholars from well-established universities in Europe and America who collaborate with them in research as well as staff and student exchange programmes. Globalisation has led to the increase in the number of international students and faculty members in Botswana's higher education institutions.

Cultural integration is encouraged as it helps people appreciate others and have a mutual understanding. The effect of globalisation of higher education in Botswana is quite visible in the area of cultural integration and association. Visiting scholars learn to adapt to the people's way of life and vice versa. Some visiting scholars to Africa have carried out research activities on African tradition and culture such as music, cultural dances, the indigenous culture, and African traditional education.

Modern technology has encouraged the creation of a global culture and global education. According to Yang (2004), with the advent of a global society driven by technology and communication systems, students are transformed into global citizens with a wide range of skills to apply in the competitive and information-based society. The universities in Botswana are equipped with modern technology, which makes it possible for both faculty members and students to have global academic engagements with their peers from other parts of the globe. This opens the doors for online learning experiences and collaboration for study and research. Ativio project was an international initiative by Botho University to connect its students with students from other parts of the globe to give them an online classroom-based international development project experience. Another laudable opportunity was a research case study initiated by University of Durham students to find out the effectiveness of Blackboard usage with Botho University students. This initiative enabled both parties to exchange both academic and cultural ideas. The fear though is that global education may diminish the cultures of smaller and poor countries.

Globalisation of higher education in Botswana is beneficial in the area of curriculum enhancement and skill transfer. Skills are highly developed through a knowledge-based society. Programme development at institutional levels involves benchmarking against other institutions in other parts of the globe to ensure that quality is maintained at different standards. One of the forces driving Botswana's National Development Plan 10 (2009–2016) is to be able to provide globally competitive graduates to drive economic growth (Botswana, 2009). This is further reinforced by the establishment of Botswana Education Hub in 2008, aimed at driving the diversification of the education system and promoting economic growth through globalisation. Claus et al, in this anthology, describe the Bologna Process as a crucial drive for the globalisation of higher education. Similarly, the Tuning Africa Project, which is an international initiative geared towards the harmonisation of African higher education could be used to actively drive the globalisation of higher education agenda in Africa. In Botswana, the University of Botswana and Botho University, used as points of reference in this chapter, are both members of the Tuning Africa project.

Challenges of globalisation of higher education in Botswana

Globalisation of higher education in Botswana is faced with some challenges emanating from the flow of staff and students from Botswana to other parts of the globe. The government sponsors citizens to go and study abroad, gain quality education, and come back to contribute to nation building. Unfortunately, some do not find it worthy to come back to their country. This is globalisation playing its role in the modern era of transformation.

Globalisation plays a role in disturbing indigenous culture, tradition, and values. People intermingle and the world system order encourages greater social inequality, where there are gaps between those who have and those who do not have. It is survival of the fittest and the weaker ones are submerged by the stronger ones. What happens to the poor who cannot afford global choices and chances? These are some burning issues.

Funding is a challenge, especially in the area of research activities. Collaboration is, therefore, encouraged to flow from the North to South to boost research activities. Institutions need financial support to be able to enjoy the academic benefits of globalisation in the area of research, quality, and standards of the institutions to compete at a global level.

There are the problems of Internet access and diversity of programmes, which affect the free flow of the globalisation agenda. Collaborations are in place but, sometimes, the diversity of programmes affect the implementation of the collaborative activity. Institutions find it difficult to partner with another institution where they do not share the same programme.

Conclusion

Developments and practices in the globalisation and internationalisation of higher education in Botswana indicate that globalisation is not a new phenomenon in Botswana. Globalisation and internationalisation of higher education in Botswana date back to the advent of the Christian missionaries and the colonial education system, which Botswana adopted until 1977 when its first national education policy was unveiled. With the current wave of globalisation of higher education, Botswana has benefited through the global and international dimensions adopted in its higher education teaching and learning processes. These are manifested in international research collaborations, recruitment of international students and academics, international strategies and engagements culminating in the establishment of branch campuses, and the role of technology in the teaching and learning processes. While these benefits are recognised and appreciated, they are not without challenges. These challenges include the issues of adapting to new cultural and social practices, curriculum development and implementation processes to suit global demands, and the difficulties in the use and maintenance of technology for teaching and learning. By and large, the benefits of globalisation in higher education in Botswana outweigh its challenges. Truly, the world is a global village!

About the Authors

Jane Iloanya is an Associate Professor and Post-Graduate Programme Co-ordinator at the Faculty of Education, Botho University , Botswana. She can be contacted at this e-mail: jane.iloanya@bothouniversity.ac.bw.

Ivy Rose Mathew is Deputy Pro-Vice Chancellor (Academics) at Botho University, Botswana. She can be contacted at this e-mail: ivy@bothouniversity.ac.bw

Bibliography

Altbatch, P. G. & U. Teichler (2001). Internationalisation and Exchange in a Globalised University, *Journal of Studies in International Education*, Vol. 5, No. 1, pp. 5–25.

Altbatch, P. G. (2002). *Perspectives on Internationalising Higher Education.* Centre for International Higher Education, Boston College.

Altbatch, P. G. & J. Knight (2007). The Internationalisation of Higher Education: Motivations and Realities. *Journal of Studies in International Education*, Vol. 2, No. 3, pp. 290–305.

Apple, M. (2010). *Ideology and Curriculum.* New York: Routledge.

Arighi, G. (2005). Globalisation in World-Systems perspectives. In R. Appelbaum & W. I. Robinson (Eds.). *Critical Globalisation Studies*, pp. 33–44. New York: Routledge.

Botswana, Republic of (1977). *Education for Kagisano: Report of the National Policy on Education.* Gaborone: Government Printer.

Botswana, Republic of (1994). *The Revised National Policy on Education.* Gaborone: Government Printers.

Botswana, Republic of (2008). *Education Hub.* Government Printers.

Botswana, Republic of (2009). *National Development Plan 10 (2009–2016).* Gaborone: Government Printers.

Carnoy, M. & D. Rhotem (2002). What Does Globalisation Mean for Educational Change? A comparative approach. *Comparative Education Review*, Vol. 46, No. 1, pp. 1–9.

Chinnammai, S. (2005). *Effects of Globalisation on Education and Culture.* Paper presented at the ICDE International Conference, New Delhi, November 19–23, 2005.

Enders, J. (2004). Higher Education, Internationalisation and the Nation State: Recent Developments and Challenges to Governance Theory. *Higher Education*, Vol. 47, No. 3, pp. 361–382.

Giddens, A. (1990). *The Consequences of Modernity.* Stanford: Stanford University Press.

Hutton, W. & A. Giddens (Eds.) (2001). *On The Edge. Living with Global Capitalism.* London: Vintage.

Iloanya, J. (2013). *Internationalisation of Higher Education and the Actualisation of Self-Reliance in Botswana's Education Philosophy.* Paper presented at Botho University's International Research Conference, Gaborone, Botswana.

Knight, J. (2008). *Higher Education in Turmoil.* The changing world of Internationalisation. Rotterdam: Sense Publishers.

Knight, J. (2004). Internationalisation Remodelled: Definition Approaches and Rationales. *Journal of Studies in International Education*, Vol. 8, No. 1, pp. 5–31.

Machingambi, S. (2014). The Impact of Globalisation on Higher Education: A Marxist Critique. *Journal of Sociology*, Vol. 5, No. 2, pp. 207–215.

Mann, M. (2013). *The Sources of Social Power: Volume 4, Globalisations 1945–2011*. Cambridge: Cambridge University Press.

Mishra, R. (2013) Globalisation and Higher Education: Threat or Opportunity? *International Journal of Humanities and Social Sciences*, Vol. 1, No. 1, pp. 39–49.

Morozov, E. (2013). To Save Everything, Click Here: Technology, Solutionism, and the urge to Fix Problems that don't exist. London: Allan Lane.

Naido, V. (2006). International Education: A tertiary-level industry update. *Journal of Research in International Education*, Vol. 5, No. 1, pp. 323–345.

Robinson, W. (2004). *A Theory of Global Capitalism: Production, Class and State in a Transnational World*. Baltimore, M.D: The John Hopkins University Press.

Sehoole, C. (2006). Internationalisation of Higher Education in South Africa: A Historical Review. *Perspectives in Education*, Vol. 24, No. 4, pp. 1–13.

Teichler, U. (2007). *Higher Education Systems: Conceptual Frameworks, Comparative Perspectives, Empirical Findings*. Rotterdam Taipei: Sense Publishers.

University of Botswana (2006). *Policy on Internationalisation*. Gaborone.

Wallerstein, I. (1998). *Utopistics: Or, Historical Choices of the Twenty-First Century*, New York: The New Press.

Yang, R. (2004). Openness and Reform as Dynamics for Development: A Case study of internationalisation of South China University of Technology. *Higher Education*, Vol. 47, No. 5, pp. 473–500.

Zeleza, P. (2013). *Internationalisation of Higher Education in Africa*. Sarua.

Chapter 4
The Native Speaker Is Alive and Kicking

Zane Siraj Sinno

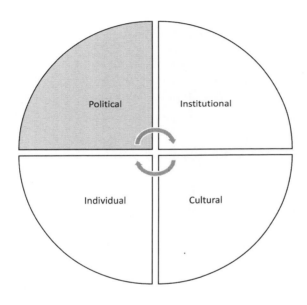

Introduction

This chapter is an important contribution to the book on Globalisation of Higher Education, as it examines globalisation relative to the role of Global English in higher education. I concentrate on globalisation, the role the English language played in globalisation, the role and employability trends of NNEST (non-native English-speaking teachers) and the NEST (native English-speaking teachers), as well as the spread of a globalised form of education through MOOCs (Massive Open Online Courses) and offshore universities. The discussion focuses primarily on the Arab world and Lebanon specifically. Reading this chapter, you will gain the following three insights into:

1. the role of the English language in the globalisation of higher education, with a focus on Lebanon and the Arab speaking part of the world.

2. discussions on the role of NEST, NNEST, NS, and NNS for both the role of the teacher and for globalisation issues.

3. reflections on further development of English-teaching as a profession.

Let me start by contextualising myself in relation to the chapter. There is one week before this chapter's due date. I ran towards work, late for my office hours. As I forged my way towards the campus, I stopped in my track when I saw a taxi parked on the sidewalk. On the back windshield of the car, in large type size, I could read, *"Taxi driver speaks very good English Tel no. ….."*

I found this very reflective of my context, Beirut, Lebanon, where multilingualism is the norm irrespective of profession or socioeconomic status. In Lebanon, Arabic is the official language with three major second languages: English, French, and Armenian.

I am by birth an Arab who grew up with English as my L1 because I was educated in American schools throughout my childhood and grew up conversing in English at home with my siblings. Relocating from one country to the other because of my father's career in the foreign service, we had to acquire a new language every 3 – 4 years, but the English language remained the main constant anchor in our lives. Notwithstanding, because English is not my language by birth, my mother tongue, I am what could be categorised as a non-native English speaking teacher (NNEST) at the American University of Beirut (AUB), teaching English to what are also known as non-native speakers (NNS) of English. In the 21st century, I am one of the 80% of NNEST (Canagarajah, 1999) and my students are among the 603 million L2 speakers of English (Ethnolgoue, 2015). For my students and me, the English language is the access key to indispensable information without which one would become irrelevant in a rapidly changing globalised world of technological advancement.

Lebanon may be too small a country (10,452 km^2) to warrant a chapter in an edited volume on globalisation in higher education. However, with an estimated population of 6,071,981 (Countrymeters, 2016) and 18 religious sects, Lebanon is an interesting country of hybridity and intersection. Located in the centre of the Middle East at the cross point of east and west, with borders with Israel and war-torn Syria, Lebanon has consistently found itself at the centre of media headlines and international interest. Dubbed as the battleground of the Middle East (Hirst, 2011), it has evidenced multiple wars, the most critical of which was a 15-year civil war (1975–1990) and is currently suffering from economic, social, and security ramifications from the spillover of the war in neighbouring Syria, as a result of which over a ballpark figure of one million Syrian refugees tax the depleted Lebanese educational, health, and social infrastructure.

Globalisation

Globalisation is a term that has been defined ad infinitum. Scholte (2000:14) confirms that the much-disputed concept of globalisation *"has become a heavily loaded word. People have linked the notion to pretty-well every purported contemporary social change, including an emergent information age, a retreat of the state, the demise of traditional cultures, and the advent of the postmodern epoch. In normative terms, some people have associated 'globalization' with progress, prosperity and peace. For others, however, the word has conjured up deprivation, disaster and doom."* Mostly, however, it is agreed that globalisation is allied with internationalisation, blurred boundaries, and the deterirtorialisation of relationships. The much contested positive or negative appraisal of globalisation is one of the main features of globalisation literature.

This elusive nature of the term in the literature on globalisation qualifies the presence of both proponents as well as opponents of globalisation. The proponents view it as the interconnection and interdependence of various cultures and countries, the creation of financial and economic webs as well as opportunities, and rapid development, primarily enabled by improved means of communication and technological advancement. This interdependence is believed by some to promote interest in peace, presumably because of common interests, improved living standards, and the generation of opportunities through what Friedman (1999:45) calls the *"democratization of technology"* and the *"democratization of finance"*.

The price tag for such valuable connectivity and rapid change is, however, as Graddol (1997) asserts, uncertainty and the loss of traditional jobs as well as much of the familiar, resulting in some alienation and opposition. Tonkin (2003:321) rightly argues that there is an ugly side to globalisation: *"the exploitation of cheap labour, the concentration of extreme wealth in a small number of hands, and the growing gap between the technological haves and have-nots."* There is the view that globalisation is the process of the Americanisation/Westernisation of the world to promote and safeguard American/Western interests, the McDonaldisation (Ritzer, 1996) of society or the creation of what Barber (1996) calls the McWorld, a world appeased by an abundance of commodities and a certain degree of affluence neither of which are equitably distributed.

Globalisation and the dominance of the English Language vs. linguistic protectionism and purism

The English language has spread throughout the world to become one of the most traded languages. In fact, *The Economist* described it as *"[i] mpregnably established as the world standard language: an intrinsic part of the global communications revolution"* (Graddol, 1997:2). A press release about the British Council's 2000 project reported that 1,400 million of the world's population live in countries where English has an official status, one-fifth of the world's population is relatively competent in English, and the other four-fifths indubitably feels the pressures of English, which has become *"the main language of books, newspapers, airport and traffic control, international business and academic conferences, science technology, diplomacy, sport, international competitions, pop music and advertising"* (Dieu, 2005:para 2). More recent statistics by Statista, a statistic portal, reveals 375 million "native speakers" to 1500 million speakers of other origins (The Most Spoken Languages, 2016).

That globalisation and language spread go hand in hand and that language is not regarded as a neutral player in the globalisation formula is obvious. The literature abounds, in particulars of how the English language was a tool for the spread of the globalisation and hence the dominance of the USA, American culture, Westernisation, and both local linguistic and cultural marginalisation.

In the Arab world, the supremacy of the English language has also been connected with the fear of the possible disintegration of the Arabic language as well as the Arab identity. Chapters in Al-Issa & Dahan's edited volume *Global English and Arabic: Issues of Language, Culture and Identity* (2011) clearly reflect this apprehension about the Arabic language's prospects with global English in the formula. In the introduction, Al-Issa & Dahan (2011:xi) underscore this *"growing problem between the spread of global English and the tendency of Arabic to lessen in prominence."* The authors voice their concern about the eclipsing of Arabic and stress the importance of bilingualism in place of global English as the medium of communication but also confirm that many academic institutions are decreasing the role of Modern Standard Arabic (MSA) in favour of increasing the role of English. This concern for the incursion on local languages is again one of the dominant universal themes in the literature on globalisation.

Troudi & Jendli (2011) recognise how their student sample was aware of the importance of proficiency in the English language for the local and global workplace but were also concerned about the prospects of Arabic in the face of English. Sinno (2008:114) also reports similar concerns for the Lebanese student sample, one of whom typically stated that *"the globalization of the English language have some disadvantages affecting the arab world and mostly Lebanon. Actually, Lebanese students in school study their math and science subjects in foreign languages; thus their Arabic skills became weaker. And as they say each language is a big part of its culture, therefore, Lebanese people are loosing a part of their culture and filling it by foreign cultures."* (Grammatical errors in the original text have been retained). In parallel, Zughol (2015) informs of how Wajeeha Al Bhareena, Chairperson of Bahrain's Women Society, complained about how the English language had taken over not only the Arabic language but also, due to the influence of the media, Arab culture and habits.

In light of the rampant concern for linguistic and cultural heritage, calls for linguistic protectionism seem to be the inevitable predictable consequence. Yasser Suleiman (2011:139) informs of the passing of linguistic protective laws in Iraq under Saddam Hussein's reign and in Syria in 2007. He explains how Kamal Muhammad, a professor of Arabic, speaks of *"linguistic and cultural Western foreignisation"* as an *"epidemic that has infected the body of the nation, leading to 'confusion and anxiety' … todayism, the acceptance of the superiority of the imported language… and the inferiority of the national heritage."* The permeation of English into Arabic has, according to Muhammad, "disfigured" Arabic and turned it into scentless "artificial flowers."

Pennigton (2014) reports that 1500 researchers and educators gathered at the International Conference for Arabic Language in Dubai to tackle the pervasive problem of disenchantment with Arabic and attraction to English. An assistant professor of Arabic, Yehiya Mohamed, complained that *"They [students] think English is cool and Arabic has nothing to do with being modern and being cool"* (Pennigton, 2014:para. 3). Mohamed added that *"We live in a completely westernised culture so students are not proud of their identity and culture."* The different voices in the conference clearly linked the Arabic language to Arab heritage, to Arab identity, perceived to have plummeted from the peak of culture and development in days of old to an all-time low. It was clearly time to address the need to regain confidence in the Arab identity and language. It must be noted, however, that Suleiman (2011) rightly warns that a proactive approach with an increased openness to change and linguistic flexibility more characteristic of the times may be more sensible than an "alarmist" approach.

Similar calls for linguistic protectionism are equally pervasive in the developed countries. The adulteration of a good number of world languages with the English language has resulted in language regulation in many countries throughout the world. Kato, a professor of linguistics at Sugiyama, claims that the integration of words from the West reveals that *"We Japanese have an inferiority complex over language which has turned into a dangerous longing ... Japanese youngsters are taking a distance from Japanese and favoring katakana words. If you go into a clothing store that caters to young people, you'll find that everything is in English"* (French, 2002:para. 12). In Japan, *Katakana* is used for writing words adopted from other languages, mostly English, but with an added local tinge. Exchanges using Katakana raised eyebrows, particularly when it flawed intergenerational and business communication. Reinhardt (n.d., para. 5) tells of a similar concern for the burgeoning infusion of the French language with English words as a growing concern for French officials and how the French Minister of Development and Francophony expressed her concern by illustrating this contamination in her humorously cautionary letter to professionals: *"Soyons clairs, je n'ai rien contre le fait de drafter des to-do list, de benchmarker sans retenue, d'établir des process par confcall et de forwarder le tout avec entrain, mais j'ai un vrai feeling: cette langue française est une chance, un atout qui mérite d'être exploité."* (Translates as *"Let's be clear, I have nothing against drafting to-do lists, benchmarking with no reservations, to establish processes by conference call, and to forward all this with pleasure, but I have a real feeling: this French language is a chance, a gift to be exploited."*). The English language, in other words, should not overpower the indigenous languages.

The Register Guard (1994) informs of how the French Parliament prohibited use of 3,500 foreign words, mostly English, among which were words like bulldozer, cheeseburger (which was to be ordered as hamburger avec fromage), chewing gum, and software. In 2013, *mot-dièse* was substituted for the trending word, *hashtag*. Likewise, Russia banned the assimilation of linguistic profanities in the arts from the English language in 2014.

NEST / NNEST / NS / NNS

One cannot discuss globalisation and language globalisation without tackling the role of the native English language speaker (NS) and the native English language teacher (NEST) with the accompanying baggage. In fact, Phillipson (1992) chronicles their role as the bread and butter of language globalisation in the creation of a business, linguistic, and cultural imperialism. In the past, the native speaker was regarded as a linguistic model. The literature attributes responsibility for this discriminatory situation to the Chomskyan (1965, 1986) portrayal of the idealised native speaker-hearer and the TESOL (Teachers of English to the Speakers of Other Languages) founding principles, which claimed ownership of the English language and set up the native speaker model as the standard for both teacher and student (Selvi, 2014). In 1985, Kachru developed the Three Circle Model to replace the native speaker, second language speaker and foreign language speaker categorisation and to classify speakers of English in what was believed to be a less hierarchal representation: the inner circle, populated by speakers whose mother tongue was English from the USA, England, Australia, Canada, and so on; the outer circle, populated by speakers colonised by Great Britain for whom English functioned as a lingua franca and an L2 but not a native tongue; and the expanding circle for whom English served as the medium for international communication and was learned as a foreign or additional language, such as in China. The inner circle is considered "norm setting," the outer circle "norm developing," and the expanding circle "norm dependent." However, such segmentations were deemed unrealistic by the facts on the ground with speakers of English eluding such a single belonging. Widdowson (1994:385) declared that English was "*not a possession which they [native speakers] lease out to others, while still retaining the freehold. Other people actually own it.*" Graddol (2014:n.p.) propitiously says, "*I don't think anyone can get away with this kind of taxonomy now. The world is much more complicated.*"

Appreciative of the rapidly changing role of English, the diverse creative ways in which it was molded and the new norms developed. McArthur (1987:97) developed the Wheel Model of World Englishes. This revision of Kachru's model with its single standard English in favour of one circle segmented into eight equal parts, each of which was further subdivided into multiple standard Englishes. At the centre of the circle is World Standard English. The eight segments are all on equal standing in McArthur's (1987) model with four standard Englishes (American Standard English, British-Irish Standard English, Canadian Standard English, and Australian, New Zealand, South Pacific Standard English) and four Standard(ising) Englishes (West, East & South(ern) African Standard(ising) English, South Asian Standard(ising) English, East Asian Standard(ising) English. Each slice contains additional subdivisions representing different Englishes. This model, unlike models conventionally covered in the literature, seems to account for the World Englishes approach by acknowledging the different versions of English gaining prominence throughout the world.

McArthur's (1987) dismantling of the three concentric circles, with its placement of the native speaker and "standard English" as the norm setter, reckoned with, for example, Kenyan English, whose norm setter is not the "native speaker" but the Kenyans themselves as they interact with their context and the global world, creating new norms as the need arises. In fact, Graddol (2014) argues there is no Standard English. One could argue, however, that standard(ising) languages and speakers are still in the process of becoming what the standard has already become. In other words, vestiges of the potentially prejudicial dichotomy between standard/native and non-standard/ standardising remain.

Yet another defining moment was Paikeday's (1985:12) *The Native*

Speaker Is Dead! and the declaration that "*the native speaker exists only as a figment of linguists' imagination.*" The term "native speaker" was gradually problematised and alternative less "othering" labels suggested by different scholars, such as *language expertise* and *language loyalty* (Rampton, 1999); *primary, proficient,* or *dominant user,* accentuating effective communication as opposed to birthplace; and *multi-competent speaker* (Cook, 1991), foregrounding the difference in operations of the learner's linguistic and cognitive resources (Andreou & Galantomos, 2009).

In the 1990s, interest in the NNS began to gain momentum. Braine (1999) published an edited volume titled, *Non-Native Educators in English Language Teaching,* including publications from the viewpoint of the NNS. Brut-Griffler & Samimy (1999:428) inform of a seminar whose purpose was to validate NNS as professionals in the field of ELT and dissolve the native-nonnative speaker divide marginalising them. They called for positioning "*the NNS professionals at the center rather than at the periphery by discarding the native-nonnative dichotomy as the main construct through which they are conceived.*"

Phillipson's (1992) *Linguistic Imperialism* further unsettled the grounds with the native speaker fallacy and in 1994 Medgyes (1994) further underscored the need to re-examine the normalised assumptions on which TESOL and ELT were based. Many scholars have queried whether the native speaker was "*intrinsically better qualified*" (Phillipson 1992:194) than the non-native speaker (e.g. Phillipson, 1992; Canagarajah, 1999). In fact, the non-native speaker is by default multilingual which certainly is conducive to a better understanding of the learners' needs. In addition, the shared cultural values and common language are invaluable advantages, making the use of students' native language / mother tongue, previously shunned in academia, an à la mode added value.

Nonetheless, preferential treatment of the NSET persisted at the expense of the NNEST. Interestingly, in a doctoral study conducted in the USA (2003), Ahmar Mahbood reports a preference for hiring NESTs in the MA TESOL programme (accounting for the low 7.9% NNESTs hire) in spite of the high number of foreign students. The study, however, also found positive and negative student perceptions of both NEST and NNEST, showing that it was not a simple preference for the native but his methodology, pedagogy, teaching practices, and cultural variables, whereas the NNEST was appreciated for other traits, like being a multicultural language learner herself. Similarly, Selvi's (2010) investigation of job postings under TESOL Career Center and Dave's ESL Café concludes that being a native speaker was the main requirement in the job market. Ruecker & Ives' (2014:750) research into the preference for the NEST in TESOL, with focus on websites announcing teaching positions in Southeast Asia, further corroborates a link between *"white privilege and native speaker privilege."* In fact, examining posts for employment on the TEFL (Teaching English as a Foreign Language) page, one immediately notes that being a native speaker is fundamental and that the term is still very actively used on the websites advertising academic positions not only for schools but also for higher education. In addition, an article posted on the British Council website informs that 70% of the employment posts are for NESTs and that some employers automatically discount NNEST applicants.

On the other hand, TEFL Equity Advocates was established in April 2014 to oppose such discriminatory practices in the TEFL (Teaching English as a Foreign Language)/TESL (Teaching English as a Second Language) industry. Crystal is quoted on the website as saying: *"If I were in charge of a language-teaching institution, I would want to know four things about applicants: are they fluent? are they intelligible? do they know how to analyse language? are they good teachers? I would not be interested in where they were born, what their first language was,"* while Jeremy Harmer notes his support for *"the ending of discrimination against more than 96% of the teachers of English in the world. Or maybe 98%... or more..."* (TEFL Equity Advocates, 2016).

Notwithstanding all these interventions in favour of the NNEST, not being a native speaker does become an issue for NNESTs who are often subject to hiring discrimination and inequitable treatment in language programmes all over the world, irrespective of competing qualifications. Medgyes (2006:432) quotes a rejection letter sent to an NNEST applicant as saying, *"I am afraid we have to insist that all our teachers are native speakers of English. Our students do not travel halfway around the world only to be taught by a non-native speaker (however good that person's English may be."* Phillipson (1992) adds that NESTs are paid higher salaries than NNEST in the periphery. Moussa & Llurda (2008) also acknowledge the staying power of the allegedly deposed native speaker misconceptions.

Such confirmations of discrepancy in hiring practices and treatment are perplexing when one also bears in mind that the ratio of NNS to NS can be approximated at 5:1 (Crystal, 2014).

Not surprisingly, this discrimination is equally typical of the linguistic landscape in the Arab world, both in schools and in institutions of higher education, and is mostly uncontested. Such biased practices in favour of the NSET are unmistakably discernible as one notes the difference in salaries, preferential treatment, and greater opportunities for professional visibility and promotion. Griffin (2014) fittingly blogs that: *"As someone from the UK who teaches English as a foreign language, the country of my birth is a huge advantage to me. As has been well documented on this blog, I am much more likely to get a job than someone from Japan, Algeria or Brazil, no matter how qualified or experienced they are. For some students, having a native speaker teacher has a certain cachet, as in most countries it is unusual and many of them think that it means they have a better teacher as a result. So, both employers and students seem to think that because I'm English, I must be a better teacher, which has got to be good for me."*

Ma's (2012) report affirms that NNESTs have not only confronted inequitable employment opportunities but have also been disrespected and had their authority questioned with explicit reservations about their qualifications. For example, Al-Issa & Dahan (2011:7) inform that the Abu Dhabi Education Council recruited 1000 native speakers in 2010 to teach alongside Arab teachers for every class. They say that the *"rationale behind the recent move is that the children must have English as part of their daily instructions from primary school. …. Not just any speaker of English is acceptable but only those who are native speakers,"* arguing that *"this is extremely worrisome, because in the UAE and the Arab world generally, a native speaker is often given carte blanche to a teaching job just by virtue of their native fluency in English. …this new batch of 1,000 has never been lauded in the news, for anything other than their native language, no one has praised or mentioned the degrees they hold or their years of teaching experience, if any, they have with young children."* Arguably, such a system implies a lesser appreciation of the local hire, which is most probably conveyed to the students.

The vociferous and representative resentment in Al-Issa & Dahan's (2011) tone speaks volumes about the underlying feelings of NNESTs in the Arab world, suffering second-rate standing from their own in favour of preferential treatment of NEST. Former President of the American University of Beirut, John Waterbury (2003:41), appositely states that *"For this market, the word 'American' is to education what 'Swiss' is to watches."*

It is relevant to underscore at this point that "native speaker norms" and "native speakerism" are still locally upheld in spite of the translingual approach as well as the conceptions of WE (World Englishes), EIL (English as an International language), and ELF (English as a lingua franca) where variations in the standard use are the norm. Linguistic proficiency and native speakerism, previously the target of language learners, metamorphosed into a non-issue for speakers of world English, the "non-native speakers", since their linguistic goal was communication and not native-speaker proficiency (Crystal, 2014). In spite of this, the NNEST teaches in the Arab world following the ousted Chompskyan ideal native speaker. It is still the trend to teach the Standard English language overlooking the fact that the standard itself has fragmented into different World Englishes that could be as different from each other as completely different languages. Also discounted is the understanding that World Englishes, EIL and ELF have inexorably become much more accommodating of different users' appropriation of the language to individual and contextual needs, of what Firth (1996) calls a "let it pass" principle where getting the bottom line message is what counts in the communication process. The NNEST tends to be more Catholic than the Pope!

Self-marginalisation and the Arab identity inferiority complex

In the 2003 TESOL conference, the terms *Non-Native Speaker* (NNS) and *Native Speaker* (NS) were used in 20 studies, mostly and surprisingly, by NNS (Llurda 2006). This usage is explained by the NNS's presumed feeling of inferiority as a speaker of English, by the lack of confidence in his own pedagogy as an NNEST in spite of the recent outpour of validation for the NNESTs. However, this issue seems more complex; I believe that there is more to this. Self-perception is naturally impacted by others' perception. I feel that what I have dubbed the Arab identity inferiority complex (Sinno, 2008) and Amin's (2006) metaphor of the *khawaja* are more reasonable explanations. Amin (2006:9) speaks of the *"khawaga or the foreigner complex (that is a feeling of interiority to Europeans or Americans) that many Arabs have, especially when victory is combined with a constant harping by the media commanded by the victors that they possess not only power but all things good. If people are not immediately fooled into thinking that the most powerful is also the best at first sight, then with time and constant trumpeting of this as truth, they likely will be."* Amin (2006:12) describes how the Arabs are impressed by Western power, affluence, and advancement to the extent that they *"ape the foreigner, and they are often ready to follow them in ridiculing the customs of their countrymen."*

It is fair to assume that such a feeling of inferiority is more prominent after 9/11, with the subsequent war on terror and rampant Islamophobia (note that everything Arab is equated with Moslem). According to one of the participants in the study *The Impact on Language Learning of Lebanese Students' Attitude Towards English in the Context of Globalization and Anti Americanism* (Sinno, 2008:125), Arabs imitated the Americans because they were the most powerful nation and the world looked up to them. *"That might be why people tend to know English more / America being the strongest country / You wanna try your best to be like them / So you speak their language and you become uhmmmmmmmmm / More widely able to communicate because many people / Try to be more American they they uhmmmmmmmm / They try to forget they are Arabs / They try to be more / Like the American people / Without the Arab origin."* Obviously, it is not becoming to be an imitator to the extent of denying what one is, explaining the self-distancing from this act by use of the third person plural. The Arab inferiority comes at a price though since participants felt stripped (*naked*) and in the dark (*shadow*): *"When you lose the economy / And you / And you as a naked / Or in the shadow / The country in the shadow / Everyone wants to be an allied to the most powerful country / So he'll give in and the language / And when he does / He's gonna / Because now he is depending on them to supply him / So really the most powerful / On the economical level / Everybody has to learn the language"* (Sinno, 2008:126).

Thus, participants explicitly expressed their perception of the English language being indirectly forced on the mediocre Arab identity (*Everybody has to learn the language*), which needs to follow the USA if it is ever to have any hope of becoming something. The fact remains that the Arab identity is poor (*naked*) and the Arab countries are in *the shadow* where they need the West for the fruits of progress: technology, education, information, and above all, the English language. Sinno (2012) corroborates this normalised acceptance of the superior status of the English language and culture.

The *Arab identity inferiority complex* is a major issue that needs to be addressed and problematised not only in globalised higher education but also in secondary education, on the levels of both NNS and NNEST. Students need to be made aware of the victim status they resign themselves to and encouraged to take charge of their own status, critically appraise and screen the causes, something only two respondents in the 2008 Sinno study did, while the rest attributed blame to others. This signals the need for student empowerment, accountability, and constructive self-enhancement.

Analogously, NNESTs need to have faith in their pedagogy and be resistant to *anglocentricity* and *professionalism* (Phillipson, 1992). Anglo centricity is when other languages are judged and viewed through the lens of the standards and norms of the English language, thereby granting the latter a superior status. The English language becomes the norm by which other languages are judged. Professionalism is the favouring of ELT pedagogy. Anglo centricity and professionalism are tools for one language (here English) to dominate other languages according to Phillipson (1992).

This empowerment of teachers is necessary so they are not "*the dupes of overpowering social structures and events, but active, reflective agents in the ongoing construction of social reality*" (Block & Cameron, 2002:4). Some administrative changes would be necessary because in Lebanon the outdated myth of the native speaker superiority remains, notably to the detriment of the local teachers and hence the students. Throughout my long career as an NNEST, I have seen different teaching practices, new buzzwords, all adopted but mostly not adapted. The NNESTs need to believe that, with faith and perseverance, they are equally capable of producing knowledge and pedagogies that are not only applicable to but more suitable for the context *they* are most familiar with.

Preference for English

As noted earlier, globalisation, the power of the USA and the UK, and the spread of global English have been linked as collaborators, partners, whether calculatedly (Phillipson, 1992) or naturally and accidentally

(Crystal, 2003; Pennycook, 1994; Kachru, 1986). This relationship has resulted in a preference for the English language mostly for utilitarian reasons. In fact, English is deemed the language of the workplace, the media, intercultural communication, and practically everything else. One of the respondents in Sinno's (2008:107) clearly expresses a need to integrate with a globalised world and says that to do so English is mandatory: "On a personal level, the English language will also help me to reach personal ambitions and success in the business and social domain. Ultimately that is why I am studying English which will in turn allow me to communicate with as much people as possible & in different places. Consequently, the English language has made the whole world largely dependent on the language itself. Various aspects of life will be extinct without the English language and that is why it will remain important for centuries to come."

Participants in the study generally showed a preference for the English language because it was associated with positive utilitarian gains, one of which is that it is believed to be the equivalent of the *metric system* for communication, an ELF. This is significant in a globalised world where intergroup communication is essential because it facilitates communication between different peoples, potentially providing the underprivileged people some equal opportunity in a conflicted world, a *key* and *passport* to access the global workplace on a par with others.

Equally important, it seems to provide a key to tolerance and understanding of the other. This is important in the context where the Arab feels substandard: "Personally, I think it's great that the world have now a united language. It helps in all ways of life and it gives opportunities to young people like us outside. But it also helps the people to get closer together despite our origins and culture. In a time of war, we can always communicate and understand each other because in the end we are all humans" (Sinno, 2008:105). Another participant says, "I, myself, being English educated, have come to see the value of my education. Knowing this language has helped open many doors in my career as well as higher education. I am able to interact with diverse people having diverse cultures through this common language. Because of my English oriented educational facilities, I have been exposed to a modern culture and been taught to accept others in their uniqueness" (Sinno, 2008:105). Table 1 summarises the participants' perception of the English language.

Communication Metric System		Self-Protection & Enhancement		Knowledge Medium	
Personal	Universal	Personal	Universal	Personal	Universal
Key to communication	Standard language	Opens	Means	Tool	Means used to transport information and studies universally
Tool of communication	Standardised code without which understanding would be much more difficult	Bridge	Bridge	Device	Role for the advancement of humanity
Connects	Reference in communication	Passport			World's international business language
Like a compass when you get lost; you will just use it, and you will sure find someone to communicate with	A tool which increases social bonds between different nations and cultures	Weapon			Most important contemporary language
	Unifies the world	Door			
	Basic necessary device in communication all over the world	Key			
	Connects				
	Breaks cultural barriers				
	Eliminates obstacles and the barriers between different people				

Table 1: Participants' perception of the English Language.

Similarly, Lindsey (2015:para.3) notes how for Hamdy, *"Learning Arabic, as an engineer, doesn't add much, but learning English adds a lot. To get into a good multinational company, for sure it's useful."* Lindsey recognises that this valuing of English as a medium of instruction is responsible for the spread of English medium teaching academic institutions of higher education in the Arab world, also adding, however, that many also recognise how this may jeopardise Arab identity and promote social inequalities. In fact, Deena Boraie, the Dean of the School of Continuing Education at the American University in Cairo, says *"English is a divider but also a dream"* (cited in Lindsey, 2015:para. 6).

Lindsey (2015) notes how, in the UAE and Qatar, English has been advanced through the subsidising of off-shore American universities and through being the medium of instruction in national universities. The uproar it created in some milieus and the prevention of access are reflective of the resistance and schism around the global role of English in academia: true some saw in the global English the unavoidable gateway to success and progress but, equally true, others feared the denunciation and renouncement of identity and roots and regarded the English language as a gatekeeper rather than a gateway. In fact, the decision to restrict the medium of instruction solely to English in Qatar was resisted for the social divide it nourished. Instruction in Arabic had to be reinstituted because English was not equally accessible to everybody. Nonetheless, Lindsey also notes the incompatibility of Egypt's public educational system with the requirements of English medium instruction in the sciences, potentially depriving students of majoring in the valued fields (engineering, medicine, and so on). This engendered an increase in private schools and universities to remedy the deficiencies in English language proficiency, further amplifying the divide because the average tuition fee of these private schools is 30 times the minimum wage. In other words, the wealthy had the opportunity to gain the education that could open doors to the global market while the economically deprived were stripped of the skill that could help them gain access to wealth.

MOOCs

Even though Massive Open Online Courses (MOOCs) are regarded by some as one of the facets of globalisation—hegemonic, ideological tools—the scope of this chapter cannot allow for more than a brief discussion of MOOCs in the Arab world. As their name indicates, MOOCs are courses delivered online to any number of registrants who want to sign up for the course. MOOCs are presented through short recorded weekly lectures, each of which consists of several 3 to 5-minute video talks. Participants attend the weekly video lectures asynchronously, complete weekly assignments, and take a weekly test. Courses last between 4 and 10 weeks and certificates of completion are awarded upon fulfilment of all the requirements. The courses are mostly free of charge, explaining the high number of registrants, typically from all over the world.

It could be said that MOOCs are the natural development or aftermath of web-enhanced courses, blended learning, and online web-based courses. Notably, MOOCs are notorious for their high dropout rates (estimated at 87% by Onah *et al.*, 2015). It is important to note, however, that the definition of course completion for MOOCs differs from the one for traditional courses, be they online, blended, web-enhanced, or face to face. Does one qualify as having completed the course if she has attended all the course lectures but has not completed the assignments and assessments? Which week of the course is considered the cut-off date for being classified as having completed the course or dropped out? How many missed assessments or activities result in failure? If one is indifferent towards being awarded a certificate but interested in the course content, completes all the lectures, mentally drafts (but does not submit) the assignments and answers the assessment questions, could we, in reality, say that he has not completed the course? Whatever the answer to such questions may be, no matter how ill-reputed MOOCs are for the high dropout rate among other criticisms, MOOCs have been considered as a possible solution to some of the problems facing educational needs throughout the world and specifically in the Arab world.

In 2013, MOOC platforms mushroomed in the Arab world with the launching of four MOOC platforms. Edraak from Jordan's Queen Rania Foundation was the first MOOC in the Arab world, in Arabic, and advertised as serving the Arab world. Edraak offers courses translated from its consortium partners as well as courses designed by Arab instructors in diaspora or regional instructors. I was privileged to be among the first from AU delivering a MOOC on Business Communication, in English. Rwaq in Saudia Arabia, MenaVersity of Lebanon, and SkillAcademy of Egypt are the three other MOOC platforms. The platforms were all Arabic content providers, except for SkillAcademy, which is in English.

It seems that MOOC providers in the Arab world felt the need to make education available for the Arab population to bridge the digital and educational gap. Additionally, the need for MOOCs is justified by what some consider as the poor quality of education in the Arab world (Edraak: Towards a Better Arab World, n.d.; El Dahshan, 2014). MOOCs would thus either supplement what academic institutions are unable to provide or provide learning opportunities. Such platforms bring the potential of higher or continued education to a population, 80% of which is fluent only in Arabic and whose general academic performance surpasses their English language proficiency (Edraak: Towards a better Arab world, n.d.). Thus, they provide prospects for the underprivileged and those who lack access to higher education (Dakak, cited in El Dahshan, 2104:para. 16).

While Edraak covers the technical support for the MOOC courses (video production, teacher or research assistants, and so on), the instructors volunteer their time to both create and deliver the content, design activities, write up the unit tests, and run the course with TA support. Preparation time (preparing and recording content), is estimated to take up to 100 hours while running the course takes between 8 and 10 hours according to Edraak. As indicated by Nafez Dakkak, founding director of Edraak, they have reached over 400,000 learners, delivered 28 courses, and granted 25,000 certificates (2015). More recent estimates approach one million learners. Edraak (n.d.) describes their venture as an attempt *"to 'get our voice back' and tell 'our' side of the story."* In 2016, The American University of Beirut announced its intention to continue its venture into MOOCs.

This contests Lane and Kinser's (2012:para.7) declaration that *"MOOCs are now at the forefront of the McDonaldization of higher education,"* that they reproduce the authority of the centre, *"play the center against the periphery,"* and *"strengthen the ivory towers by enabling a few elite institutions to broadcast their star courses to the masses from the comfort of their protected perches."* It is true that the Arab MOOC platforms also provide access to courses from the Ivy League platforms. Nonetheless, the production of local courses by local scholars to satisfy the needs of the region seems to be an act of resistance, or what Widdowson (1997), Canagarajah (1999), and Appardurai (1996) would consider an act of appropriation and resistance. Leber (2014) confirms that these providers have been *"translating, adapting, and creating MOOCs to fit their own unique needs"* thus breaking the cycle of dependence on the West for content. However, some see US MOOC providers such as Coursera and edX, with which most Arab MOOC providers collaborate, as potentially a new form of imperialism. That Arabic is one of the two fastest increasing MOOCs in the West (Tucker, 2014) may corroborate that. However, it does seem that MOOCs in the Arab world are on the right track of tailoring education to the needs of the Arab world. From my perspective, such initiatives are worthy of respect and encouragement.

Offshore universities

Another feature of the globalisation of higher education is the offshore universities or what I think of as a form of the franchising of higher education. In the past decade, there has been a massive proliferation of off-shore universities in the Arab world. Hanauer & Phan (2011) estimate that approximately 30% of satellite or branch universities are in the Persian Gulf and Qatar. According to Maslen (2015), the United Arab Emirates is the largest "importing" country at 33 universities. Often funded by the Arab host country, the USA, France, and England have established several branches of their Ivy League universities across the world. Bridgestock (2015) speaks of the rising preference of some Arab students to remain in the region and with the development of educational centres making that possible, the option to resort to local alternatives may be inviting. That "preference" may also be explained by stricter visa measures after 9/11 and the widespread Islamophobia.

Arnold, a former president of the American University in Cairo, has referred to this trend as the *"gold rush"* in higher education, with many universities seeking business opportunities outside of the home campus, reminding one of the business model when large corporations developed into transnational corporations (TNCs) and enjoyed a larger segment of the market at the expense of the smaller ventures they overshadow. Altbach (2007) warns that *"it is important to ensure that globalization does not turn into the neocolonialism of the 21st century."* Bridgestock (2015) predicts that, even though Western supremacy in the Arab world remains unthreatened, it will most likely be maintained through education, consultation, and business. Many such offshore universities though have closed down (e.g. George Mason) or risk closure due to low enrolment or oversaturation as universities rushed to open branches.

Conclusion

The American University of Beirut (AUB) seems to be heading in the direction of the globalisation of higher education on several levels. In 2016, the president of AUB informally announced in a town meeting that AUB was considering the opening of international branches. Mention of further developments in online courses and MOOCs has also been made. With globalisation also comes the porous walls as AUB reaches for improved connections with other local and regional academic institutions. Similarly, in the Arab world, globalisation of higher education has been manifested through the dominance of the English language, which resulted in the region's concern for the Arabic language; the prevalence of MOOCs; and the franchising of Western offshore universities in the Arab world that also exported the native educator with the franchise.

In this chapter, I argued that in the Arab world, specifically in Lebanon, the picture of globalisation and the role of the English language are different from what the literature portrays. The realities of globalisation and L2 in higher education are partially uplifting but also daunting. In Lebanon and most of the Arab world, the myth of the NS and the NEST is still alive and kicking along with the discrimination against the NNS and NNEST. We suffer from what Kumaravadivelu (2007) labels as the *"process of self-marginalization,"* and what Sinno (2012:344) identifies as the *"process of internalized colonialism."* I also contend that native speaker norms and native speakerism are still locally upheld in spite of the translingual approach paradigm shift where communication and not mastery of the language is the goal, where *"language norms are open to negotiations"*, and the *"strong ethic of collaboration"* are paramount for the accommodation of linguistic and cultural differences that characterise most communication in the global age (Canagarajah 2013:180). The Arab world would benefit from recognition of the paradigm shift in language teaching, which accommodates the negotiation of meaning as well as the conceptions of WE, EIL, and ELF where variations in the standard use are the norm. In academia, we remain far from Salman Rushdie's (1983, cited in Crystal, 2003:185) belief that *"The people who were once colonized by the language are now rapidly remaking it, domesticating it, becoming more and more relaxed about the way they use it."* The NNEST, as well as the NNS, needs to break from the dependency on and idealisation of the NS, the NEST, and Kachru's three famous circles of speakers of English (Inner, Outer, Expanding).

On a more positive note, I would like to conclude by noting that a new syndrome is currently emerging. The American University was established 150 years ago. In January 2015, it inaugurated its first president of Lebanese origin, Dr. Fadlo Khuri. Formerly a professor and chair of the Department of Hematology Medical Oncology at Emory in Atlanta, USA, Khuri swam against the tide of Lebanese doctors flocking to the USA, or as Salem (2013) would say, Lebanese "doctor in diaspora." The president's inauguration speech is very telling. The main themes were related to much more than simply manufacturing workers endowed with 21st century workplace skills. The message was mainly a call to join hands and collaborate with local, regional and global institutions of higher education; to extend into the community and give back; to create leadership; to reach out into the community and tear down the walls of the ivory tower.

Most interesting though is that Khuri calls for *"mentor[ing] the next generation of giants who will build and rebuild a new Arab world."* His belief in the capabilities of the Arabs and the AUB community is clear as he invokes that *"We have to make AUB a sustainable example of the great 21st Century University, a standard bearer of Arab Liberal Thought, a graduator of university presidents and NGO founders, and changers of businesses, peoples and nation-states and genres. We have to develop new micro-economies in the Arab world, and in Lebanon we have to focus on all of our constituencies equally, irrespective of their ability to pay. If we can accomplish what we have set out to do, I think we can have, I know we can have, a transformative effect on Lebanon, on higher education and in the Arab world."* It is clear that President Khuri is not only the first Lebanese president at AUB, but also one who believes we can restore Arab pride and both Lebanese and Arab leadership. In other words, what I see developing is a new form, not of globalisation, but of glocalisation of higher education. And, yes, we can do it.

About the Author

Zane Siraj Sinno is a lecturer at the Department of English at the American University of Beirut. She can be contacted at this e-mail: zs00@aub.edu.lb

Bibliography

Adham, R. S. & K. O. Lundqvist. (2015). MOOCs as a method of distance education in the Arab World—A review paper. *European Journal of Open, Distance, and E-Learning,* Vol. 18, No. 1, pp. 123–139.

Al-Issa, A. & L. S. Dahan (2011). Global English and Endangered Arabic in the United Arab Emirates. In A. Al-Issa & L. S. Dahan (Eds.), *English and Arabic: Issues of Language, Culture, and Identity.* Bruxelles, BEL: Peter Lang AG, pp. 1–22.

Al-Issa, A. & L. S. Dahan (Eds.) (2011). *Contemporary Studies in Descriptive Linguistics, Volume 31: Global English and Arabic: Issues of Language, Culture, and Identity.* Bruxelles, BEL: Peter Lang AG.

Alseweed, M. A. (2012). University Students' Perceptions of the Influence of Native and Non-native Teachers. *English Language Teaching,* Vol. 5, No. 12, pp. 42–53.

Altbach, P. G. (2007). Globalization and the University: Realities in an Unequal World. Testimony to the Committee on Science and Technology U.S. House of Representatives. *International Handbook of Higher Education.*

Amin, G. (2006). Illusions of Progress in the Arab World: A Critique of Western Misconstruction. Cairo: American University in Cairo Press.

Amin, N. (2001). Nativism, the Native Speaker Construct, and Minority Immigrant Women Teachers of English as a Second Language. *CATESOL Journal,* Vol. 23, No. 1, pp. 89–107.

Amin, N. (1997). Race and the Identity of the Nonnative ESL Teacher. *TESOL Quarterly,* Vol. 31, pp. 580–583.

Andreou, G. & I. Galantomos (2009). The Native Speaker Ideal in Foreign Language Teaching. *Electronic Journal of Foreign Language Teaching,* Vol. 6, No. 2, pp. 200–208.

Appadurai, A. (2001). Globalization. Durham, NC: Duke University Press.

In D. Block & D. Cameron (Eds.), *Globalization and Language Teaching.* London and New York: Routledge.

Braine, G. (Ed.) (1999). *Non-native Educators in English Language Teaching.* Mahwah, NJ: Erlbaum.

Bridgestock, L. (2015). Middle Eastern students abroad: In numbers. *QS Top Universities*. Online Resource: http://www.topuniversities.com/blog/middle-eastern-students-abroad-numbers [Accessed 9 November 2016].

Brutt-Griffler, J. & K. Samimy (1999). Revisiting the Colonial in the Postcolonial: Critical Praxis for Nonnative-English-Speaking Teachers in a TESOL Program. *TESOL Quarterly*, Vol. 33, pp. 413–431.

Canagarajah, S. A. (1999). *Resisting Linguistic Imperialism in English Teaching*. Oxford New York: Oxford University Press.

Canagarajah, S. A. (2013). *Translingual Practice: Global Englishes and Cosmopolitan Relations*. New York: Routledge.

Chomsky, N. (1965). *Aspects of the Theory of Syntax*. Cambridge, Massachusetts: The M.I.T. Press.

Chomsky, N. (1986). *Knowledge of Language: Its Nature, Origin, and Use*. USA: Praeger Publishers.

Cook, V. (1999). Going Beyond the Native Speaker in Language Teaching. *TESOL Quarterly*, Vol. 33, No. 2, pp. 185–209.

Crystal, D. (2003). *English as a Global Language*. Cambridge: Cambridge University Press.

Crystal, D. (2014). Interview with David Crystal. *Tefl Equity Advocates*. Online Resource: http://teflequityadvocates.com/2014/07/06/interview-with-david-crystal/ [Accessed 1 December 2016].

Dakkak, N. (2015). *HAW Talks 2015*. Online Resource: https://www.youtube.com/watch?v=dcxS6TE8UPA [Accessed 1 December 2016].

Davies, A. (1991). *The Native Speaker in Applied Linguistics*. Edinburgh: Edinburgh UP.

Edraak (2015). *Towards a better Arab world*. Online Resource: http://sites.nationalacademies.org/cs/groups/pgasite/documents/webpage/pga_153278.pdf [Accessed 9 November 2016].

El Dahshan, M. (2014). How do you say "MOOC" in Arabic? *Foreign Policy*. Online Resource: http://foreignpolicy.com/2014/03/11/how-do-you-say-mooc-in-arabic/ [Accessed 9 November 2016].

Firth, A. (1996). The Discursive Achievement of English and Conversation Analysis. *Journal of Pragmatics*, Vol. 26, pp. 237–260.

Firth, A. & J. Wagner (1997). On discourse, communication, and (some) fundamental concepts in SLA research. *Modern Language Journal*, No. 81, pp. 285–300.

Frech, H. (2002). To Grandparents, English Word Trend Isn't "Naisu." *The New York Times*. Online Resource: http://www.nytimes.com/2002/10/23/international/asia/23TOKY.html [Accessed 8 October 2016].

Graddol, D. (1997). *The Future of English: A guide to forecasting the popularity of English in the 21st century*. London: The British Council.

Graddol, D. (2005). Spoken Everywhere but at What Price. *The Guardian*. Online Resource: http://www.theguardian.com/theguardian/2005/apr/20/guardianweekly.guardianweekly11 [Accessed 10 December 2016].

Graddol, D. (2014). *IATEFL Harrogate Online 2014*. Online Resource: http://blog-efl.blogspot.com/2014/04/iatefl-harrogate-online-2014-david.html [Accessed 22 November 2016].

Hanauer, E. & A.-H. Phan (2011). *MIDDLE EAST: Global higher education's boldest step*, The Book, p. 185.

Hirst, D. (2011). *Beware of Small States: Lebanon, Battleground of the Middle East*. New York: Nation Books.

Internet World Stat (2015). Online Resource: http://www.internetworldstats.com/stats5.htm [Accessed 9 November 2016].

Kachru, B. B. (1986). *The Alchemy of English: The spread, functions, and models of non native Englishes*. Oxford: Permagon.

Khuri, F. R. (2016). *Presidential Inauguration Ceremony Speech*. Online Resource: https://www.aub.edu.lb/president/Documents/inauguration-speech-fadlo-khuri.pdf [Accessed 14 December 2016].

Kiczkowiak, M. (2014). *Native English-speaking Teachers: Always the right choice?* British Council. Online Resource: https://www.britishcouncil.org/voices-magazine/native-english-speaking-teachers-always-right-choice [Accessed 18 November 2016].

Kumaravadivelu, B. (2007). Cultural Globalization and Language Education. New Haven: Yale University Press.

Lane, J. & K. Kinser (2012). MOOCs and the McDonaldization of Global Higher Education. *The Chronicle of Higher Education*. Online Resource: http://www.immagic.com/eLibrary/ARCHIVES/GENERAL/CHRON_HE/C120928L.pdf [Accessed 20 November 2016].

Lebanon Population (2016). *Countrymeters*. Online Resource: http://countrymeters.info/en/Lebanon [Accessed 2 November 2016].

Lebanon Net Migration Rate. Online Resource: http://www.indexmundi.com/lebanon/net_migration_rate.html [Accessed 2 November 2016].

Leber, J. (2014). *MOOCs Are No Longer a Cultural Export of the West*. Online Resource. http://www.fastcoexist.com/3033132/moocs-are-no-longer-a-cultural-export-of-the-west [Accessed 2 November 2016].

Lee, J. (2005). The Native Speaker: An Achievable Model? *Asian EFL Journal*, Vol. 7, No. 2, pp. 56–65.

Lindsey, U. (2015). How Teaching in English Divides the Arab World. *The Chronicle of Higher Education*. Online Resource. http://search.proquest.com/docview/1692051388?accountid=8555 [Accessed 2 November 2016].

Linguistic Protectionism Eugene (1994). *Register-Guard*. Online Resource: https://news.google.com/newspapers?nid=1310&dat=19940711&id=t t9WAAAAIBAJ&sjid=ousDAAAAIBAJ&pg=3705,2589477&hl=en [Accessed 2 November 2016].

Llurda, E. (2006). *Non-native Language Teachers: Perceptions, Challenges and Contributions to the Profession*. Springer Science & Business Media. New York: Springer.

Ma, L. P. F. (2012). Advantages and Disadvantages of Native- and Non-Native-English-speaking Teachers: Student Perceptions in Hong Kong. *TESOL Quarterly*, Vol. 46, No. 2, pp. 280–305.

Mahboob, A. (Ed.) (2010). *The NNEST Lens in The NNEST Lens: Non-Native English Speakers in TESOL*. NewCastle Upon Tyne: Cambridge Scholars Publishing.

McArthur, A. (1987). The English language. *English Today* 11, 9–13.

Pennycook, A. (1994). The Cultural Politics of English as an International Language. London & New York: Longman.

Maslen, G. (2015). While Branch Campuses Proliferate, Many Fail. University World News, No. 355.

Medgeyes, P. (2014). An Interview with Peter Medgyes—A Teaser. Tefl Equity Advocates. Online Resource: https://teflequityadvocates.com/2014/04/16/an-interview-with-peter-medgyes-a-teaser/ [Accessed 28 November 2016].

Medgyes, P. (2006). Native and Non-native English Speaking Teachers in Vietnam: Weighing the Benefits. *TESL-EJ*, Vol. 6, No. 12.

Medgyes, P. (2014). When the Teacher Is a Non-native Speaker. In M. Celce-Murcia (Ed.), *Teaching English as a Second or Foreign Language*. Beijing: Foreign Language Teaching and Research Press, pp. 429–442.

MOOCs, The Next Arab Spring (2015). Edraak. Online Resource: http://sites.nationalacademies.org/cs/groups/pgasite/documents/webpage/pga_153278.pdf [Accessed 15 November 2016].

MOOCs as a Method of Distance Education in the Arab World—A Review Paper 2015. Online Resource: http://www.eurodl.org/?p=current&article=689 [Accessed 15 November 2016].

Moussu, L. & E. Llurda (2008). Non-native English-Speaking English Language Teachers: History and Research. *Language Teaching*, Vol. 41, No. 3, pp. 315–348.

Mugila, C. (2015). *Moise A. Khayrallah Center for Lebanese Diaspora Studies*. Online Resource: http://lebanesestudies.news.chass.ncsu.edu/2015/02/04/

methods-of-finding-population-statistics-of-lebanese-migration-throughout-the-world/ [Accessed 15 November 2016].

Paikeday, T. (1985). *The Native Speaker Is Dead!* Toronto: Paikeday Publishing Inc.

Pennington, R. (2014). Cool Factor Boost Needed to Ensure Arabic's Survival. *The National.* Online Resource: http://www.thenational.ae/uae/education/cool-factor-boost-needed-to-ensure-arabics-survival [Accessed 15 November 2016].

Phillipson, R. (1992). *Linguistic Imperialism.* Oxford: Oxford University Press.

Reinhardt, L. P. (n.d.). *Anglicisms in France: The French Business World to Blame.* Online Resource: https://e2f.com/5172/ [Accessed 1 December 2016].

Ritzer, G. (1996). *The McDonalization Thesis.* London: Sage.

Salem, P. A. (2013). *The Lebanese doctor in diaspora.* Online Resource: http://www.pasalem.com/articles/newsletter/the-lebanese-doctor-in-diaspora [Accessed 15 November 2016].

Scholte, J. A. (2000). *Globalization: A Criticial Introduction.* New York: Palgrave.

Selvi, A. F. (2014). Myths and Misconceptions About Nonnative English Speakers in the TESOL (NNEST) Movement. *TESOL Journal,* Vol. 5, No. 3.

Sinno, Z. (2008). *The Impact on Language Learning of Lebanese Students' Attitude Towards English in the Context of Globalization and AntiAmericanism.* Unpublished thesis submitted for the degree of Doctor of Education at the University of Leicester. Online Resource: https://lra.le.ac.uk/bitstream/2381/4234/1/2008SirajSinnoZedd.pdf [Accessed 15 November 2016].

Sinno, N. (2012). Navigating the linguistic imperialism, cultural hybridity, and language pedagogy. In A. Al-Issa & L. S. Dahan (Eds.), *English and Arabic: Issues of Language, Culture, and Identity.* Bruxelles, BEL: Peter Lang AG, pp. 335–354.

Statista (2016). *The most spoken languages worldwide.* Online Resource. http://www.statista.com/statistics/266808/the-most-spoken-languages-worldwide/ [Accessed 15 November 2016].

Suleiman, Y. (2011). *Arabic, Self and Identity: A Study in Conflict and Displacement.* Oxford University Press, USA.

TEFLE (2014). *Equity Advocates for Equal Employment Opportunities for Native and Non-native English Speakers in ELT.* Online Resource: https://teflequityadvocates.com/2014/05/11/only-nests-can-provide-a-good-language-model-really/ [Accessed 15 November 2016].

Taylor, J. (2014). *Why I Wish I Was Born a Non-native English Speaker.* Online Resource. http://teflequityadvocates.com/2014/05/20/why-i-wish-i-was-a-non-native-english-speaker-by-james-taylor/ [Accessed 15 November 2016].

Troudi, S. & A. Jendli. (2011). Emirati Students' Experiences of English as a-Medium of Instruction. In Al-Issa, A. & Dahan, L. S. (Eds.), *Contemporary Studies in Descriptive Linguistics, Volume 31: Global English and Arabic: Issues of Language, Culture, and Identity*. Bruxelles, BEL: Peter Lang AG, pp. 23–48.

Tucker, D. (2014). *MOOC List*. Online Resource. https://www.mooc-list.com/instructor/tucker-balch?static=true [Accessed 2 November 2016].

W³ Techs (2016). Online Resource. http://w3techs.com/technologies/overview/content_language/all [Accessed 2 February 2016].

Waterbury, J. (2003). *Hate Your Policies, Love Your Institutions. Foreign Affairs*. Online Resource: https://www.foreignaffairs.com/articles/middle-east/2003–01–01/hate-your-policies-love-your-institutions [Accessed 1 March 2016].

Widdowson, H. G. (1997). The Forum: EIL, ESL, EFL: Global Issues and Local Interests. *World Englishes*, Vol. 16, No. 1, pp.135–146.

Widdowson, H. G. (1994). The Ownership of English Author(s). *TESOL Quarterly*, Vol. 28, No. 2, pp. 377–389.

Zughol, M. R. (2015). *Globalization, the American Empire and the Cultural Politics of English in the Arab/Muslim World*. Online Resource: http://www.ayk.gov.tr/wp-content/uploads/2015/01/ZUGHOUL-Muhammad-Raji-GLOBALIZATION-THE-AMERICAN-EMPIRE-AND-THE-CULTURAL-POLITICS-OF-ENGLISH-IN-THE-ARAB-MUSLIM-WORLD.pdf [Accessed 1 December 2016].

Chapter 5

Globalisation of Higher Education: A Chinese Perspective

Xiaobin Li & Xiaoyang Wang

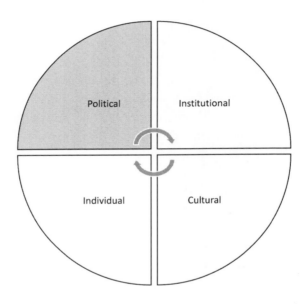

Introduction

This chapter is an important contribution to this book on globalisation of higher education, as understanding a Chinese perspective is meaningful. With 37 million students, the Chinese higher education system is the largest in the world, and it continues to grow (Ministry of Education, 7 April 2016). The Chinese economy is the second largest in the world and is expected to be the largest in a few years. Rudd (2015) assumes the Chinese economic growth rate exceeding 6 percent is probable for the next decade. China is the biggest contributor to peacekeeping missions among the UN Security Council's five permanent members (The Economist, 2014) and the biggest exporter of cultural goods in the world

(UNESCO, 2016). China is the most important source of international students (OECD, 2015). At the same time, it is becoming one of the most important international student destinations (Postiglione, 2015). As more Chinese are interested in learning from developed countries, more people in other countries are interested in learning about China. Like another chapter in this volume (see Iloanya & Mathew, this volume), the focus of this chapter is at the national level.

A gradual globalisation of Chinese higher education began after China opened up to the world in 1978, which brought great transformation to almost all facets of China (He, 2016). In recent years, an increasing number of Chinese scholars have called for the further globalisation of Chinese higher education (Li & Zhao, 2008). Since globalisation is multi-centred, multi-formed, and multi-causal (Kauppinen, 2013), an understanding of world higher education globalisation without a Chinese perspective is incomplete. Throughout the West, knowledge of Chinese higher education has been somewhat limited over the years (Ji, 2014). It is useful to have an understanding of a Chinese perspective on globalisation.

Globalisation is the process of forming the global dimension in higher education, consisting of world systems of knowledge and information flow, networks, and people movement between systems, marked by the quickening of global awareness (Marginson, 2011a). In this chapter, globalisation of higher education is defined as interaction among staff and students from different countries, driven by desires of raising institutional reputation, generating revenues, engaging in academic exchange, studying at renowned foreign institutions, acquiring international experiences, improving one's employability, and immigrating to a country with a better quality of life. The process of globalisation is facilitated by information technology. With the above definition of globalisation, some discussion of higher education internationalisation can be had. An analysis of data from the IDP Australia Database of Research on International Education indicates that "globalisation" is one of the keywords showing steady usage in research on international education published in 2011, 2012, and 2013 (Proctor, 2016). However, globalisation of higher education, at least, must be interaction among higher education systems from different languages, different cultures, and ideally different continents. Growing up in Canada but working in the United States cannot be considered globalisation.

When reading this chapter, you will gain the following three insights:

1. the context of Chinese higher education globalisation;

2. the process, extent, and effects of higher education globalisation in China, and

3. a Chinese perspective on globalisation. The findings of this chapter will contribute to helping us have a better understanding of the globalisation of higher education in the world.

Context

One of the impacts of the discourse about globalisation is to regard services as tradable (Scott, 2016). Economic relations play an important role in education relations (He, 2016), and the General Agreement on Trade in Services includes education as services. When China joined the World Trade Organization and signed the General Agreement on Trade in Services, it stated that it would gradually open its higher education markets, with certain conditions. In many ways the Chinese people have been learning from developed countries since 1978. Most people working in Chinese higher education welcome globalisation, believing it is conducive to Chinese catching up with developed countries (Li & Zhao, 2008). In 2015, 397,635 foreigners went to China to study (Ministry of Education, 2016), and there are also foreigners working in Chinese institutions. In 2015, 523,700 Chinese went overseas for education (Sun & Shi, 2016). In addition, universities from Britain, America, Australia, and other developed countries have established branch campuses or joint programs in China, collaborating with Chinese institutions.

Twenty-first-century globalisation has significantly increased the international dimension of universities (Yang, 2014). There is a growing economisation of education (Robertson & Dale, 2015), and there is a tendency to utilise the conceptual frame of economic globalisation and the increasing trade in educational services worldwide (Svensson & Wihlborg, 2010). There is also a common assumption that universities are primarily promoters of national economic competitiveness (Kauppinen, 2012). There are similarities between globalisation in other countries and in China. Embracing the above tendency and assumption, many Chinese scholars call for increasing the globalisation of Chinese higher education (Feng, 2013; Li & Zhao, 2008). The Chinese leadership also recognizes that outstanding universities can be engines of economic growth (Yang, 2014).

While there are similarities, there are differences because China has its unique geography, history, culture, as well as social and political context. Higher education is always a part of its society (Valimaa & Nokkala, 2014), and it is extremely difficult to detach political and economic rationales from higher education (Lo & Wang, 2014). Nations attempt to provide quality education so that their students can meet the needs of a competitive global economy in different ways (Cheung & Chan, 2010). Unlike most countries in the world, as a Confucian education nation, China has a strong nation-state shaping of structures, funding, and priorities (Marginson, 2011b). China's central government exercises strong regulation over higher education (Gao, 2015), where the ultimate authority to issue degrees does not reside in institutions but belongs to the state (Feng, 2013). The Chinese model for development denotes a central role of the state and places emphasis on efficiency for the sake of accelerating economic growth, which finds its expression in universities (Zha *et al.*, 2015). The moment of the politics of education (Robertson & Dale, 2015) is different in China. In addition, the Chinese culture emphasises a broad interpretation of the meaning of knowledge, while adhering to the Confucian ethical and philosophical tradition (Altbach, 2016; Chen, 2009). Chinese universities reflect a distinctiveness that is different from their Western peers (Zha, 2016). The Chinese welcome globalisation in higher education for reasons that are similar to and different from other countries'.

Although China has a long history of education if Confucius (551–479 BCE) is considered the beginning of Chinese education, at 18 percent the 2012 Chinese entry rate into tertiary-type A education is lower than 58 percent, which is the average of OECD countries (OECD, 2015). In June 2015, approximately 9.4 million Chinese took the higher education entry examination, but only about 7 million would be admitted into various programs in the autumn (CCTV 4, 9 June 2015). It seems that the current supply is not meeting demand. To meet the increasing demand for higher education and to learn from developed countries, globalisation of Chinese higher education continues (van der Wende, 2015).

The Chinese higher education system does poorly on quality indicators

(Postiglione, 2015); China is still a norm taker (Lo & Wang, 2014), facing difficulties in the move from the periphery to the centre (Li & Chen, 2011). There are five "inadequacies" in higher education (Ministry of Education, April 7, 2016), and there is a long way to go for China to become an internationally influential part in the world (Huang, 2015). Building world-class universities became an important policy in China since 1998 (Yang, 2014), and the Chinese are working on improving the quality of education. In 2015, the State Council issued "The Overall Plan to Promote the Construction of World-Class Universities and Disciplines". The Ministry of Education (January 15, 2016) declared that the focus of work in 2016 is to improve the quality of education. As an integral part of China's nation-building project, higher education is a critical element in Chinese strategic policy initiative of building national strength through science and education (Yang & Welch, 2012). It is believed that the further globalisation of higher education is introducing quality education resources from developed countries into China and that going overseas for study is helping the Chinese learn from developed countries.

China is undergoing significant changes as it is further integrating into the world economy. Increasingly, things happening in China have global consequences, as illustrated by the stop of trading in Chinese stock exchanges in early January. As globalisation increases, Chinese higher education is more exposed to international influences, and China is attracting more international students and scholars.

Methodology

To provide a Chinese perspective on the globalisation of higher education, we conducted an extensive literature review in China National Knowledge Infrastructure (CNKI), searching for articles reporting research findings on the globalisation of higher education from a Chinese perspective. CNKI is the most comprehensive database in the country containing Chinese academic journals, doctoral dissertations, master's theses, and proceedings from conferences. We also examined Chinese laws that affect globalisation. We reviewed journals for articles on the globalisation of higher education written by Chinese scholars and scholars familiar with Chinese higher education. In addition, we reviewed books on the globalisation of higher education.

A Chinese Perspective

In 1978, the Ministry of Education sent its first group of 52 Chinese visiting scholars to the United States (Zhang, 2008). Shortly thereafter the Chinese could go overseas individually for education. In 1981, China adopted the American style of academic degrees (Ma & Wen, 2013). The number of Chinese going abroad for education has been increasing every year over the last three and a half decades, reaching 523,700 in 2015. Since 1978, over 4 million Chinese have gone overseas for education, and of these 4 million 2.2 million have returned (Ministry of Education, March 25, 2016). During the same period, Chinese universities admitted more foreign students, with the number reaching 397,635 in 2015.

The Higher Education Act stipulates that foreigners may enter Chinese institutions to study, conduct research, participate in academic exchange, or teach, and their lawful rights and interests shall be protected by the government (National People's Congress, 1998). In 2003, the Ministry of Education launched "the Overseas University Leadership Program" to promote international professional development for university leaders. Selected leaders from top-ranked universities visited foreign universities that have the best reputations, where they learned and observed university practices (Yu, 2014). In 2004, the Ministry of Education promulgated a decree: The Implementation of the Regulation on Chinese-Foreign Collaborative Education, which states that the government encourages Chinese institutions to collaborate with foreign institutions that have their quality universally recognized. From a supplement, Chinese-foreign education cooperation became a component of Chinese education (He, 2016).

Currently, there are over 2,000 Chinese-foreign collaborative institutions and programs in China, which have approximately 550,000 students and from which over 1.5 million people have graduated (Jiang & Cai, 2015). The presence of foreign universities is an important part of China's ongoing experiment in higher education expansion and reform (Conning, 2016). The perceived benefits from a collaborative institution, according to Chinese students in one Sino-British university, include greater employability, higher status, integration into the global knowledge economy, and the development of desirable skills such as critical thinking, team working, and intercultural awareness (Moufahim & Lim, 2015).

China is accelerating its efforts to globalise higher education through joint ventures with universities in developed countries (Feng, 2013). The State Council (2015) encourages international exchanges to introduce quality international resources into Chinese teaching and research. The first UK-China Education Policy Week concluded in March with the announcement of a statement of principles that will inform transnational education programmes between the two countries (The Quality Assurance Agency for Higher Education, 2016).

English is seen as having a crucial part to play in China's ambitious development agenda to strengthen its access to cutting-edge knowledge, enhance its competitive edge in international economic activity, and fully integrate into the world system (Hu & Lei, 2014). Flagship universities have made a substantial investment in developing English courses (Gao, 2015). The use of English language has become widespread in China, making English education one of the important industries (Rai & Deng, 2016).

In China, all international branch campuses (IBCs) such as the University of Nottingham Ningbo and New York University Shanghai are organized as formal Sino-foreign partnerships, with the Chinese partner in the lead. These IBCs are recognized as new Chinese universities that are considered independent entities within the Chinese system (Kinser & Lane, 2016). In addition to IBCs, there are Sino-foreign cooperation programmes where international pedagogies, teaching materials, and instructors are introduced. These cooperative institutions and programmes have been well-accepted by the Chinese government, higher education institutions, and students (He, 2016). Most Chinese scholars summarise Sino-foreign cooperation in education using three categories: the integration model, the grafting model, and the relaxed model (Zhang, 2014).

Engaging in international cooperation in education has helped the Chinese bring in high-quality foreign resources, upgrade education philosophies, and develop versatile talent that meets international standards (Zhang, 2014). Some Hong Kong universities of very high quality are more international, and these universities have been playing a positive role in the globalisation of Chinese higher education. The effects of the globalisation of higher education are: Chinese educators and students are more aware of international resources, philosophies, pedagogies, practices, standards (He, 2016), and a global perspective. While the Chinese participate more in international assessments to measure students' learning outcomes, it is unlikely that Chinese learning will be standardised with one international measurement because, with a long history and an influential tradition, the Chinese are culturally different. Globalisation has increased the choices Chinese students have. They can receive higher education at home, but also internationally. Chinese students want to study internationally for these reasons: higher quality education, international employability, higher employability, higher income, possibility of immigration to a developed country, and parents' decision.

The globalisation of Chinese higher education is not only meaningful for China but also for the whole world. How many Chinese students will be studying internationally 10 years from now? The answer is important, as many universities around the world have a high dependency on recruiting Chinese students (Kemp, 2016). In some countries, it is partly a consequence of the reduction in the domestic demand. As globalisation increases, whether people like it or not, influences from higher education systems in different countries are increasingly intertwined (see Rasmussen *et al.*, this volume).

Conclusion

Chinese scholars have been involved in research on the internationalisation and globalisation of higher education (Lo & Wang, 2014; Zhang, 2014). Shanghai Jiao Tong University is a partner in two global networks in higher education research: The Global Centers for International Higher Education Studies and the Centre for Global Higher Education (de Wit, 2016). Many Chinese scholars contend that Chinese higher education should increase its globalisation (Feng, 2013; Li & Zhao, 2008).

The Chinese government indicates that it encourages international collaboration between Chinese institutions and world-class foreign counterparts to introduce quality international resources into China, hoping that Chinese institutions work together with international counterparts in educating high-level talent. Chinese institutions should actively participate in major international scientific projects, create favourable environments for international staff and students, and increase Chinese right of international discourse and competitiveness (State Council, 2015).

National strategies surrounding IBCs need to be taken seriously as exhibitions of national sovereignty in education (Kinser & Lane, 2016). By extension, national strategies surrounding the globalisation of higher education need to be taken seriously as exhibitions of national sovereignty. The globalisation of Chinese higher education has to take national strategies seriously so that Chinese benefits are considered. To receive understanding, the Chinese need to participate more in international activities and have a strategic vision appropriate for the Chinese context. This vision needs to manifest Chinese higher education's value orientation and reflect unique Chinese knowledge, including its service goals and evaluation criteria (Xie & Wen, 2015). In globalising, Chinese institutions should actively contribute towards China's economic development, political democracy, cultural advancement, national defence modernisation, and social harmony. Of the three positions distinguished by Held *et al.* (1999, cited in Marginson, 2011a) - hyper-globalists, sceptics, and transformationalists - most Chinese scholars are close to transformationalists, believing that nations have been relativised by the global dimension but remain important.

Today more Chinese receive overseas education, more of them return after study, more foreigners go to China to study and work, and more courses in China use English as the medium of instruction. Indications are that the globalisation of Chinese higher education, which is on the verge of a new era (Sadler, 2015), will continue to increase (Government of China, 2016). With the understanding that globalisation touches everyone's life (Connell, 2016), we believe the further globalisation of Chinese higher education is beneficial for both China and the whole world. It is beneficial for China to catch up with the developed countries and for the world to have a better understanding of China. In the emergence of a global culture (see Dawson, in this volume), higher education should play a positive role.

About the Authors

Xiaobin Li is associate professor in the Faculty of Education at Brock University, St. Catharines, Ontario, Canada. He can be contacted at this e-mail: xli@brocku.ca

Xiaoyang Wang is associate professor in the Higher Education Research Institute at Tsinghua University, Beijing, China. He can be contacted at this e-mail: wangxiaoyang@sino-education.org

Bibliography

Altbach, P. (2016). The Many Traditions of Liberal Arts—and Their Global Relevance. *International Higher Education*, No. 84, pp. 21–23.

CCTV 4. News (2015). 9 June 2015.

Chen, P. (2009). 大学有精神 [*The Spirit of University*]. Beijing: Peking University Press.

Cheung, H. & A. Chan (2010). Education and Competitive Economy: How Do Cultural Dimensions Fit in? *Higher Education*, Vol. 59, No. 5, pp. 525–541.

Connell, C. (2016). The Ascent of Global Learning. *International Educator*, Vol. 25, No. 2, pp. 16–23.

Conning, A. (2016). Establishing a Presence in China: Lessons for University Leaders. *The Observatory on Borderless Higher Education*. Online Resource: http://www.obhe.ac.uk/documents/view_details?id=967 [Accessed 10 November 2016].

The Economist (2014). What China Wants? *The Economist*, 412(8901), p. 9.

De Wit, H. (2016). Higher Education Research Goes Global. *International Higher Education*, Vol. 85, pp. 8–10.

Feng, Y. (2013). University of Nottingham Ningbo China and Xi'an Jiaotong-Liverpool University: Globalization of Higher Education in China. *Higher Education*, Vol. 65, No. 4, pp. 471–485.

Gao, Y. (2015). Constructing Internationalisation in Flagship Universities from the Policy-Maker's Perspective. *Higher Education*, Vol. 70, No. 3, pp. 359–373.

Government of China. (2016). 中共中央办公厅、国务院办公厅印发 《关于好新时期教育对外开放工作的若干意见》 [*The Chinese Communist Party Central Committee Office and the State Council Office Distribute "Opinions on Enhancing the Opening up of Education to the World in a New Era"*]. Online

Resource: http://www.gov.cn/home/201604/29/content_5069311.htm [Accessed 10 November 2016].

He, L. (2016). Transnational Higher Education Institutions in China: A Comparison of Policy Orientation and Reality. *Journal of Studies in International Education*, Vol. 20, No. 1, pp.79–95.

Hu, G. & J. Lei (2014). English-Medium Instruction in Chinese Higher Education: A Case Study. *Higher Education*, Vol. 67, No. 5, pp. 551–567.

Huang, F. (2015). Building the World-Class Research Universities: A Case Study of China. *Higher Education*, Vol. 70, No. 2, pp. 203–215.

Ji, B. (2014). Foreword. In R. Rhoads; X. Wang; X. Shi & Y. Chang (Eds.), *China's Rising Research Universities: A New Era of Global Ambition*, Baltimore: Johns Hopkins University Press, pp. vii-ix.

Jiang, N. & T. Cai (2015, April 27). 中外合作办学毕业生已超过150万人 [1.5 *Million People Have Graduated from Chinese-Foreign Collaborative Institutions and Programs*]. *People's Daily Overseas Edition*, 1.

Kauppinen, I. (2012). Towards Transnational Academic Capitalism. *Higher Education*, Vol. 64, No. 4, pp.543–556.

Kauppinen, I. (2013). Academic Capitalism and the Informational Fraction of the Transnational Capitalist Class. *Globalisation, Societies and Education*, Vol. 11, No. 1, pp.1–22.

Kemp, N. (2016). The International Education Market: Some Emerging Trends. *International Higher Education*, No. 85, pp.13–15.

Kinser, K. & J. Lane (2016). International Branch Campuses: Evolution of a Phenomenon. *International Higher Education*, No. 85, pp. 3–5.

Li, X. & L. Zhao (2008). Globalization and Chinese Higher Education. *Globalization*, 7. Online Resource: http://globalization.icaap.org/content/special/Li_Zhao.html [Accessed 10 December 2016].

Lo, W. & L. Wang (2014). Globalization and Regionalization of Higher Education in Three Chinese Societies: Competition and Collaboration. *Chinese Education and Society*, Vol. 47, No. 1, pp. 3–6.

Li, M. & Q. Chen (2011). Globalization, Internationalization and the World-Class University Movement: The China Experience. In R. King; S. Marginson & R. Naidoo (Eds.), *Handbook on Globalization and Higher Education*, Cheltenham, UK: Edward Elgar, pp. 241–255.

Ma, W. & J. Wen (2013). The Chinese Academic Profession: New Realities. In P. Altbach; L. Reisberg; M. Yudkevich; G. Androushchak & Y. Kuzminov (Eds.), *The Global Future of Higher Education and the Academic Profession: The BRICs and the United States*, New York: Palgrave Macmillan, pp. 126–159.

Marginson, S. (2011a). Imagining the Global. In King, R.; S. Marginson & R. Naidoo (Eds.), *Handbook on Globalization and Higher Education*, Cheltenham, UK: Edward Elgar, pp.10–39.

Marginson, S. (2011b). Higher Education in East Asia and Singapore: Rise of the Confucian Model. *Higher Education*, Vol. 61, No. 5, pp. 587–611.

Ministry of Education (2004). 中华人民共和国中外合作办学条例实施办 [*The Implementation of the Regulation on Chinese-Foreign Collaborative Education in the People's Republic of China*]. Online Resource: http://www.crs.jsj.edu.cn/index.php/default/news/index/6 [Accessed 10 December 2016].

Ministry of Education (2016). 全面提高教育质量,加快推进教育现代化: 2016年全国教育工作会议召开 [*Comprehensively Raise the Quality of Education to Accelerate Modernisation: 2016 National Education Working Conference Held*]. Online Resource: http://www.moe.gov.cn/jyb_xwfb/gzdt_gzdt/moe_1485/201601/t20160115_228038.html [Accessed 17 November 2016].

Ministry of Education (2016). 《中国留学回国就业蓝皮书 2015》情况介绍 [*A Briefing on "The 2015 Blue Book of Overseas Chinese Returning for Employment"*]. Online Resource: http://www.moe.edu.cn/jyb_xwfb/xw_fbh/moe_2069/xwfbh_2016n/xwfb_160325_01/160325_sfcl01/201603/t20160325_235214.html [Accessed 27 November 2016].

Ministry of Education (2016, April 7). 系列高等教育质量报告首次发布 [*The First Higher Education Quality Report Published*]. Online Resource: http://www.moe.gov.cn/jyb_xwfb/xw_fbh/moe_2069/xwfbh_2016nxwfb_160407/160407_sfcl/201604/t20160406_236891.html [Accessed 7 April 2016].

Ministry of Education (2016, April 14). 2015年全国来华留学生数据发布 [*The Data of 2015 Foreign Students in China*]. Online Resource: http://www.moe.gov.cn/jyb_xwfb/gzdt_gzdt/s5987/201604/t201604 14_238263.html [Accessed 15 April 2016].

Moufahim, M. & M. Lim (2015). The Other Voices of International Higher Education: An Empirical Study of Students' Perceptions of British University Education in China. *Globalisation, Societies and Education*, Vol. 13, No. 4, pp. 437–454.

OECD. (2015). *Education at a Glance 2014: OECD Indicators*. Online Resource: http://www.oecd.org/edu/Education-at-a-Glance-2014.pdf [Accessed 23 November 2016].

National People's Congress (1998). 中华人民共和国高等教育法 [*The People's Republic of China Higher Education Act*]. Online Resource: http://www.moe.

gov.cn/publicfiles/business/htmlfiles/moe/moe_619200407/1311.html [Accessed 23 November 2016].

Postiglione, G. (2015). Chinese Higher Education: Future Challenges. *International Higher Education*, No. 80, p. 14.

Proctor, D. (2016). The Changing Landscape of International Education Research. *International Higher Education*, No. 84, pp. 19–21.

The Quality Assurance Agency for Higher Education (2016). *UK and China Agree Principles for High Quality TNE*. Online Resource: http://www.qaa.ac.uk/en/Newsroom/Pages/UK-China-principles-TTNE.aspx#.Vv6zjXpmrme [Accessed 1 April 2016].

Rai, L. & C. Deng (2016). Glocalisation and English Language Education in Chinese Context. *Globalisation, Societies and Education*, Vol. 14, No. 1, pp. 127–144.

Robertson, S. & R. Dale (2015). Towards a "Critical Cultural Political Economy" Account of the Globalising of Education. *Globalisation, Societies and Education*, Vol. 13, No. 1, pp. 149–170.

Rudd, K. (2015). U.S.-China 21: *The Future of U.S.-China Relations Under Xi Jinping*. Online resource: http://asiasociety.org/files/USChina21_English.pdf [Accessed 10 November 2016].

Sadler, D. (2015). The Challenges Facing Chinese Higher Education— And Why They Matter. *The Observatory on Borderless Higher Education*. Online Resource: http://www.obhe.ac.uk/documents/view_details?id=954 [Accessed 1 April 2016].

Scott, P. (2016). International Higher Education and the "Neo-Liberal Turn". *International Higher Education*, No. 84, pp. 16–17.

The State Council. (2015). 统筹推进世界一流大学和一流学科建设总体方案 [*The Comprehensive Plan for Promoting the Construction of World Class Universities and Disciplines*]. Online resource: http://www.gov.cn/zhengce/content/2015–11/05/content_10269.htm [Accessed 29 November 2016].

Sun, X. & Y. Shi (2016). 去年出国留学人员52万 [Last Year over 520,000 Chinese Went Overseas for Education]. *People's Daily Overseas Edition*, 4.

Svensson, L. & M. Wihlborg (2010). Internationalising the Content of Higher Education: The Need for a Curriculum Perspective. *Higher Education*, Vol. 60, No. 6, pp. 595–613.

UNESCO (2016). *The Globalisation of Cultural Trade: A Shift in Consumption*. Online Resource: http://www.uis.unesco.org/culture/Documents/international-flowscultural-goods-report-en.pdf [Accessed 28 November 2016].

Valimaa, J. & T. Nokkala (2014). The Dimensions of Social Dynamics in Comparative Studies on Higher Education. *Higher Education*, Vol. 67, No. 4, pp. 423–437.

Van der Wende (2015). 全球视野下的中国高等教育: 世界一流大学建设运动的 领跑者还是追随者？ [*Chinese Higher Education with a Global Perspective: A Leader or Follower in the Movement of Building First Class Universities in the World?*]. Online Resource: http://www.zuihaodaxue.com/Article.jsp?id=kaac1MsBjCLPlqwkpCnLkUjBi4wJY [Accessed 24 November 2016].

Xie, W. & W. Wen (2015). 中国高等教育的独立自主性—中国特色高等教育研 究话语体系的意义分析 [The Independence and Self-Reliance of Chinese Higher Education]. *Chinese Higher Education Research*, Vol. 8, No. 1, pp. 1–2.

Yang, R. (2014). Going Global: Contemporary International Networking in Chinese Mainland Universities. *Chinese Education and Society*, Vol. 47, No. 1, pp. 27–43.

Yang, R. & A. Welch (2012). A World-Class University in China? The Case of Tsinghua. *Higher Education*, Vol. 63, No. 5, pp. 645–666.

Yu, H. (2014). Building Leadership Capacity in China: The Overseas University Leadership Program. *Chinese Education and Society*, Vol. 47, No. 2, pp. 3–7.

Zha, Q. (2016). China Calls for Smarter Standards for Its World-Class Universities. *International Higher Education*, Vol. 86, pp. 10–11.

Zha, Q.; J. Shi & X. Wang (2015). Is There a Chinese Model of a University? *International Higher Education*, Vol. 80, pp. 27–29.

Zhang, X. (2008). 30 Years of Progress and Achievements of Chinese Going Overseas for Education. *China Scholars Abroad*, pp. 4–7.

Zhang, Y. (2014). Discussion of Sino-Foreign Cooperation Models for Higher Vocational Institutions. *Chinese Education and Society*, Vol. 47, No. 5, pp. 86–94.

Chapter 6
Transnational Higher Education

John Branch

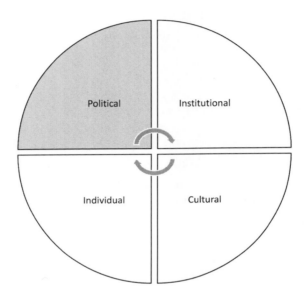

Introduction

This chapter is an important contribution to this anthology on the globalisation of higher education, because it explores a new, and relatively unknown, phenomenon—transnational higher education. Reading this chapter, you will gain the following three insights:

1. transnationalisation is a deviation from the broader and long-running internationalisation of higher education;

2. transnationalisation follows a different logic than internationalisation;

3. transnationalisation is an issue of importance (and concern) for a number of stakeholders.

The purpose of this chapter is to survey transnational higher education. I begin the chapter by defining transnational higher education, contrasting it in particular with a more historic view of the internationalisation of higher education. I then describe the logic of transnational higher education, highlighting both its rationales and incentives. Finally, I outline the significance of transnational higher education, enumerating its benefits and underlining its importance (and concern) for stakeholders.

The Internationalisation of Higher Education

According to the Institute of International Education (2014), 2013 was a record year for both international students studying in the United States and Americans studying abroad—819,644 and 283,000 students, respectively. But the internationalisation of students is nothing new. Indeed, international student mobility dates back to the 4th century BCE (Chadee & Naidoo, 2009). The University of Oxford welcomed its first international student, Emo of Friesland, in 1190 (University of Oxford, 2014). Sultan Ulug Beg, the 14th-century ruler of a vast area of Central Asia from Kyrgyzstan to Afghanistan, built one of the world's first observatories in Samarkand along the Silk Road, thereby attracting scholars from far and wide to study astronomy and geometry (Golden, 2011).

Viewed more broadly, the internationalisation of higher education as a whole might be considered as old as the university itself. In medieval Europe, scholars often spent their sabbaticals abroad, enjoying time in *"Oxford, Tübingen or the Sorbonne to pursue their scholarly activities and access the vast resources of the university libraries"* (Harris, 2008:352). Latin, which was the *lingua franca* of higher education until the Renaissance, facilitated the itinerant scholar's rambling from *studium* to *studium* (de Ridder-Symeons, 1992). It is not surprising, therefore, that the European Union chose the name ERASMUS (European Community Action Scheme for the Mobility of University Students) for its student exchange programme, a nod to one of the most famous academic "wandering minstrels" of the Middle Ages.

At the end of the Middle Ages, however, the university lost its academic universalism, becoming an instrument of the state. Indeed, its newfound purpose was to serve the ideological and professional needs of the emerging nation-states of Europe (Scott, 2000). Kerr (1994:27) characterised this period as the "convergence model" in which *"education, and higher education, not only came to serve the administrative and economic interests of the nation-state but became an essential aspect of the development of national identity"*. It was during this period that the university also gained its new identification with science and technology.

As these emerging nation-states gained power, national systems of higher education also began to emerge, and these systems were subsequently exported. Johns Hopkins University in Baltimore, for example, adopted the German discovery-oriented approach to higher education and became the model for the modern American research university (A Brief History of JHU, 2014). The export of national systems of higher education, however, was more often another facet of the European colonisation of Africa, Asia, and Latin America (Knight & de Wit, 1995). Although primarily in the service of national interests, it also led to the sharing of scientific ideas and reignited academic exchanges.

The years immediately following World War II triggered an explosion in higher education. Indeed, half of the world's universities have been established since 1945. In the United States, in particular, higher education became linked to a broader social equity movement which aimed to expand educational opportunity and access, and which led to the "massification" of higher education. But as highlighted by Scott (2000), the "golden age" of universities also coincided with the height of the Cold War and was correspondingly linked to a kind nationalism, which, he argued, led to a kind of (using Kerr's [1994] language) re-convergence. Higher education during this period took on an almost "Fordist" assembly line approach to teaching and research.

The 1960s and 1970s, however, saw a rekindling of the internationalisation of higher education, despite—or perhaps because of—the Cold War. Both the United States and the Soviet Union began to support international exchange for economic and political motivations, resulting in a new form of educational imperialism. Consider the legions of African and Latin American engineers, doctors, and scientists who were educated in universities and institutes across the Soviet Union. The People's Friendship University (now of Russia), for example, was founded in the U.S.S.R. in 1960, with the express purpose of educating citizens of developing nations.

The internationalisation of higher education in the 1960s and 1970s was also spurred by the de-colonisation of the developing world, the rapid expansion of higher education globally, and the changing role of the university from a centre of intellectual pursuit to a training facility for human resources (Knight & de Wit, 1995). This internationalisation took on a decidedly north-south geographical axis, with students moving (usually one-way) from south to north, and staff and technical assistance in the opposite direction. The consequences were both positive (scientific development) and negative (brain drain).

The forces of globalisation, which erupted in the 1980s, prompted a new twist on the internationalisation of higher education. Indeed, the sense of urgency that accompanied these forces resulted in more internally-oriented international activities at higher education institutions which, in turn, it was hoped, would nurture the internationalness of staff and students. This urgency was captured concisely in *A Nation at Risk*, the landmark federal evaluation of American public elementary and secondary education which was commissioned by then President Ronald Reagan: "*Our unchallenged preeminence in commerce, industry, science, and technological innovation is being overtaken by competitors throughout the world*" (National Commission on Excellence in Education, 1983, p.1). In higher education, more specifically, the concern over America's global competitiveness led directly to the Center for International Business Education (CIBE) programme, "*created under the Omnibus Trade and Competitiveness Act of 1988 to increase and promote the nation's capacity for international understanding and economic enterprise*" (Centers for International Business Education Program, 2016:np).

The 1990s, however, ushered in the newest era in the internationalisation of higher education—an era in which education itself is considered a product which can be packaged and sold abroad (Cudmore, 2005). Now known most commonly as transnational higher education, this international trade of higher education was triggered in the United Kingdom, for example, by Tony Blair, who launched a worldwide campaign to increase the number of foreign students in British universities (Ayoub & Massed, 2007). Likewise, government changes in higher education funding encouraged Australian universities to begin offering their degrees internationally, especially in the "markets" of Southeast Asia. The inclusion of education as a tradable product in the World Trade Organization's 1995 General Agreement on Trade in Services (GATS)—the culmination of the Uruguay Round of negotiations which began in 1986—gave "additional momentum to the process" (Anandakrishnan, 2008:199).

Transnational higher education is now a multi-billion-dollar industry (Alderman, 2001); trade in higher education accounts for 3% of global services exports (Vincent-Lancrin, 2005). Recent decades have witnessed an explosion in the number of universities "going abroad". Consider Weill Cornell Medical College, which was opened in Qatar by the American institution Cornell University in 2001. The Open University Business School of the United Kingdom now has more than 30,000 students studying by distance education in more than 107 countries (Open University, 2014). And higher education ranks as Australia's fourth largest export behind coal, iron ore, and gold (Group of Eight, 2014).

Transnational Higher Education

According to the Council of Europe (2002), transnational higher education—sometimes also called cross-border higher education or borderless higher education (Bennett *et al.*, 2011)—includes *"all types of higher education study programmes, or sets of courses of study, or educational services (including those of distance education) in which the learners are located in a country different from the one where the awarding institution is based"* (Council of Europe, 2002). For some experts, it also includes foreign student mobility (Naidoo, 2009), which is consistent with many governments that consider services delivered to foreign nationals within the country as exports. But, in short, transnational higher education is about the international trade of higher education, and it is now a widely-recognized concept and a fast-growing global phenomenon (Chen, 2015). Its impact can be seen, for example, in the number of students studying internationally (Husain, 2007) which the OECD (2013) predicts will reach 6.7 million by 2020.

For Yang (2008), the emergence of transnational higher education signalled a dramatic change in the nature of higher education. Indeed, it switched the emphasis from the internationalisation of *higher education* to the *internationalisation* of higher education. It moved from *making* higher education international to *taking* higher education international.

Knight & de Wit (1995), for example, noted that the internationalisation of higher education has historically followed four different approaches:

1. activity—the internationalisation of curricular and extra-curricular activities such as international exchanges and joint research;

2. ethos—the creation of an international culture in an institution;

3. competency—the development of international skills and attitudes among students and staff;

4. process—the integration of an international dimension in all university programs, policies, and procedures.

Similarly, Homeric (1999) suggested that the internationalisation of higher education has historically focused on:

1. international studies—the study of internationalization as an academic subject (area studies or cultural studies, for example);

2. facilitation of interaction—the furnishing of opportunities for shared experiences (study abroad and foreign student recruitment, for example);

3. international assistance—the provision of foreign aid (instructor exchanges, for example);

4. preparation of students—the instigation of the "global citizen" (internationally-themed dormitories, for example);

Transnational higher education, on the contrary, views the internationalisation of higher education through a product lens. Indeed, in contrast to the historical view of the internationalisation of higher education in which an international dimension is injected into university teaching/training, research, or service functions (Knight, 1997), transnational higher education considers higher education as a product that "can be manufactured, bought, and sold" (Muller, 1995)—that which Galway (2000) called the "commodification of higher education". It acknowledges that commercial forces have a legitimate, if not dominant, role in higher education (Altbach & Knight, 2007).

This new product lens is mirrored in the significant, if subtle, semantic shift of terminology. The historical view of the internationalisation of higher education resulted in various descriptors of higher education, including international, comparative, cross-cultural, global, and multi-cultural, all of which allude to the potential internationalness of higher education. Transnational higher education instead takes the nation as its defining unit, which, when combined with the Latin prefix *trans*—which means across or beyond—intimates the very tangible movement of higher education across national boundaries.

The Logic of Transnational Higher Education

It is evident that transnational higher education also follows a different logic for internationalisation. Knight & de Wit (1995) argued that the internationalisation of higher education has historically been driven by economic and political rationales, and by cultural and educational rationales. Economic and political rationales include:

1. economic growth and investment in the future economy—the internationalisation of higher education has a positive effect on international trade, bilateral economic relations, country competitiveness, and technological development;

2. human resources globalisation—the internationalisation of higher education is necessary, in order to equip students for a global labour market;

3. foreign policy—the internationalisation of higher education is a form of soft diplomacy, improving a nation's "brand image";

4. revenue generation—the internationalisation of higher education earns additional income, especially with full fee-paying foreign students;

5. educational demand—the internationalisation of higher education serves students from nations which have limited capacity.

Cultural and educational rationales include:

1. cultural function—the internationalisation of education spreads social values;

2. development of the individual—the internationalisation of higher education is necessary, in order for students to learn about

themselves by confronting alternative world-views;

3. internationalising research and teaching—the internationalisation of higher education reflects the universal human enterprise of advancing knowledge and understanding;

4. institution-building—the internationalisation of higher education strengthens the structures and systems of an institution;

5. quality improvement—the internationalisation of higher education can enhance the content and delivery of teaching and can increase the rigor of research.

The latent incentives of these rationales are principally altruistic and humanistic in nature. They exhibit very clearly a selfless and disinterested concern for student welfare, national progress, and human development. Even the revenue generation and institution-building rationales, which at first glance appear to be motivated more by selfishness and prejudice, ought to be considered relatively benign—and perhaps even benevolent—in origin.

Transnational higher education, on the contrary, is premised on a different set of rationales (and correspondingly a different set of incentives). Transnational higher education is most often associated with marketisation, neo-liberalism, and globalisation (Moutsios, 2008). As summarised by Sidhu & Christie (2013:182), higher education has now embraced "*neo-liberal funding regimes, marketisation, cross-border movements of students as well as institutions, the centrality of information and communications technology, and the challenges of a knowledge economy more generally.*"

Marketisation

Beginning with the marketisation of higher education, it is clear that transnational higher education has embraced—perhaps even accelerated—the paradigmatic shift from government-controlled systems of higher education, in which higher education is for the public good, to a market-based system in which higher education is a good for the public (Jongbloed, 2003; Altbach & Knight, 2007). It exploits the commodification of higher education (ESIB, 2004), spurring universities to "market" their wares (Alexander & Rizvi, 1993). It is certainly not isolated to the Western world; indeed, there is evidence of the marketisation of higher education in Russia (Hare & Lugachev, 1999), Eastern and Central Europe (Czarniawska & Genell, 2002), Israel (Oplatka, 2002), Asia (Gray *et al.*, 2003), and Africa (Ivy, 2001; Maringe, 2004; Maringe & Foskett, 2002). In summary, it re-defines the economic narrative of higher education. *"Instrumental reasoning, new regimes of accountability, and strict adherence to the economic imperative are the defining features of the contemporary university. Competitiveness, excellence, and performance are central to its survival."* (Harris, 2008: 347).

Stromquist (2002) argued that this marketisation of higher education can be explained partly from a social equity perspective—state-funded higher education typically benefits the upper and middle classes of society and, consequently, it is intrinsically unfair. Similarly, Altbach & Davis (1999) observed that governments have increasingly viewed higher education as an individual, not social, benefit and held, therefore, that individuals ought to bear the cost of higher education. Kerlin & Pollack (2010), drawing on institutional theory, proposed that the rising commercial activity among universities is due to the broader exogenous environmental forces that influence all not-for-profit organisations. Carroll & Stater (2009) suggested that revenue diversification in not-for-profits can lead to greater financial stability.

Viewed through a policy lens, the marketisation of higher education (and the transnational higher education that it engenders) appears to be more the result of pro-active decisions made by governments in recent decades. Consider the Australian case, for example. As mentioned previously, the Conservative government in Australia deregulated and de-funded education in the late 1980s and early 1990s, opening the way for full fee-paying foreign students (Alexander & Rizvi, 1993). The total number of foreign students increased from 17,248 in 1987 to 39,490 in 1992, with full fee-paying foreign students rising from 1,109 to 30,296, most coming from Hong Kong, Malaysia, and Singapore (National Report on Australia's Higher Education Sector, 1993). By 2013, however, almost 300,000 foreign students were enrolling at Australian universities, contributing $15 billion to the Australian economy (Group of Eight, 2014).

Cudmore (2005) reported on the marketisation of the Colleges of Applied Arts and Technology (CAATs) in Canada, which were created in the 1960s in order to support the economic development of the province of Ontario. He noted that in 2002 the government rewrote the mandate for the CAATs in order *"to meet local, regional, and global marketplace demand"* (Cudmore, 2005:38, my emphasis). Subsequently, the CAATs have attempted to internationalise, with the recruitment of foreign students, the internationalisation of the curriculum through foreign languages, overseas academic programmes, faculty exchanges, and technical assistance to other countries.

Several nations have explicitly declared their intentions (often accompanied by government-led incentives) to become educational "hubs" within a global educational market (Chen, 2015). Singapore (Mok, 2008) and Malaysia (Gill, 2009), for example, have both been highlighted because of the national higher education strategies of their governments which aim not only to attract foreign students but also to lure branch campuses of foreign universities (George, 2006). The United Arab Emirates and Qatar, which now boast 40 and 9 branch campuses, respectively, are also mentioned frequently, particularly due to the generous financial and infrastructure support from their governments (Becker, 2010). Twenty-two of the 40 branch campuses in the United Arab Emirates are located in Dubai, specifically within the so-called Dubai International Academic City, which offers 100 percent foreign ownership, tax exemption, and repatriation of profits. In Qatar, the government bears all development costs for educational infrastructure.

Perhaps the most obvious examples of a government's pro-active decisions to market higher education can be found within the European Union. In 1987, the ERASMUS programme was developed by the European Union in order to support student exchanges within the Union (Enders, 1998). In the 20 years since its inception, more than 2 million students have participated. In 1999, however, the European Union undertook an even bolder initiative. Named the Bologna Accord after the Italian city in which the declaration was signed into effect, it aimed to create a single transparent and competitive higher education market out of the diverse higher education systems of 46 nations, by adopting a standardised bachelor-master-doctoral 3 cycle progression and a common credit transfer system (Bennett *et al.*, 2010). The result has been the emergence of the "European Area of Higher Education", the educational equivalent of Europe's currency-based *Eurozone*.

Neo-liberalism

Continuing with neo-liberalism, the marketisation of higher education which transnational higher education has embraced appears to have grown in tandem with a broader neo-liberal economic agenda, which likewise has left an imprint on transnational higher education. Neo-liberalism is an economic philosophy which advocates consumer agency, free markets, and private property. It eschews government participation and market interference. Furthermore, it underpins modern views of economic growth and globalisation (WHO, 2014). As summarised by Dudley (1998:25), *"[t]he claim of globalization is that national economies are being increasingly subsumed into a global economy and that the discipline of international markets and money markets, rather than national, social, and/ or political priorities, should determine public policy. These policies, almost without exception, require states to reduce public spending, deregulate capital and labour markets, minimize welfare provision, and either eliminate or privatize as much as possible of the welfare state."*

Neo-liberalism is evidenced in higher education at the general level in a number of ways. Chen (2015), for example, suggested that entrepreneurship has become an important activity of the modern university—a method of generating funding for research and teaching support, student services, and infrastructure maintenance and growth. Harris (2008) noted that neo-liberalism is also reflected in the mission statements of today's universities, and in the aggressive promotion that they perform. Slaughter & Rhoades (2004) even proposed that "academic capitalism" can explicate the global dominance of the American university.

With respect to transnational higher education specifically, neo-liberalism is manifest in the policy of the World Trade Organization, which promotes trade liberalisation, including in educational services (Naidoo, 2010)—that which Rikowski (2001:3) characterises *"as the facilitation of the business takeover of education through its commercialization, privatization, and capitalization"* and which has led to a kind of invisible hand of education (Chen, 2015) and a *"single global marketplace of ideas, data, and communication"* (Knight & de Wit, 1995:8).

Neo-liberalism has also ushered in a new level of competition in higher education. As summarised by Lowrie & Hemsley-Brown (2012:1081), *"competition will define higher education and its being in the world*". This competition, however, consists not only of other universities but also of non-university providers (Lourtie, 2001) and "corporate universities" (Husain, 2007). According to Lorange (2002), higher education has always had competition—universities competed for resources, including money, faculty, facilities, and students. But, with globalisation, he continued, they are now also competing globally for students, with foreign institutions, and with commercial education providers. In its 2008 report, for example, the US Council of Graduate Schools underlined the efforts that Europe was making to retain its students and to recruit more international students.

Chen (2015) maintained that transnational higher education is also a response to the growing global demand for higher education (and education in general), especially from emerging economies. According to UNESCO (2009), student numbers rose 125% between 1990 and 2007. This growth is due, Chen hinted, to rising incomes, changing demographics, both domestically and internationally, and labour shortages. Bloom (2002) added that higher education has simply become a necessity; higher education is to today's knowledge economy as secondary education was to the industrial economy.

Many national higher education systems, however, are simply unable to meet this new demand. The leading providers of technical, medical, and commercial training in India, for example, can only serve about 1% of the market (Anastasios, 2011). To exacerbate the issue, according to Colucci *et al.* (2009), demand for higher education is outpacing (traditional) supply. They quoted Sir John Daniel who, in 1996, claimed that a sizable new university would need to be created every week merely to sustain the participation rates in higher education at the time. This excess demand, argued Alam *et al.* (2013), can only be met by transnational higher education.

Consequently, many higher education institutions have shifted their financial support for emerging economies and begun to serve full fee-paying foreign students—they have shifted "from aid to trade". For many of these universities, these students have become an important source of income, especially as public budgets have withered (Altbach & Knight, 2007).

In the neo-liberal competitive global market for higher education, reputation has also become increasingly salient. Consider the importance now ascribed to university league tables, such as the Shanghai Academic

Ranking of World Universities (See www.shanghairanking.com.). From a transnational higher education perspective, the level of a university's internationalisation has also become a measure of its excellence (Harris, 2008). Indeed, both students and sponsors alike consider it to be a contributing factor in a university's brand image (Naidoo, 2010).

Globalisation

Complementing marketisation and neo-liberalism is the notion of globalisation. It is evident that the emergence of transnational higher education has also mirrored the acceleration of globalisation which was triggered in the 1980s by the opening of the global economy. According to Sidhu & Christie (2013:182), one of the most important effects of globalisation *"has been to crack open existing territorialities to enable different local actors to participate in international arenas that were once open only to nation states."* Consequently, higher education has de-monopolised, de-institutionalised, and de-nationalised (Kampf, 2002). It is impossible to understand transnational higher education, therefore, without understanding it in the context of the forces of globalisation (Singh *et al.*, 2007).

According to the IMF (2008), globalisation is primarily an economic phenomenon, involving the increasing integration of national economies through the growth of international trade, investment, and capital flows. It implies the reduction or elimination of national barriers, temporal limits, and spatial boundaries. In the words of Friedman (1999:14), author of bestsellers "The Lexus and the Olive Tree: Understanding Globalization" and "The World is Flat: A Brief History of the 21st Century", globalisation is the *"inexorable integration of markets, nation-states, and technologies to a degree never witnessed before—in a way that is enabling individuals, corporations, and nation-states to reach around the world farther, faster, deeper, and cheaper than ever before."*

In the context of transnational higher education, Haug (2000:par. 3) emphasised that *"what is genuinely new and explains the growth of transnational education is that students are less and less restricted to what their national system is prepared to offer"*. This reduction of restrictions is due, in part, to the new opportunities for transnational higher education which are afforded to students by information technologies (Husain, 2007). Indeed, the internet has completely transformed the notion (and reputation) of distance learning from the days during which distance learning meant "correspondence school". The University of London International Programmes, for example, which was chartered by Queen Victoria in 1858, now has more than 54,000 students in 180 nations who follow courses on their own time and in their own locations (University of London, 2014). The reduction in temporal limits and spatial boundaries has been accelerated further by the *"emergence of 'global English' as an alternative to the national language for the acquisition of higher education qualifications"* (Haug, 2000:par. 5) and as the lingua franca of modern higher education (Altbach, 1989).

The impact of globalisation on higher education is most pronounced in emerging economies, which often have unmet demands (Naidoo, 2010) or face other distinctive challenges (Husain, 2007), including:

1. the inability to offer degrees in certain disciplines;

2. a lack of curricula and teaching materials in local languages;

3. limited domestic expertise;

4. restrictive social customs (access to higher education for women, for example).

As summarised by Lourtie (2001:6), the growth of transnational education to emerging economies is *"a sign that the national systems are not responding to the needs of potential students"*.

The Significance of Transnational Higher Education

Now, it ought to be obvious that the latent incentives of transnational higher education are consistent with the incentives of marketisation, neo-liberalism, and globalisation, with which it is most often associated. Indeed, transnational higher education follows the precepts of laissez-faire and self-interested capitalism, subscribing to the belief in the power of the market to improve both the efficiency and effectiveness of higher education globally. The logic is straightforward—emancipate higher education from government participation and interference, furnish students with the dignity of economic choice, and allow the invisible hand of economics to work its magic (Chan & Mok, 2011). The result will be a common (global) market of higher education, which provides students with services more effectively, which diffuses knowledge more equitably, which holds institutions of higher education more accountable, and which uses scarce resources more efficiently. In other words, higher education is now subject to, and supportive of, a kind of economic Darwinism.

Although this economic narrative has come to dominate discussions of transnational higher education, other rationales with less "soulless" incentives have been proffered. Universities are, by their nature, committed to the advancement of human knowledge. Kerr (1994) argued that this academic universalism was usurped by the nation states of the 19th and 20th century Europe when they co-opted universities to serve their national agenda. But according to Brown (1950:12), *"the universities of the world are today aspiring to return to one of the basic concepts of their origin—the universality of knowledge"*, thereby increasing access to students worldwide, and strengthening mutual understanding (Naidoo, 2010).

Whichever rationales (and corresponding incentives) have indeed underpinned the logic of transnational education, it is anticipated that transnational higher education will continue to grow and consequently change the nature and scope of higher education. Husain (2007) suggested that student exchanges will eventually be eclipsed by student mobility. Adams (2001) predicted that in the long-term, more and more programmes will be offered by universities in foreign nations; the capital investment of a foreign entity might be high, he admitted, but after it is recuperated, he reasoned, marginal costs are relatively low and profits, therefore, are attractive. Wood *et al.* (2005) were even more dramatic, envisaging the death of the traditional university and the birth of a global and most likely virtual higher education industry.

Whatever the precise future of higher education, the economic, societal, and scientific benefits of transnational higher education have frequently been cited (See Dam, 2001; Alam *et al.*, 2001; Husain, 2007; Nadir, 2010; Shams & Huisman, 2011, for example.). These include:

+ local skill development;

+ higher standards of living;

+ knowledge and technology transfer;

- increased access to education;

- increased competitiveness of local institutions;

- higher national education level;

- reduction of skills migration and brain drain;

- capacity-building;

- new research opportunities;

- more innovation;

- less capital outflow;

- less pressure on local education systems;

- higher quality.

Writing about transitional economies broadly and about Russia specifically, Saginova & Belyansky (2008) suggested that transnational higher education can facilitate the development of the university sector in nations that are in transition, which in turn can make positive contributions to society.

Transnational higher education, however, has not been without its critics. The first and, perhaps, most passionate critique of transnational higher education mirrors the more general critique of the marketisation of higher education overall (de Vita and Case, 2003; Levidow, 2002; Lynch, 2006). Indeed, to purists, *"education is a public good and never a commodity, let alone a free trade"* (Cheung, 2006:n.p.). Harris (2006:356) conceded that great universities must internationalise, but she argued that this internationalisation must *"be a cultural rather than economic internationalisation because such an internationalisation degenerates into instrumentalism, and this robs higher education of what should be essential to it"*. As in the case of public versus private elementary and secondary education in the United States, this instrumentalism could also lead to educational "haves and have-nots".

At a more operational level, critics of transnational education also lambaste universities for simply losing sight of their primary purpose—for pursuing profits instead of progress. Hodges (2007:1) chronicled the number of British universities that appeared to be chasing Chinese students with *"pound signs in their eyes"*, neglecting, she charged, their domestic responsibilities of teaching and research. Critics contend, therefore, that universities ought to *"stick to their knitting"* (Shattock, 2007:1). Other criticisms (Adam, 2001; Alam *et al.*, 2001) include the over-Westernisation of local culture and unfair competition.

Despite—perhaps, because of—these criticisms, and considering both its growth and cited benefits, transnational higher education is unquestionably an issue of importance (and concern) for a number of stakeholders (Adam, 2001). Transnational higher education is "big business" (Healey, 2012), which is both an "enormous opportunity" (Wood *et al.*, 2005) and a "risky venture" (Wilkins & Huisman, 2012). Consequently, it has the potential to have an enormous impact on governments, accreditation bodies, institutions, funders, instructors and, of course, students.

From a public policy perspective, governments must be watching transnational higher education with a mixture of both trepidation and jubilation. How does transnational higher education, for example, affect the economy? Which influences will it have on society? More pragmatically, what does it mean for taxes and spending? Think about the Kingdom of Saudi Arabia, for example, a relatively young nation with a conservative domestic political and social climate. An argument could be made—based on the theory of comparative advantage—that the Kingdom ought to have foregone its own higher education system, focusing its efforts instead on the petroleum industry in which it performs "comparatively better". In order to educate its citizens, the theory would hold, the Kingdom of Saudi Arabia ought to have engaged in the international trade of higher education as it does with petroleum, perhaps by providing educational credits for students to study abroad with a kind of higher education "voucher" programme.

Indeed, since the founding of the Kingdom of Saudi Arabia, tens of thousands of Saudi students have studied at international universities, most recently under the King Abdullah Foreign Scholarship Program (Ministry of Higher Education, 2014). Granted, the Kingdom has developed its own universities and colleges, three of which rank among the top 500 universities globally (www.topuniversities.com). But today the petroleum industry (and the Kingdom overall) is doubtless more industrially and scientifically advanced as a result of these students, if less culturally homogeneous.

Governments must also be concerned about the loss of educational sovereignty and control over traditional educational values and national identity. Consider, for example, the potency of courses such as History of the Communist Party of the Soviet Union and Marxist/Leninist Philosophy, which were required of all university students in the Soviet Union (Cunningham, 2002). The "academic capitalism" of transnational higher education also raises fundamental questions about regulatory issues, including standards and consumer rights. Governments will certainly want to protect the public by eradicating "degree mills" and bogus institutions, malpractice, and fraud (Adam, 2001).

In a similar way, transnational higher education also calls into question the role of accreditation bodies, whose traditional purview has been to "scrutinize colleges, universities and programs for quality assurance and quality improvement" (Eaton, 2012:1). Perhaps presaging the global competition now experienced by many business schools, the American Association of Collegiate Schools of Business (AACSB) changed its name (but not its acronym) in 2001 to the Association to Advance Collegiate Schools of Business (AACSB, 2014). More pertinently, it has itself internationalised, accrediting some 716 business schools in 48 countries. It is now commonly referred to as AACSB International, and its slogan reads Advancing Quality Management Education Worldwide.

The global competition now experienced by many business schools as a result of transnational higher education has also been realised at the institutional level. Consequently, administrators (at all levels) now face not only fundamental questions about the purpose of their institutions, but also serious strategic management decisions about such competitive issues as positioning, branding, product offerings, and pricing (Taylor, 2004). As summarised by Naidoo (2010:20), transnational higher education mandates that "universities operating in a changing international education landscape be more market oriented for them to be successful".

Transnational higher education, as intimated previously in the discussion of governmental concerns, also challenges traditional views of higher education funding. If a global marketplace for students is indeed emerging, then who is responsible for financing higher education? Perhaps a "sign of the times" is the recent announcement of the Schwarzman Scholars programme, a $350 million endowment which was created by Stephen Schwarzman, CEO and co-founder of one of the world's largest private equity firms, and which promises to rival the long-established and prestigious Rhodes Scholarships to the University of Oxford. Billed as A LANDMARK SCHOLARSHIP FOR THE DEFINING CHALLENGE OF OUR TIME, the programme *"will give the world's best and brightest students the opportunity to develop their leadership skills through a one-year Master's Degree at Tsinghua University in Beijing"* (Schwarzman Scholars, 2014:n.p.).

The Schwarzman Scholars programme also hints at the concerns which transnational higher education raises for instructors. Competition for university posts, for example, could increase, with candidates coming from all four corners of the world and, paralleling that which has occurred in labour-intensive industries, reducing instructor salaries. The new types of programmes and forms of delivery, which transnational higher education fuels could be threatening to many instructors, requiring them to re-tool or become obsolete. Like Latin in the Middles Ages, English has become the *lingua franca* of modern higher education teaching and research, in effect shutting out those instructors who have not mastered it.

Finally, and most importantly, transnational higher education has many implications for students. Adherents to the neo-liberal rationale, which was described previously, would argue that transnational higher education will benefit students, at the most basic level, with increased access. But extending the argument points to more choice in institutions and a broader range of subjects which are of higher quality and with lower prices. The logical conclusion for students is an increase in their competitiveness, with commensurate increases in mobility, salaries, and living standards.

Students ought to be wary of this argument, however. They might first reflect on the claim of subject breadth. Transnational higher education has occurred most commonly in subjects like information technology and business, which are easiest to sell (Naidoo, 2009). Most courses and programmes offered internationally are also fee-based and are almost always more expensive than government-funded local options. Students could easily fall prey to unscrupulous institutions if programme quality goes unchecked and because it is difficult for students to evaluate accurately. If English does become the *lingua franca of* modern higher education, some students might be left behind. Students also ought to know that the qualifications which they earn might not be recognised internationally.

Conclusion

Trade among humans has occurred for thousands of years. And international trade now accounts for more than 25% of the gross world product. It ought not to be surprising, therefore, that higher education has also come to be traded internationally. Called transnational higher education, this international trade of higher education is a fast growing and important phenomenon. The growth of transnational higher education is spurred by the marketisation of higher education, a neo-liberalist economic agenda, and the forces of globalisation. It has the potential to have an enormous impact on governments, accreditation bodies, institutions, funders, instructors, and, of course, students.

About the Author

John Branch is Academic Director of the part-time MBA programmes and Assistant Clinical Professor of Business Administration at the Stephen M. Ross School of Business, and Faculty Associate at the Center for Russian, East European, & European Studies, both of the University of Michigan in Ann Arbor, U.S.A. He can be contacted at this e-mail: jdbranch@umich.edu

Bibliography

JHU (n.d). *A Brief History of JHU*. Online resource: http://webapps.jhu.edu/jhuniverse/information_about_hopkins/about_jhu/a_brief_history_of_jhu/ [Accessed 1 October 2016].

AACSB (2014). *Frequently Asked Questions*. Online resource: www.aacsb.org [Accessed 9 November 2016].

Adam, S. (2001). Transnational Education Project Report and Recommendations. *Confederation of European Union Rector's Conference*, 2001.

Alam, F.; Q. Alam; H. Chowdhury & T. Steiner (2013). Transnational Education: Benefits, Threats and Challenges. *Procedia Engineering*, Vol. 56, pp. 870–874.

Alderman, G. (2001). The Globalization of Higher Education: Some Observations Regarding the Free Market and the National Interest. *Higher Education in Europe*, Vol. 26, No. 1, pp. 47–52.

Alexander, D. & F. Rizvi (1993). Education, Markets and the Contradictions of Asia-Australia Relations. *Australian Universities' Review*, Vol. 36, No.2, pp. 16–20.

Altbach, P. (1989). The New Internationalism: Foreign Students and Scholars. *Studies in Higher Education*, Vol. 14, No. 2, pp. 125–136.

Altbach, P. & T. Davis (1999). Global Challenge and National Response: Note of Baan International Dialogue on Higher Education. In Altbach, P. & P. Peterson (Eds.), *Higher Education in the 21st Century. Global Challenge and National Response*. Annapolis Junction: Institute of International Education Books, pp. 3–10.

Altbach, P. & J. Knight (2007). The Internationalization of Higher Education: Motivations and Realities. *Journal of Studies in International Education*, Fall/Winter, pp. 290–304.

Anandakrishnan, M. (2008). Promises and Perils of Globalized Higher Education. *Journal of Educational Planning and Administration*. Vol. 22, No. 2, pp. 199–211.

Anastasios (2011). *Transnational Education in India: Opportunities and Challenges for UK Institutions*. Online resource: http://anastosioslife.blogspot.com [Accessed 2 December, 2016].

Ayoubi, R. & H. Massoud (2007). The Strategy of Internationalization in Universities: A Quantitative Evaluation of the Intent and Implementation in UK universities. *International Journal of Educational Management*, Vol. 21, No. 4, pp. 329–349.

Becker, R. (2010). International Branch Campuses: Trends and Directions. *International Higher Education*, No. 58, pp. 3–5.

Bennett, P.; S. Bergan; D. Cassar; M. Hamilton; M. Soinila; A. Sursock; S. Uvalic-Trumbic & P. Williams (Eds.) (2010). *Quality Assurance in Transnational Higher Education. Lifelong Learning Programme of the European Union*. European Association for Quality Assurance in Higher Education: Helsinki, Finland.

Bloom, D. (2002). *Mastering Globalization: From Ideas to Action on Higher Education Reform*. Online document http://www.tfhe.net/resources/mastering_globalization.htm [Accessed 28 November 2016].

Brown, F. (1950). Universities in World-Wide Cultural Cooperation. In M. Chambers (Ed.). *Universities of the World Outside USA*. Washington: American Council on Education, pp. 11–21.

Carroll, D. & K. Stater (2009). Revenue Diversification in Nonprofit Organizations: Does it Lead to Financial Stability? *Journal of Public Administration Research and Theory*, Vol. 19, No. 4, pp. 947–966.

Centers for Business Education Program. http://www2.ed.gov/programs/iegpscibe/index.html [Accessed 12 January 2016].

Chadee, D. & V. Naidoo (2009). Higher Educational Services Exports: Sources of Growth of Asian Students in US and UK. *Service Business: An International Journal*, Vol. 3, No. 2, pp. 173–187.

Chan, D. & K. Mok (2001). Educational Reforms and Coping Strategies Under the Tidal Wave of Marketisation: A Comparative Study of Hong Kong and the Mainland. *Comparative Education*, Vol. 37, No. 1, pp. 21–41.

Chen, P. (2015). Transnational Education: Trend, Modes of Practices and Development. *International Journal of Information and Education Technology*, Vol. 5, No. 8, August, pp. 634–637.

Cheung, P. (2006). Filletting the Transnational Education Steak. *Quality in Higher Education*, Vol. 12, No. 3, pp. 283–285.

Colucci, E.; M. Van Rooijen & P. Ueker (Eds.) (2009). *Off-Shore Campuses and Programmes – A Mainstream Activity for Europe's Universities?* Online document http://www.obhe.ac.uk/what_we_do/events/conference_presentations [Accessed 28 November 2016].

Council of Europe (2002) http://www.coe.int/t/dg4/highereducation/recognition/code%20of%20good%20practice_EN.asp [Accessed 20 October 2016].

Cudmore, G. (2005). Globalization, Internationalization, and Student Recruitment of International Students in Higher Education, and in the Ontario Colleges of Applied Arts and Technology. *The Canadian Journal of Higher Education*, Vol. XXXV, No. 1, pp. 37–60.

Cunningham, H. (2002). Moscow University, 1977–1978. http://www.cyberussr.com/rus/mgu-core-e.html [Accessed 26 October 2016].

Czarniawska, B. & K. Genell (2002). Gone shopping? Universities on their Way to the Market. *Scandinavian Journal of Management*, Vol. 18, No. 4, pp. 455–475.

de Ridder-Symeons, H. (1992). Mobility. In H. de Ridder-Symeons (Ed.), *A History of the University in Europe. Vol. 1.* Cambridge, England: Cambridge University Press, pp. 280–304.

de Vita, G. & P. Case (2003). Rethinking the Internationalisation Agenda in UK Higher Education. *Journal of Further and Higher Education*, Vol. 27, No. 4, pp. 383–398.

Dudley, J. (1998). Globalization and Education Policy in Australia. In J. Currie & J. Newson (Eds.), *Universities and Globalization: Critical Perspectives.* London: Sage, pp. 21–44.

Eaton, J. (2012). *An Overview of U.S. Accreditation.* Washington: Council for Higher Education Accreditation.

Enders, J. (1998). Academic Staff Mobility in the European Community: The ERASMUS Experience. *Comparative Education Review,* Vol. 42, No. 1, pp. 46–60.

ESIB (2004). *European Student Handbook on Transnational Education.* European Student Union.

Friedman, T. (1999). *The Lexus and the Olive Tree: Understanding Globalization.* New York, U.S.A.: Picador.

Galway, A. (2000). *Going Global: Ontario Colleges of Applied Arts and Technology, International Students Recruitment and the Export of Education.* Toronto, Canada: Ontario Institute for Studies in Education, University of Toronto.

Gill, J. (2009). *Malaysia: Full of Western promise. The Times Higher Education.* Retrieved from http://www.timeshighereducation.co.uk/story. asp?storycode=407873 [Accessed 27 August 2016].

George, E. (2006). Positioning Higher Education for the Knowledge Based Economy. *Higher Education,* Vol. 52, No. 2, pp. 589–610.

Golden, P. (2011). *Central Asia in World History.* Oxford, England: Oxford University Press.

Gray, B.; K. Fam & V. Llanes (2003). Cross Cultural Values and the Positioning of International Education Brands. *Journal of Product, & Brand Management,* Vol. 12, No. 2, pp. 108–19.

Group of Eight (2014). *International Students in Higher Education and Their Role in the Australian Economy.* https://go8.edu.au/publication/international-students-higher-education-and-their-role-australian-economy [Accessed 21 October 2016].

Hamrick, J. (1999). *Internationalizing Higher Educational Institutions: Broadening the Approach to Institutional Exchange.* Paper presented at: Managing Institutional Change and Transformation Project, Center for the Study of Higher and Postsecondary Education, University of Michigan. http://www-personal.umich.edu/~marvp/facultynetwork/whitepapers/jimhamrick.html [Accessed 18 October 2016].

Hare, P. & R. Lugachev (1999). Higher Education in Transition to a Market Economy: Two Case Studies. *Europe-Asia Studies,* Vol. 51, No. 1, pp. 101–122.

Harris, S. (2008). Internationalising the University. *Educational Philosophy and Theory,* Vol. 40, No. 2, pp. 346–357.

Haug, G. (2000). *Response to Professor Sergio Machado's Presentation 'Introducing the Theme of Transnational Education'*. Delivered at the Conference of the Directors General for Higher Education and Heads of the Rectors' Conferences of the European Union, Aveiro, Portugal.

Healey , N. (2012). *Overview of the Global Market in Transnational Education*. Presentation at: 8th QS-APPLE Annual Conference 15 November 2012. http://www.dreducation.com/2013/02/global-transnational-education-market.html [Accessed 29 November 2016].

Husain, I. (2007). Transnational Education: Concept and Methods. *Turkish Online Journal of Distance Education*, Vol. 8, No. 1, pp. 163–173.

IMF (2008). *Globalization: A Brief Overview*. https://www.imf.org/external/np/exr/ib/2008/053008.htm [Accessed 23 October 2016].

Institute of International Education (2015). *Open Doors Report on International Education Exchange*. www.iie.org [Accessed 16 February 2016].

Ivy, J. (2001). Higher Education Institution Image: A Correspondence Analysis Approach. *The International Journal of Educational Management*, Vol. 15 No. 6, pp. 276–82.

Jongbloed, B. (2003). Marketisation in Higher Education, Clarke's Triangle and the Essential Ingredients of Markets. *Higher Education Quarterly*, Vol. 57 No. 2, pp. 110–135.

Kampf, K. (2004). *The Internationalization of German Higher Education*. Dissertation: University of Mainz.

Kerlin, J. & T. Pollak (2011). Nonprofit Commercial Revenue: A Replacement for Declining Government Grants and Private Contributions? *The American Review of Public Administration*, Vol. 41, No. 6, pp. 686–704.

Kerr, C. (1994). *Higher Education Cannot Escape History: Issues for the Twenty-First Century*. Albany, U.S.A.: Sunny Press.

Knight, J. (1997). Internationalization of Higher Education: A conceptual framework. In J. Knight & H. de Wit (Eds.), *Internationalization of Higher Education in Asia-Pacific Countries*. Amsterdam: European Association for International Education.

Knight, J. & H. de Wit (1995). Strategies for Internationalization of Higher Education: Historical and Conceptual Perspectives. In H. de Wit (Ed.), *Strategies for Internationalization of Higher Education: A Comparative Study of Australia, Canada, Europe and the United States of America*. Amsterdam, Netherlands: European Association for International Education, pp. 5–33.

Levidow, L. (2002). Marketizing Higher Education: Neoliberal Strategies and Counter-Strategies. In K. Robins & F. Webster (Eds.), *The Virtual University?: Knowledge, Markets and Management*. Oxford, England: Oxford University Press, pp. 227–248.

Lorange, P. (2002). *New Vision for Management Education: Leadership Challenges*. Oxford, England: Pergamon.

Lourtie, P. (2001). *Furthering the Bologna Process. A Report to the Ministers of Education of the Signatory Countries*. Prague http://www.ehea.info/Uploads/Documents Lourtie Report-FromBolognatoPragueMay2001.pdf [Accessed 20 May 2016].

Lowrie A. & J. Hemsley-Brown (2011). This Thing Called Marketisation. *Journal of Marketing Management*, Vol. 27, No. 11–12, pp. 1081–1086.

Lynch, K. (2006). Neo-Liberalism and Marketisation: The Implications for Higher Education. *European Educational Research Journal*, Vol. 5, No. 1, pp. 1–17.

Maringe, F. (2004). Vice Chancellor's Perceptions of University Marketing: A View from Universities in a Developing Country. *Higher Education Review*, Vol. 36, No. 2, pp. 53–68.

Maringe, F. & N. Foskett (2002). Marketing University Education: The South African Experience. *Higher Education Review*, Vol. 34 No. 3, pp. 35–51.

Moutsios, S. (2008). International Organisations and Transnational Education Policy. *Compare: A Journal of Comparative and International Education*, Vol. 39, No. 4, pp. 1–12.

Ministry of Higher Education (2014). *King Abdullah Foreign Scholarship Program*. http://www.mohe.gov.sa/en/aboutus/Institutions/Pages/Emission-of-the-outer.aspx [Accessed 9 November 2016].

Mok, K. (2008). Singapore's Global Education Hub Ambitions: University Governance Change and Transnational Higher Education. *International Journal of Educational Management*, Vol. 22, pp. 527–546.

Muller, S. (1995). Globalisation of Knowledge. In K. Hanson & J. Meyerson (Eds.), *International Challenges to American Colleges and Universities: Looking Ahead*. Phoenix, U.S.A.: Oryx Press, p. 75.

Naidoo, V. (2009). Transnational Higher Education: A Stock Take of Current Activity. *Journal of Studies in International Education*, Vol. 13, No. 3, pp. 310–330.

Naidoo, V. (2010). Transnational Higher Education: Who Benefits? *International Higher Education*, No. 58, pp. 6–7.

National Commission on Excellence in Education (1983). *A Nation at Risk: The Imperative for Educational Reform*. Washington, U.S.A.: United States Government.

Department of Employment, Education and Training. Higher Education Division (2003). *National Report on Australia's Higher Education Sector*. Canberra, Australia.

OECD (2013). *Education Indicators in Focus. July*. New York, U.S.A.: OECD.

Open University. *The Open University Business School.* http://www.open.ac.uk/ business-school/about/global-study-international-students [Accessed 9 September 2016].

Oplatka, I. (2002). Implicit Contradictions in Public Messages of 'Low-Stratified' HE Institutions: The Case of Israeli Teacher Training Colleges. *The International Journal of Educational Management,* Vol. 16 No. 5, pp. 248–56.

Rikowski, G. (2002). *Globalization and Education.* A paper presented to the House of Lords Select Committee in Economic Affairs - Inquiry into the Global Economy. London. http://www.leeds.ac.uk/educol/ documents/00001941.htm [Accessed 17 October 2016].

Saginova, O. & V. Belyansky (2008). Facilitating Innovations in Higher Education in Transition Economies. *International Journal of Educational Management,* Vol. 22, No. 4, pp. 341–351.

schwarzmanscholars (2014). *Program.* http://schwarzmanscholars.org/ program/ [Accessed 10 November 2016].

Scott, P. (2000). Globalisation and Higher Education: Challenges for the 21st Century. *Journal of Studies in International Education,* Vol. 4, No. 1, Spring, pp. 3–10.

Shams, F. & J. Huisman (2012). Managing Offshore Branch Campuses: An Analytical Framework for Institutional Strategies. *Journal of Studies in International Education,* Vol. 16, No. 2, pp. 106–127.

Shattock, M. (2007). A New Agenda in Higher Education? *Higher Education Quarterly,* Vol. 49, Iss. 2, pp. 97–98.

Sidhu, R. & P. Christie (2014). Making Space for An International Branch Campus: Monash University Malaysia. *Asia Pacific Viewpoint,* Vol. 55, No. 2, August, pp. 182–195.

Singh, M.; F. Rizvi & M. Shrestha (2007). Student Mobility and the Spatial Production of Cosmopolitan Identities. In K. Gulson & C. Symes (Eds.). *Spatial Theories of Education. Policy and Geography Matters.* New York, U.S.A.: Routledge, pp. 195–214.

Slaughter, S. & G. Rhoades (2014). *Academic Capitalism and the New Economy: Markets, States and Higher Education.* Baltimore, U.S.A.: Johns Hopkins University Press.

Stromquist, N. (2002). *Education in a Globalized World: The Connectivity of Economic Power, Technology and Knowledge.* Lanthan, England: Rowman & Littlefield Publishers.

Taylor, J. (2004). Toward a Strategy for Internationalisation: Lessons and Practice from Four Universities. *Journal of Studies in International Education,* Vol. 8, No.2 , Summer 2004, pp. 149–171.

UNESCO (2009). *Institute of Statistics, UIS Database.* http://unctad.org/fr/Docs/gdscsir20041_en.pdf [Accessed 12 April 2016].

University of London (2014). *Our History.* http://www.londoninternational.ac.uk/our-global-reputation/our-history [Accessed 25 October 2014].

University of Oxford (2014). *International Applicants.* http://www.ox.ac.uk/admissions/undergraduate/international-students/international-applicants [Accessed 1 September 2014].

Vincent-Lancrin, S. (2005). Building Capacity Through Cross-Border Tertiary Education. *Observatory on Borderless Higher Education,* March.

WHO (2014). *Neo-Liberal Ideas.* http://www.who.int/trade/glossary/story067/en/ [Accessed 23 October 2014].

Wilkins, S. & J. Huisman (2012). The International Branch Campus as Transnational Strategy in Higher Education. *Higher Education,* Vol. 64, No. 5, pp. 627–645.

WTO (2016). *Education Services.* https://www.wto.org/english/tratop_e/serv_e/education_e/education_e.htm [Accessed 15 February 2016].

Wood, B.; S. Tapsall & G. Soutar (2005). Borderless Education: Some Implications for Management. *International Journal of Educational Management,* Vol. 19, No. 5, pp. 428–436.

Yang, R. (2008). Transnational Higher Education in China: Contexts, Characteristics and Concerns. *Australian Journal of Education,* Vol. 52, No. 3, pp. 272–286.

Chapter 7

The Internationalisation of the Stockholm School of Economics

Diana Pauna & John Branch

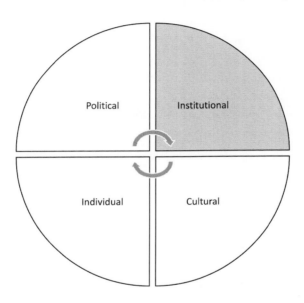

Internationalisation Versus Globalisation

According to Mitchell & Nielsen (2012), internationalization is seen as something which higher education institutions do while globalization is something that is happening to them. Indeed, as introduced by Branch *et al.* (in this volume), globalisation is a process of economic and political integration. It concerns the increasing interaction between countries, and the reduction or elimination of their boundaries. And, perhaps most germane to Mitchell & Nielsen's logic, it is exogenous to institutions. That is to say, globalisation exists independent of any single institution.

Internationalisation, on the contrary, is endogenous. It is something which is undertaken by an institution...the result of specific decisions which have been made within an institution. And it is purposeful, part of an institution's 'strategy'. Knight (1999:16) captures its spirit and activities with the following: *"internationalization of higher education is the process of integrating an international/intercultural dimension into the teaching, research, and service functions of the institution"*.

Higher education institutions, however, differ dramatically in terms of their size and scope, their resources and rankings, their missions and mandates, their courses and constraints. Simply stated, each institution is unique. Consequently, the internationalisation of each institution is correspondingly unique. That is to say, an international/intercultural dimension is integrated into the teaching, research, and service functions differently in different institutions.

Researchers, however, have attempted to identify discernible patterns of institutional internationalisation. Indeed, they have looked for commonalities in the steps, stages, or strategies which institutions follow when integrating an international/intercultural dimension into teaching, research, and service functions. One such attempt was made by Chan & Dimmock (2008), who concluded that three distinct models of institutional internationalisation exist which differ in terms of their internationalisation locus, activities, aims, and focus: 1. the internationalist model, 2. the translocalist model, and 3. the globalist model.

The purpose of this chapter is to explore the internationalisation of the Stockholm School of Economics in Riga, with a view to identifying whether or not it follows a specific model of institutional internationalisation as per Chan & Dimmock (2008). It begins by describing the three models of institutional internationalisation which were proposed by Chan & Dimmock (2008). It then documents the evolution of the Stockholm School of Economics in Riga, with a particular emphasis on its internationalisation. Finally, it discusses the internationalisation of the Stockholm School of Economics in Riga with respect to the three models of institutional internationalisation which were proposed by Chan and Dimmock. Reading this chapter, you will gain the following three insights:

1. Different institutions internationalise differently;

2. The differences in institutional internationalisation result from different contextual circumstances;

3. The differences in institutional internationalisation result in different institutional strategies (policies and infrastructure) and programmes (curriculum).

Three Models of Institutional Internationalisation

The premise of the article by Chan & Dimmock (2008:189) is not unlike that of this chapter—that different institutions internationalise differently. Indeed, they began with the basic assumption that *"the meanings and interpretations of internationalization in higher education shift according to various rationales, incentives, activities, and the political and economic circumstances within which it takes place"*. And consequently, they continued, institutional internationalisation will differ in terms of both the institution's strategies (policies and infrastructure) and its programmes (curriculum).

In order to explore their logic, Chan & Dimmock (2008) conducted a comparative case study of the internationalisation of two institutions: the first, a medium-sized, research-oriented British university with an international reputation, and the second an undergraduate teaching-oriented university which is located in Hong Kong and which primarily serves the local community. They followed an interpretive research approach, using data which was collected from institutional documents and through in-depth interviews with 24 participants (12 from each institution).

Analysis of the data supported the notion that the meanings and interpretations of internationalisation differed as a result of the differences in institutional circumstances. Additionally, the analysis also buttressed the corresponding claim that internationalisation strategies and programmes subsequently differ. For example, because internationalisation is a foundational national goal of Great Britain, internationalisation in the British university included the idea of fostering inter-cultural understanding, and likewise led to the active recruitment of foreign students. The relatively small number of foreign students who were enrolled in the Hong Kong university, on the contrary, mirrored the cultural homogeneity of the

Chinese Special Autonomous Region, and also the government's regulation which limited foreign student enrolment.

The differences between the institutional internationalisation of the British and Hong Kong universities, however, also led Chan & Dimmock (2008) to propose that these two uniquely different versions of internationalisation might also represent two generic models of institutional internationalisation: 1. the internationalist model and 2. the translocalist model. Although their comparative study was limited to only these two universities, they also surmised that a third generic model of institutional internationalisation—the globalist model—might also exist. The characteristics of these three models of institutional internationalisation are summarised below in Table 1.

The Stockholm School of Economics in Riga

SSE Riga was the brainchild of Staffan Burenstam Linder, who served as the Rector of SSE from 1986 to 1995, and who believed that it was Sweden's duty to help its Baltic neighbour following the independence of Latvia in May 1990. Although the idea for a Riga-based branch of SSE was proposed in 1991, the project began in earnest in January 1992 (See Table 2.), when a group of students from SSE surveyed business administration and economics programs at 6 national universities in Estonia, Latvia, and Lithuania. In parallel, Staffan Burenstam Linder started networking with key decision-makers and opinion-leaders in both Sweden and Latvia, in border to gain political support for the idea.

Subsequently, the Swedish government funded a feasibility study to be conducted by a professional consultant, in accordance with the SSE Riga Guiding Principles which were developed in July 1993, and which outlined the School's objectives, level of autonomy, the language of instruction, instructor and student goals, recruitment plans, and facilities demands. The feasibility study included visits to Riga, meetings with education professionals, and examination of the Latvian higher education 'climate'. It also included discussions of curricular designs, calculations of costs, and debates about student recruitment. In December 1992, the feasibility study was submitted to the Ministry of Foreign Affairs of Sweden.

In early 1993, the SSE Riga management team was formed with the appointment of the Rector, the Pro-rector (of Latvian descent), and a Professor of International Business, all from Sweden. In March 1993, the Parliament of Sweden formally approved funding for a three-year period, and tentatively for a ten-year period. The Cabinet of Ministers of the Republic of Latvia approved the establishment of SSE Riga, and assigned the building at Strēlnieku iela 4a. The legal ownership framework was signed on 20 June 1993, with SSE holding 75% of share and the Ministry of Education and Science of the Republic of Latvia holding the remaining 25%. Reconstruction work of the building began in December 1993.

	Internationalist	Translocalist	Globalist
Locus	Most likely found in developed economies with a multicultural population, especially English-speaking countries enjoying the monopolistic position of the English language, and the existence of a global education market.	Most likely found in less developed economies (post-colonial countries, for example) with culturally-homogeneous populations where nation-building is a priority or at least a concern.	Most likely found in developing economies with a large number of foreign businesses and/or growing populations of local elites aspiring for upward mobility both at home and abroad.
Activities	Well-established, research-intensive, and comprehensive institutions with significant numbers of international faculty members and students, international research, and an international standing.	Primarily teaching institutions, a large proportion of faculty members who are local but maybe trained overseas, a small number of international students, and serving the local community.	International institutions engaged in transitional education (including those of distance education) catering to the demand for internationally-recognised educational qualifications.

Aims	Aim for international positioning, research at an international level, academic excellence, and world-class status.	Aim to be good national universities providing quality education, cultivating a national and global perspective among students, within the context of nation-building and student employment in the competitive global market.	Aim only for unilateral benefits of national or institution self-interests.
Focus	Focused on internationalisation abroad: global delivery of courses, international alliances, and development partnerships, with internationalisation-at-home being attempted at the discretion of individual departments and faculty members.	Focused on internationalisation at home, such as internationalising the curriculum through the injection of an international dimension on campus and, in the case of non-English-speaking countries, the creation of an English-speaking environment, supplemented by some internationalisation-abroad efforts such as study abroad and overseas partnerships.	Focused on the global delivery of national or international programmes of study while eschewing intercultural understanding, open-mindedness, foreign language proficiency, or mutually-beneficial international and inter-institutional cooperation.

Table 1: Three Models of Institutional Internationalisation. Adapted from Chan & Dimmock (2008).

During the period October to December 1993, the SSE Riga Rector began recruiting instructors who were provided with a special course about Latvian culture, history, politics, language, and economics. In February 1994, these instructors also visited Riga, meeting various ministers in the government and professors at the University of Latvia. Both the course and the visit helped to strengthen the camaraderie of the SSE Riga instructors.

Timing	Steps
January 1992	SSE students visited Tallinn Technical University and Tartu University in Estonia, University of Latvia and Riga Technical University in Latvia, and Vilnius University and Kaunas Technical University in Lithuania.
January 1992 to June 1992	Meetings were held with key decision makers and opinion leaders in Sweden and Latvia, including the Prime Minister of Sweden, Ministers of Education in Latvia and Sweden, and the Minister of Foreign Affairs of Sweden.
February 1992	Three SSE leaders travelled to Estonia, Latvia, and Lithuania to establish contacts with education institutions, ministries, and Swedish embassies.
July 1992	The guiding principles of SSE Riga were formulated, including the objectives, level of autonomy, the language of instruction, instructors and students, recruitment, and facilities.
July 1992 to December 1992	A feasibility study was conducted.
January 1993 to February 1993	Rector and Pro-Rector were hired.
February 1993 to March 1993	The Parliament of Sweden formally approved funding for a three-year period, and tentatively for a ten-year period.
March 1993	The Cabinet of Ministers of the Republic of Latvia approved the establishment of SSE Riga, and assigned the building at Strēlnieku iela 4a.
30 June 1993	The agreement between the Ministry of Education and Science of the Republic of Latvia and the Stockholm School of Economics was signed.
October 1993 to December 1993	Instructors attended a course about Latvian culture, history, language, politics, and economy.
December 1993 to November 1994	Reconstruction of the building began, funded by the Swedish partners, and performed by a Swedish construction company.
February 1994	SSE Riga instructors visited Latvian ministries, authorities, and companies, and met professors at the University of Latvia.
January 1994 to February 1994	Promotion of the B.Sc. program was launched throughout Latvia.
January 1994 to June 1994	The local administrative team and local instructors were recruited.

Timing	Steps
March 1994	Admission tests and interviews were conducted.
8 July 1994	The first cohort of 56 students started the B.Sc. Economics and Business programme at the nearby School of Geography of the University of Latvia.
8 November 1994	SSE Riga was inaugurated by the King of Sweden Carl XVI Gustaf and the President of the Republic of Latvia Guntis Ulmanis.

Table 2: Key Steps in the Founding of SSE Riga.

The final steps in the founding of SSE Riga were the promotion of the new B.Sc. in Business and Economics programme, recruitment of students, and, of course, its launch. Newspaper advertisements, radio spots, and a Latvia-wide road show led to more than 750 applicants for the planned 50 seats in the B.Sc. Admission tests were held in order to assess logical aptitude, plus mathematics and English-language skills. The top candidates were then invited for interviews at which they could demonstrate their character, their experiences, and their motivation to study economics and business. 58 candidates were offered seats; 56 students enrolled in B.Sc. which began 8 July 8 1994. The official inauguration of SSE Riga in the presence of the King of Sweden Carl XVI Gustaf and the President of the Republic of Latvia Guntis Ulmanis occurred 8 November 1994.

SSE Riga, however, has changed significantly since its founding in 1991. Indeed, its history is a more elaborate tale of specific decisions, activities, and events, which together chronicle the evolution of SSE Riga and which culminate in its current incarnation (See Table 3.).

Instructors, Students, and the Curriculum

Following the guiding principles of SSE Riga, the professorial corps has been international in nature. In the early years, instructors were 'imported' from SSE. Over the years, however, additional instructors have been drawn from business schools of other countries, including the United States. More recently, Latvia-born instructors, almost always with 'Western' education and/or experience, have been added to the mix.

Financially, this international professorial crops has been the most

most expensive component of the SSE Riga project. Indeed, remuneration, travel expenses, and accommodation all add significantly to the cost of 'running the business'. In order to minimise accommodation expenses, a special SSE Riga apartment was created, where the visiting instructors could also meet each other and socialise during their stay in Riga.

A second significant challenge of the in-sourced instructor model has been ensuring interaction with students. In contrast to traditional universities in which instructors are available for meetings with students regularly and over long periods of time, SSE Riga instructors only spend short intensive periods in country to deliver their courses. The instructors have typically been available every day during their stay in Riga, and most have an open door policy. Consequently, and despite the brevity of the courses, students have developed close relationships with their instructors.

SSE Riga is the only international business school in the Baltic countries with English as the language of instruction. Combined with the Western-style of education, the reputation of SSE, and the merit-based recruitment, SSE Riga has earned the reputation as the leading business school in the region, and is now ranked among the best in all of Europe. It is unsurprising that the number of applicants has increased year-on-year, since the inaugural 1995 cohort.

Timing	Activity	Outcome
1994–1997	A two-year condensed program 8-week Summer Program, including a two week trip to Sweden that started in July	The first graduates in June 1996
1995 January-March	To connect with the labor market and develop income channels to financially support the undergraduate program, executive education was launched.	The first executive education program launched
1995, spring	A group of three international experts were invited to assess the study program, including the curriculum, the faculty and students, and the learning environment.	Quality assessment
1995, March	The entrance test and interviews were organized in the locations: Riga, Tallinn, and Vilnius	Selection of students from three Baltic countries

Timing	Activity	Outcome
1995, July	The first students from Estonia and Lithuania admitted (78 from Latvia, 12 from Lithuania, 10 from Estonia)	The full class of 100 students
1995, August 16–18	The conference on "Micro-level Studies of Transition in the Baltic Countries" was organized, attended by 50 international scholars.	Putting SSE Riga on the map as a research institution
1995, October 5	To address the differences between the legal terms and conditions on higher education institutions in Latvia such as the length of the program and the language of instruction and obtain recognition of the study program from the Ministry of Education and Science of the Republic of Latvia, a special law was adopted. It was essential to work towards the first graduating class to be awarded with legally approved diplomas.	Law on Stockholm School of Economics in Riga adopted by the Parliament of the Republic of Latvia
1995, November	The first Career Days organized by the SSE Riga Student Association to engage with the job market and provide jobs for the graduating class.	The first Career Days organized to put SSE Riga on the map for potential employers
1996, January – May	SSE Riga was chosen as the first higher education institution in Latvia to be accredited during a pilot accreditation project, engaging three international experts from the United Kingdom.	National accreditation of SSE Riga and the B.Sc. in Economics and Business study program.
1996, May	Based on the national accreditation of SSE Riga and the B.Sc. study program, it is also formally recognized in Estonia and Lithuania.	The SSE Riga diploma recognized in all three Baltic countries
1996, July 2	Out of 56 students who started the program,	The first graduating class of 46 students
1996, August	Ten top students from the graduating class were offered studies in an international graduate program (IGP) at SSE in Stockholm, providing them with full scholarships.	The initial steps for raising potential resident faculty for SSE Riga

Timing	Activity	Outcome
1996, fall	A decision is made to extend the study program to three years in order to provide students with more knowledge and experiences by adding a few more courses and internships	A three years B.Sc. study program being developed
1997, June	The first class of 89 students from Estonia, Latvia and Lithuania graduated from SSE Riga.	The objectives of SSE Riga graduating students from all three Baltic countries fulfilled
1997, August	A three-year program was started by 100 students (84 from Latvia, 8 from Lithuania, 8 from Estonia), and the Summer Program was transferred to a 6-week long Preparatory Semester.	A three-year B.Sc. program launched

Table 3: The Evolution of SSE Riga.

The difficulty of studying in a foreign language, however, is exacerbated by the rigour of the B.Sc. programme, and for many students, by the stress of leaving home. The transition from secondary school to university and the additional demands of higher education—from the more substantial workload to the additional requirements for academic work—can also be troublesome for some students. In response, SSE Riga developed a student safety net scheme, which includes social counselling, alumni-student mentoring, and peer support.

Following the guiding principles of SSE Riga, the curriculum of SSE Riga has always been similar to that of SSE. Initially, the programme took the three-year SSE bachelor of science degree and condensed it into two years, separated with only a four-week summer break between the first and second years. Individual courses were condensed into four-five week modules in order to accommodate visiting instructors. But admittedly it was very demanding for students. The accreditation committee subsequently recommended extending the program to three years in order to provide more time for students to digest (and master) the curriculum.

In 1997, therefore, the decision was made to extend the program to 2.5 years as of 1997, gradually reaching three years by the year 2000. The extension was accomplished by lengthening some of the courses (Macro-economics. for example, was lengthened from 4 to 6 weeks and Financial Economics was lengthened from 4 to 8 weeks); adding a few courses such as Econometrics, Advanced Accounting, and Applied Economics; and providing time for project work, study abroad, and internships. Extending the program also provided additional time for students to work on a thesis which is a graduation requirement.

In order to address the Latvia legal requirements for higher education institutions (length of the program, for example, and the language of instruction), and to obtain recognition of the program from the Ministry of Education and Science of the Republic of Latvia, the 'Law on Stockholm School of Economics in Riga' was adopted by the Parliament of the Republic of Latvia in October 1995, which provided SSE Riga with a special status within the Latvian higher education system. At the time, it was considered particularly important to have this legal recognition so that the diplomas of the first graduates would also be recognised.

SSE Riga was also chosen as the first higher education institution in Latvia to be accredited, during a pilot accreditation project which was launched in the mid-1990s using three experts from the United Kingdom. In Spring 1996, SSE Riga and the B.Sc. in Economics and Business study program in Latvia were accredited; shortly thereafter both were recognised in Estonia and Lithuania. On 2 July 1996, therefore, the first cohort—46 students in total—was awarded the official degree of Bachelor of Science in Economics and Business from the accredited SSE Riga.

Research and Executive Education

The mission of most institutions of higher education is not only to disseminate knowledge but also to create knowledge. In the Autumn of 1995, therefore, SSE Riga made its first foray into academic research, by hosting an interdisciplinary conference: Micro-level Studies of the Transition in the Baltic States. The conference was attended by fifty international scholars, and resulted in a book with the title 'Transition in the Baltic State: Micro-Level Studies'. The book was edited by Neil Hood, Roberts Kilis, and Jan-Erik Vahlne, and was published in 1997 by St. Martin's Press.

At that same time, the Rector of SSE Riga also began thinking about the development of a new generation of scholars who would explore Baltic business and economic phenomena, and who could eventually replace the in-sourced instructors. A scholarship programme was launched, therefore, to sponsor the top ten students from the graduating cohort to continue their studies at the graduate level at SSE.

1995 also marked the introduction of an executive education department, whose aim was to contribute to the development of management expertise in the Baltic region, by conducting open-enrolment and customised training programmes on its own and with partner institutions, for public and private organisations from Latvia and elsewhere. In 2006, for example, a programme was developed in cooperation with Telia-Sonera Corporation for 20 high-level managers from Estonia, Denmark, Latvia, Lithuania, Norway, and Sweden. The programme consisted of two modules (4 days in total); sessions were led by eight international instructors. The success of this programme made SSE Riga a kind of hub for executive education for multinational companies in the Baltic region.

The EMBA Programme

For almost a decade, the B.Sc. in Business and Economics was the only degree programme offered at SSE Riga. But in 2002, an Executive MBA (EMBA) programme was launched, in response to market demand and also in service of the Baltic business community. Likewise taught entirely in English, the EMBA was designed for managers who had reached executive-level positions in commercial or public organisations, and was structured in a modular format with courses meeting over a four-day weekend once per month.

The first cohort had 21 students: 20 Latvians and 1 Lithuania. 80% of the students were male, with the average age was 34. Over time, as the EMBA gained momentum, the pool of applicants became more international, with students hailing from Argentina, Croatia, Denmark, Estonia, Finland, France, Germany, Israel, Lithuania, Netherlands, Russia, Spain, Taiwan, Ukraine, the United Kingdom, and the United States. Male to female ration has also improved, and the diversity of industry and educational backgrounds has broadened.

Instructors for the EMBA are drawn from leading international business schools, and from industry. Not unlike in the B.Sc., 80% of the

EMBA instructors are in-sourced. Many of the in-sourced instructors have been affiliated with SSE Riga for years. John, for example, started teaching there in 2004.

The EMBA curriculum is relatively 'traditional' in nature, but is also supplemented with international study trips which combine lectures and seminars, company visits, social activities, and cultural visits. Unsurprisingly, these study trips have included journeys to SSE and to its third satellite campus—the Stockholm School of Economics in Saint Petersburg. But over the years, other study trips have also ventured further abroad, to such destinations as Belgium (2003), Luxembourg (2004), Buenos Aires in Argentina (2007), Shanghai in China (2008), and Hong Kong (2009–2015).

The study trips were always co-organised with local partner schools: Solvay Business School and the University of Liege/HCE business school in Belgium, IAE Business School in Buenos Aires, the Shanghai Maritime University in China, and both the Hong Kong City University and HKUST in Hong Kong. In some instances, students from the SSE Riga EMBA and the partner university worked jointly on an international project. In addition to the curricular goals, these study trips also provided SSE Riga EMBA students the opportunity to compare themselves to students of other EMBA programmes, and to network with international colleagues.

Erasmus and Institutional Partnerships

A significant achievement in the evolution of SSE Riga paralleled Latvia's accession to the European Union in 2004. Indeed, preparation for Erasmus student mobility began with the development of a document "SSE Riga and the Bologna Process", which provided policies and processes for comparable degrees, the ECTS grading system, international mobility, and international partnerships. ECTS grades were introduced in 2003, and the graduating class of 2004 received new transcripts which included both SSE Riga grades and ECTS grades, thereby providing better comparability and recognition of the SSE Riga diplomas internationally.

The number of partnership agreements with other institutions also grew dramatically after European Union accession. In 6 years, the 5 partnerships which SSE Riga had in France, Norway, and Sweden of 2004, which provided placements for 5 outgoing SSE Riga students and one incoming student from Sweden, mushroomed to 35 Erasmus partnerships in 17 European Union member states and Norway by 2010, providing 30 mobility placements and 10 internship spots. Internationalisation was enhanced further with the Higher Education Support Program (HESP) which created partnerships in Armenia, Azerbaijan, Kazakhstan, Moldova, and Russia. Bilateral agreements were also signed with universities in Buenos Aires, Hong Kong, Mexico, and Israel. By 2010, SSE Riga had more than 60 partnerships in 34 countries. It hosted 43 incoming students and sent 40 SSE Riga students abroad to study.

The Erasmus Program also provided a framework for instructor and administrator mobility. And SSE Riga began hosting a number of international student groups from Denmark, Germany, the Netherlands, Norway, Sweden, and the United States. SSE Riga likewise designed study trips for its undergraduates, in order to reinforce the international dimension and to activate knowledge and understanding of international business. In 2004, for example, students visited Nürnberg-Erlangen and Freiburg, and in 2005 Stralsund.

Academic Partnerships

At this time, SSE Riga also began accelerating its scientific activities, first by by joining Central and East European Management Development Association (CEEMAN) and the European Institute for Advanced Studies in Management (EISAM). In 2004, TeliaSonera endowed the TeliaSonera Professorship at the SSE Riga, and funded the TeliaSonera Institute at SSE Riga whose mission was to conduct policy-oriented research in the fields of entrepreneurship, telecommunications, and information technology. The Baltic Institute of Economic Policy Studies (BICEPS) was established at SSE Riga, and, together with the Stockholm Institute of Transition Economics (SITE) at SSE, received funding in Spring 2007 from the Swedish Institute to support various network activities with partners in Sweden, Russia, Ukraine, and Poland.

SSE Riga also participated in several applied research projects which were financed by external sources, in many cases various European Union funds, and nearly all involving international partners. For example, SSE Riga engaged in the European Union INTERREG IIIC and INTERREG IVC programmes which focused on interregional cooperation across Europe. One project which was entitled 'Best Practice Guidelines for Instrument of Regional Development and Spatial Planning in an Enlarged EU' (GRIDS, 2004–2006) was led by Cardiff University in Wales, but also engaged ministries, regional and city administrative units, and other institutions from Ireland, Flanders, Latvia, and Lithuania. Similarly, SSE Riga instructors' members grew professionally from their participation in the European Community 6th Framework Program for Research, Technological Development and Demonstration, notably the project on 'Accommodating Creative Knowledge – Competitiveness of European Metropolitan Regions within the Enlarged Union' (ACRE, 2006–2009), which was managed by the University of Amsterdam. Smaller-scale projects within the Leonardo da Vinci and Nordplus frameworks also provided instructors opportunities to develop innovative practices in higher education and lifelong learning.

SSE Riga also became an arena for international academic and policy debate, particularly surrounding issues related to European Union accession. In Spring 2005, for example, SSE Riga hosted a conference 'Human Development in EU accession countries', which engaged academic and professional speakers from the European Commission and universities in Croatia, Cyprus, the Czech Republic, Denmark, Estonia, France, Germany, Macedonia, Mexico, the Netherlands, Poland, Romania, the United Kingdom, and the United States. And in September 2006, a conference on the European Union project 'Stepwise Environmental Product Declaration (EPD) featured speakers from Denmark, Portugal, and Sweden. SSE Riga also played host to a number of conferences which were organised in cooperation with the Latvian Ministry of Culture, Ministry of Economics, Ministry of Finance, Ministry of Foreign Affairs, Ministry of Environmental Protection and Regional Development, and Ministry of Welfare.

Academic partnerships also led to new executive education offerings. SSE Executive Education (then IFL) often served as a broker, bringing new customers to SSE Riga. In 2006, a partnership with the William Davidson Institute at the University of Michigan was established, and a new product—Strategic Management Program (SMP)—was offered. Thirty-six executives, senior managers, and high-potential managers attended the 2-week programme which explored the most recent theoretical developments in management. The success of this programme all resulted in the launch of several additional executive education offerings, including the Marketing Professionals Program (October 2008) and HR Professionals Program (February 2009).

Change of Ownership

2010/2011 witnessed the completion of a 'change of ownership', with SSE Riga transitioning from a joint Swedish and Latvian government-funded institution, to a private-held non-for-profit institution which operates under a licensing agreement with SSE. Amendments related to the administrative and organisational structures, procedures, and functions of SSE Riga were also made to the Law on Stockholm School of Economics in Riga. As a consequence of the change of ownership, the SSE Riga Foundation with its Supervisory and Management Boards were established to provide oversight and governance of SSR Riga.

Academically, the change of ownership meant 'business as usual'. But it resulted in new policies related to the license agreement and the governance structure to specifically, the use of the SSE name, and compliance with quality standards. These new policies subsequently resulted in new procedures which were initiated and managed by new organisational units, including the Programme Directors' Task Force and the Faculty and Programme Board. The change of ownership also triggered a new emphasis on grants and external fund-raising. Indeed, in 2010, the Center for Media Studies was established, and two years later in 2012 the Center for Sustainable Business opened its doors.

The Swedish Grant Programme

In September 2010, the Swedish Government (through the Swedish Ministry of Foreign Affairs) announced a grant programme to finance up to 20 students from Belarus, Moldova, Georgia, and Ukraine (with a preference for students from Belarus and Moldova) for the 3-year SSE Riga B.Sc. degree. The programme was initially planned for a period of five years, but would be extended to the present day if results were acceptable.

The grant programme changed the complexion of the student body significantly, with 20 of the 120 students of each incoming SSE Riga cohort now arriving from outside the Baltic states. It also added a new dimension to SSE Riga promotion and admissions activities elevated communication, for example, with both the Ministries of Education and the Swedish Embassies in Belarus, Moldova, Georgia, and Ukraine. The new non-European Union students also led to the development of new SSE Riga routines regarding student integration, visa requirements, visa processing, residence permits, dormitory space, and summer internship placements.

The grant programme, by all measures, has been very successful. Indeed, the number of applicants has grown year-on-year (See Table 4.), as both the grant programme and SSE Riga become better known in Belarus, Georgia, Moldova, and Ukraine, not only because of expanded SSE Riga promotional activities but also because of increased social media 'buzz'. Students from the four countries are exceptionally good, representing 40% of the most recent top 10 graduates. On the whole, they are also more socially-active, and are often elected into leadership positions in student government and student associations.

	2011	2012	2013	2014	2015
	Admits/ Applicants	Admits/ Applicants	Admits/ Applicants	Admits/ Applicants	Admits/ Applicants
Belarus	8/36	8/74	11/69	10/99	7/85
Georgia	1/9	1/9	1/16	1/6	2/8
Moldova	9/53	8/74	9/66	8/111	7/54
Ukraine	2/6	2/36	2/20	2/15	2/23

Table 4: Students from Belarus, Georgia, Moldova, and Ukraine.

The grant programme has also benefitted other units of SSE Riga, and spurred additional eastward activities. At B.Sc. road shows and annual education fairs in Chisinau, Kiev, Tbilisi, and Minsk, for example, the School is able to promote the SSE Riga EMBA. In 2013, SSE Riga was also able to secure Swedish Government support to train 25 journalists from Armenia, Azerbaijan, Belarus, Georgia, Moldova, and Ukraine in the art and science of investigative journalism, with a special emphasis on business and economics. In 2014, a similar programme was offered in concert with the Riga Graduate School of Law for civic leaders and public administrators from Armenia, Azerbaijan, Belarus, Georgia, Kazakhstan, Kosovo, Kyrgyzstan, Moldova, Tajikistan, Turkmenistan, Ukraine, and Uzbekistan.

Discussion

It ought to be obvious from this short description of the evolution of SSE Riga that its internationalisation has indeed been unique. That is to say, its internationalisation has reflected its unique circumstances. Or paraphrasing Chan & Dimmock (2008), the internationalisation of SSE Riga has differed in terms of both its strategies (policies and infrastructure) and its programmes (curriculum), precisely because the meanings and interpretations of internationalisation have shifted according to its various rationales, incentives, and activities, and to the political and economic circumstances within which the internationalisation of SSE Riga occurred. But does the internationalisation of SSE Riga follow one of the three generic models of institutional internationalisation which were proposed by Chan & Dimmock (2008)?

To begin, it must be stated that SSE Riga has lived a sort of schizophrenic existence, operating as both a satellite of the SSE 'mothership' in Stockholm, and as a self-supporting, self-sustaining entity. As such, its internationalisation must be viewed from both perspectives. First, it can be argued that SSE Riga was in fact the outcome of the transnationalisation of SSE. As such, it could be considered as the product of SSE's adherence to the globalist model of institutional internationalisation. Indeed, at the time of the founding of SSE Riga, Latvia was a developing economy, with a growing population of elites (economic and academic) who aspired to 'break the shackles' of the Soviet Union and its antiquated educational system, especially in the fields of business and economics. Although it is claimed that the motives for the founding of SSE Riga were altruistic in nature—Sweden's sense of duty to help its Baltic neighbour—doubtless SSE Riga has benefited both SSE and the Swedish economy. That SSE Riga was required to deliver the SSE curriculum in whole simply reinforces that SSE Riga was the outcome of the transnationalisation of SSE.

Chan & Dimmock's (2008) model breaks down, however, when it comes to intercultural understanding, foreign-mindedness, foreign language proficiency, or mutually-beneficial international and inter-institutional cooperation. Whereas Chan & Dimmock (2008) suggest that an institution eschews these factors in favour of a more standard-ised export approach, SSE Riga, on the contrary, adopted the notion that successful graduates of economics and business had to be part of the global economy. Now to be fair, Chan & Dimmock's (2008) research was situated at the university level, and globally-minded citizens are not always a priority. In most business schools, however, globalisation, global markets, cross-cultural competence, etc. have become commonplace curriculum components. In this sense, therefore, the globalist model of institutional internationalisation still holds true.

If SSE Riga is viewed not as the outcome of the transnationalisation of SSE, however, but as its own institution in the throes of internationali-sation, then it can be argued that SSE Riga has followed the translocalist model of institutional internationalisation. Again, at the time of its founding (and still to this day to some degree), Latvia was a developing economy. The relatively small population was culturally-homogeneous, notwithstanding the strife between ethnic Latvian and Russian citizens, and nation-building, both politically and economically, was a concern. SSE Riga's primary function was to train a new cadre of business profes-sionals. It drew heavily on instructors from abroad. Its international student population was limited. And its activities were intended to serve the local (Baltic) community.

Its aim was to become an institution of excellence among Latvian (and Baltic) institutions of higher education, providing the best quality economics and business education. As mentioned before, it cultivated a global perspective among its students, by teaching in English, insourcing foreign professors, facilitating study-abroad options, and offering a curriculum which embraced globalisation. It strove to graduate students who were competitive not only nationally but internationally, and who could help contribute to the development of Latvia and the Baltic.

More recently, and especially since the change of ownership, SSE Riga also appears to be adopting more of an internationalist model of institutional internationalisation. During the Soviet times, Latvia (and also Estonia and Lithuania) were always viewed as more advanced, more 'Western'. But today, its standing among countries to the East (Belarus, Moldova, Georgia, and Ukraine, for example) has risen, especially since its accession to the European Union. Consequently, SSE Riga enjoys a strong reputation among students from these countries, augmented by the SSE brand, its instruction in the English language, and its academic excellence which is supported by its ranking in the European business school league tables. It looks and acts like a 'serious' business school, with international partnerships, international instructors, and growing scientific output.

Conclusion

In the words of Friedman (1999:14) globalisation is the *"inexorable integration of markets, nation-states, and technologies to a degree never witnessed before—in a way that is enabling individuals, corporations, and nation-states to reach around the world farther, faster, deeper, and cheaper than ever before"*. It is against this backdrop of globalisation, that institutions find themselves internationalising—integrating an international/intercultural dimension into their teaching, research, and service functions.

Different institutions, however, internationalise differently in response to globalisation, but more importantly as a result of different contextual circumstances. Chan & Dimmock (2008) proposed three generic models of institutional internationalisation: 1. the internationalist model, 2. the translocalist model, and 3. the globalist model. The Stockholm School of Economics Riga, Latvia which was founded in 1993 as a satellite of the Stockholm School of Economics in Sweden, appears to follow each of these models of institutional internationalisation, at different times throughout its evolution.

About the Authors

Diana Pauna is Dean of Arts & Sciences at University of Central Asia, and the former Pro-Rector of the Stockholm School of Economics in Riga, Latvia. She can be contacted at this e-mail: diana.pauna@ucentralasia.org

John Branch is Academic Director of the part-time MBA programmes and Assistant Clinical Professor of Business Administration at the Stephen M. Ross School of Business, and Faculty Associate at the Center for Russian, East European, & European Studies, both of the University of Michigan in Ann Arbor, U.S.A. He can be contacted at this e-mail: jdbranch@umich.edu

Bibliography

Chan, W. & C. Dimmock (2008). The Internationalization of Universities: Globalist, Internationalist, and Translocalist Models. *Journal of Research in International Education*, Vol. 7, No. 2, pp. 184–204.

Friedman, T. (1999). *The Lexus and the Olive Tree: Understanding Globalization.* New York, U.S.A.: Picador.

Knight, J. (1997). Internationalization of Higher Education: A Conceptual Framework. In J. Knight & H. de Wit (Eds.), *Internationalization of Higher Education in Asia-Pacific Countries.* Amsterdam: European Association for International Education.

Chapter 8

International Virtual Exchange: An Example from Health Education

Nicola Bartholomew, Geraldine Nevin,
Hannah Abbott, Deborah Pittaway & Robyn Nash

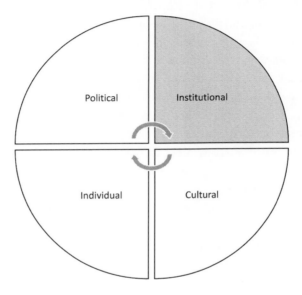

Introduction

This chapter is an important contribution to the book on Globalisation of Higher Education as it explores our experience of designing and delivering an international virtual exchange programme for students on healthcare courses as a collaboration between Birmingham City University (BCU) in England and Queensland University of Technology (QUT) in Australia. This initiative was a response to the globalisation of both healthcare and higher education. This is reflected locally by the strategic aim for internationalisation at both universities through a range of activities including overseas student placements and increased globalisation of the curricula. Traditionally, these objectives have been achieved via a range of strategies such as Erasmus opportunities or shorter observational overseas experiences; however, these present a number of challenges for the pre-registration health professional courses due to professional/regulatory requirements relating to placement or the lack of an equivalent profession overseas. In addition to this, we recognised the financial and practical implications of an overseas experience and that consequently these opportunities would not be accessible to all students. In order to address these challenges and offer a practical opportunity for international student mobility, we developed a "virtual exchange" with QUT as a partner university and will explore our experiences within this chapter.

Health provision was traditionally nationally focused (WHO, 2016); however, this has changed significantly within the last 15 years, and in the current clinical setting globalisation is evidenced by increasing international mobility as overseas practitioners are actively recruited in the UK, most commonly nurses (WHO, 2016). This is mirrored in Australia where the governmental workforce strategy includes the need to recruit skilled practitioners from overseas (Australian Bureau of Statistics, 2013; Parker and McMillan, 2007), including both nurses and allied health professionals. This diversity in the healthcare workforce is particularly evident in London (Hutt and Buchan, 2005) and other large cities. It has been shown, however, that these multicultural healthcare teams can present challenges resulting in stress for both the host and immigrant practitioners (Xiao et al., 2015), and it is, therefore, essential to preparing practitioners and students for practice in a diverse clinical setting so they are able to work effectively within a multicultural team for the provision of safe patient care. In addition to working within a diverse healthcare setting within their country of origin, registrant health professionals may also decide to practice in another country during their career. The most frequent destination for UK health professionals wishing to practice overseas is Australia, followed by other English-speaking countries, for example, the United States of America, Canada and New Zealand (Tjadens et al., 2013). Similarly, Australian health professionals will also seek opportunities to practice overseas, including South Africa, the Middle East and New Zealand. Consequently, the international virtual exchange allowed students to also consider the potential for overseas practice as part of their professional careers and a number of students had cited this as contributing to their motivation to participate.

This virtual exchange project, therefore, explored the globalisation of healthcare from both the service user and the practitioner perspectives, academic staff and students were encouraged to consider the wider context of health and social care within their discussions. In order to participate in the project, the students engaged in discussions within an online learning environment and consequently this supported a secondary aim of developing students' collaborative and digital literacy skills, which are important factors for globalised education.

From reading this chapter, you will be able to:

+ discuss the educational and professional drivers for embedding globalisation in pre-registration healthcare education;

+ explain the key considerations when developing a virtual exchange project;

+ discuss the advantages and challenges of virtual exchange as an educational opportunity;

+ consider the different opportunities and implementation strategies for virtual exchange.

Project Context

The challenge of moving health and social care curricula forward to reflect national change and development remains a constant [Quality Assurance Agency (QAA), 2015]. The challenge of ensuring that curricula reflect globalisation and the inter-professional nature of health and social care is similarly crucial. Thus, ensuring that service delivered is based on cultural sensitivity and the development of a workforce well equipped to deliver such high-quality care [Australian Health Practitioners Regulating Authority (AHPRA), 2014; Brownie et al., 2014; Connor, 2003; Health and Care Professions Council (HCPC), 2016; Nursing and Midwifery Council (NMC), 2015]. This demands that courses offer exposure to opportunities to develop and enhance such skills. Certainly, in some health professions such exposure is advocated and integral to course outcomes and knowledge; indeed, they can no longer be ignored if courses are to remain sustainable (Bradbury-Jones, 2009).

Rising to such challenges places the onus on course teams to seek out new opportunities to expose students to experiences, both at home and overseas, that raise their understanding of a how an appreciation of global contexts can have a positive impact on their experiences. This inclusion of transnational education (TNE) within the curriculum is considered to become increasingly important in the development of students and staff as 'global citizens' (Parkes & Hayes, in this volume). Traditionally, these global/international experiences have been generated through travel abroad programmes, such as the Erasmus (Milne & Cowie, 2013) and other university initiatives like QUT's Study Abroad and Exchange programmes. However, the global economy has placed additional pressures on students and often these opportunities are now limited, not by lack of enthusiasm or desire, but rather by a paucity of personal funding streams. Course teams recognise this and set about developing other "means" of global exposure with some advocating periods abroad (NMC, 2010).

The idea of virtual exchange is not new, and experience of such tools to assist in developing a more in-depth understanding of globalisation and to enhance life-long learning skills have demonstrated its value at creating community learning globally (Doerry et al., 2004; Edwards et al., 2007; Todhunter et al., 2013). Such an "exchange" possibility was felt to offer students across the Faculty and professions the opportunity to explore the concept of globalisation and inter-professional working with another similar international provision. The notion of exchange in this programme was the students' exchange of experiential knowledge related to their own university and clinical practice context and this reflects the concept of culture posed by Dawson (in this volume), which considers universities as both "scientific and cultural institutions". This virtual exchange, therefore, encouraged students to compare and contrast the culture of the higher educational experience between the different institutions.

The project team at Birmingham City University (BCU) identified Queensland University of Technology (QUT) as a partner offering comparable programmes of study in health and social care, with similar student demographics. Early discussions with the teams identified similar needs to enhance international and interdisciplinary opportunities for students, particularly those unable to commit finances to physical exchanges and placements overseas (BCU, 2014; QUT, 2014). Previous experience of using a virtual learning community further confirmed the "fit" with the project plan (Edwards *et al.*, 2008). A "letter of intent" was agreed between the two teams to outline the project aims and the focus of the experience. The early collaboration meetings were held using Skype as a communication medium. These synchronous discussions proved invaluable in developing working relationships. Early lessons were had in relation to the impact that time differences would have on the collaboration and the impact that technology can have and, indeed, is having on the student experience, particularly in social networking sites.

It was agreed that the BCU Moodle virtual learning environment would be the home of the virtual exchange. Moodle, as an open source virtual learning platform, has been utilised within BCU since 2004 and offered the team an ideal site to launch the project. The forum activity within Moodle is simple to use and offers users, both enrolled BCU students and invited guests, a valuable and accessible resource, enabling students and staff to engage in the learning environment wherever and whenever they chose. (Salmon, 2011) The exchange site was designed to be as user-friendly as possible, an uncluttered introduction page with obvious navigation guide and information clearly reflecting both universities to ensure that students from QUT felt welcomed into this new environment (ibid). IT support and access, both during the development phase and during the project, was agreed and seen as pivotal to success.

Welcome emails were sent to all participants with easy to follow instructions for joining the discussion forums. The site was structured around agreed learning objectives for the project and adherence to the BCU Moodle Code of Conduct agreed for all activity and discussions within the VLE (BCU 2015). Leads from each Faculty recruited students from across the range of health and social care programmes with a maximum number of 10 from each Faculty seen as the ideal. Such an interdisciplinary approach to the recruitment was seen as vital. The need for students to become more confident in a multi-professional forum is evident and serves to enhance care delivery for patients and clients (Thistlewaite, 2012; Wakeley *et al.*, 2013). It was felt that this number would enable staff to facilitate meaningful dialogue whilst "testing" the exchange learning outcomes.

The project was designed as an extracurricular activity, and there was some real concern regarding this issue and whether recruiting adequate numbers to make the project viable would be achievable. Students are busy balancing hectic lives, and adding one more activity with no perceived credit value was a risky proposition. Often, in spite of encouragement to participate in such activities, particularly in relation to the acquisition of further employability skills, students remain reticent (Gerard & Billington, 2014). However, after an initial mail shot poster outlining the project, sufficient numbers were recruited to make the project viable.

Learning objectives previously agreed by the team were to be launched on a weekly basis, and discussion forums were structured around the subsequent dialogue generated by these topics. A gentle, "light-touch" approach was taken in the first week in order to facilitate the introduction of both the students and the Faculty leads. This type of "light-touch" approach is advocated (Todhunter et al., 2013) and enables students to feel comfortable in the VLE and develop an understanding of how the asynchronous discussion forums would be managed. For the next four weeks, each learning objective was launched at an agreed date and time. This structure and schedule enabled students to plan their asynchronous contribution to these forums. It was agreed that given that students would be contributing something "extra" to their current curricula and that there was a nine-hour time difference, an expectation that synchronous discussion would be possible was perhaps too ambitious in this initial un-credited activity. It was intended that Faculty leads would engage in the forum to ensure discussions were developed, as in any "classroom" setting, but it was agreed that this was of particular significance in the VLE. It was felt that facilitation in this arena would be crucial to engage students in the discussion and maintain the discussion flow.

Project Evaluation and Conceptual Framework

In the early stages of project planning, focus was directed towards the proposed topics for discussion, the "content", and this influenced the development of content-driven project objectives to frame discussions. The discussion themes prompted participants to explore the challenges of local health and social care from the perspective of both countries, to consider how geographical position impacts on determinants of health and to analyse their own professional roles within a global health and social care context. These discussion objectives influenced the subsequent evaluation of the project to an extent; however, an emergent evaluation focus steered us towards exploring levels of collaboration and shared understanding within the online forum. If we aim to prepare our students for work in the 21st century, with its heightened emphasis on the global economy, then we have a responsibility to foster essential 21st-century skills. Pellegrino and Hilton (2012) identify such skills as being cognitive, interpersonal, which includes communication and collaboration, and intrapersonal in nature. Upvall *et al.* (2014), citing Hunter *et al.* (2013), note that nurses, as health advocates and diplomats, could be key players in forging global partnerships; however, globalisation is dependent on the construction of networks, interactions and interdependent participants supported by information and communication technologies to enable information and knowledge exchange (Cornali *et al.*, 2012). Jisc (2015) also acknowledge communication, collaboration and participation to be integral digital literacy skills. With this heightened reliance on ICT and its influence on the globalisation of education, the development of digital literacy skills to enable students to work in a digital society is essential.

Saadé and Huang (2009) propose that learning networks, constructed via computer-mediated communications, provide opportunities for gathering and sharing information. Indeed, they emphasise the inherent benefits of online networks to enable the construction of relationships in a *"culturally diverse global environment"*. However, Kear (2010) highlights the significance of building a social presence within online learning communities as the text-based, asynchronous and potentially impersonal nature of online discussion forums can easily lead to disengagement of participants. Salmon (2011) also promotes the importance of effective design and facilitation of these virtual learning spaces to encourage socialisation and to scaffold learning. Collaborative learning in an online context may be defined as a *"communicative process directed towards knowledge construction among peers with similar skills in a virtual scenario of positive interdependence"* (Tirado *et al.*, 2011). Our student participants/peers were all studying at a similar level and within a healthcare context, but they were reliant on each other to share their backgrounds and experiences from across the globe. The role of the forum facilitators would be important here to maintain an open, "friendly" and supportive learning environment, whilst encouraging reciprocity, the exchange of ideas and the progression of discussion threads.

Drawing from the collaborative, cognitive and interpersonal themes of 21ˢᵗ-century learning, a conceptual framework was duly constructed as part of the project evaluation strategy (table 1), and this framework was aimed to convey markers indicating levels of student engagement with the project. The discussions within the online forum would provide the data for discourse analysis, framed by these concepts, and with a coding system applied to identify relevant markers of engagement. Participants were issued with an evaluation form as the project concluded, and this feedback was also included within the data set. The framework analysis is summarised in table 2.

Concept	Generated through	Markers
Digital literacy	Participant evaluations	Ease of access to Moodle, navigation of VE site
Participation	Forum logs	Number and or length of posts, Transnational information exchange relating to project objectives, contributions across both institutions
Social presence	Discourse analysis of forum threads Participant evaluations	Depictions of "real" people through expressions of feeling, self introductions, jokes, compliments, greetings (Angeli et al, 1998), emoticons, emphasis of expression
Collaboration	Discourse analysis of forum threads	Peer to peer and tutor to peer contributions, offering opinions, acknowledging others, replying to peers, seeking agreement (Bartholomew, 2015), posing general questions, shared resources
Cognitive skills	Discourse analysis of forum threads	Critical thinking, argument, reflection, concept reinforcement, shared language, analysis, researching new ideas, posing subject questions

Table 1: Conceptual framework adapted from Saade et al. (2012).

Digital literacy

An initial stumbling block to engagement could be associated with problems accessing and navigating the online environment. Salmon (2011) identifies the importance of quick and easy access to maintaining positive attitudes towards online learning. In relation to the design and navigation of the project space, 75% of students felt the Moodle layout was "clear", "simple", and "easy to navigate". However, two students felt the site was "cluttered" and "confusing". Such polarised views can render the design of effective online learning environments challenging; however, Jisc acknowledges that effective (online) learning is likely to occur when opportunities to learn involve the "right learners" (Jisc, 2004). Students' prior experience, motivations and expectations of a course, in addition to support for ICT competence, must be addressed from the outset to encourage effective engagement. One respondent did acknowledge that he would have found navigation easier if he had accessed the site more often and this is perhaps suggestive of low motivation, although self-efficacy with the online medium must also be considered. Jisc (2016) acknowledges that although students may be digitally aware, they will not necessarily be used to learning within virtual environments. Students, as the future workforce, must be well prepared for this mode of learning and be offered opportunities to develop digital literacy skills so they may contribute effectively to the global economy.

Student Engagement

Saade *et al.* (2012) citing Schrire (2006) posit that social discourse, as a cognitive process, emerges from interactions within discussion forums whilst also contributing to these interactions. Participation and information exchange, the "content" of discussions, need to be established for meaning-making (through collaboration) to occur. The conceptual framework considers the characteristics of participant contributions and the extent to which project objectives (topic themes) had been discussed.

Concept	Number of examples of markers
Digital capability	100% of participants able to access VLE easily
	75% of participants
Levels of participation	Week 1: 24 posts (9 from staff, 15 from students)
	Week 2: 13 posts (4 from staff, 7 from students)
	Week 3: 10 posts (4 from staff, 6 from students)
	Week 4: 1 posts (1 staff)
	Week 5: 12 posts (6 from staff, 6 from students)
	20 incidents of information exchange (relating to topics)
Social presence/interpersonal skills	60 incidents in week 1 (including photos)
	34 incidents across weeks 2–5
Collaboration	36 incidents
Cognitive skills	38 incidents

Table 2: Markers for collaboration: Results of sampled data

A review of forum postings revealed that activity was variable across the duration of the project. During week 1, all 15 students from both institutions contributed equally to the welcome discussion; however, four students (two from each institution) subsequently disengaged from the project. Students who remained within the project responded fairly consistently across threads except for the anomalous week 4 where no contributions were offered. Student evaluations indicate that "other commitments" and "illness" were factors influencing engagement. Furthermore, the nature and facilitation of discussion themes may have been causative factors for diminishing engagement, and while several students offered full and insightful responses, others felt "unequipped to answer some questions". This was associated with the broad and indirect nature of discussion themes and with themes becoming focused around one professional discipline and being "too evidence-based". While open-ended discussion questions to develop critical, higher-order thinking skills are to be encouraged, they could be too challenging for some students, especially around subject areas outside of their own discipline. This would impact on student confidence and their capacity to achieve, leading to isolation within the online environment. Direct Socratic-style probing and problem-based/task orientated activities may help to maintain momentum (Haugen *et al.*, 2001; Xia *et al.*, 2013). Student feedback is also sympathetic to this view.

"Perhaps in future years, more stringent tasks and more specific questions could be allocated."

"Maybe a few more direct questions would have helped to break the discussions up."

The timing of facilitator intervention is also critical as responding too early with comments can potentially shut down student discussion (Mazzolini & Maddison, 2007, p.2004), but delayed feedback can also lead to reduced motivation and disengagement. An asynchronous forum was deliberately chosen as a vehicle for discussion, and Shi *et al.* (2006) advocate the allocation of a week per discussion theme for online asynchronous forums, which was factored into the project plan. However, the 10-hour time difference could still have hampered engagement somewhat, with certain students quick to post and monopolising discussions to a degree. Facilitation is key here. Shi *et al.* (2006) advocate the distribution of participation rules to outline the expected frequency of participation. Although the discussion themes were made clear, and responses to themes were invited on a week-by-week basis, we did not indicate how often they were expected to participate in a given thread. Many students often submitted single responses to threads, which limited the discussion a little. However, time constraints also need to be acknowledged here and it transpired that the project overlapped with an exam schedule at QUT. Participation rules could also include a rotating list of students to spearhead discussions (ibid). Faculty development is also an essential consideration in the use of VLE discussion forums. The delivery of content in a dynamic way takes on greater importance, especially for curriculum development of health professional programmes, and there is a need for sufficient training and ongoing administrative support for these forums to be successful (Claman, 2015).

Establishing a strong social scaffold is also critical to online forum engagement (Salmon, 2011). The light-touch week of "getting to know one another" enabled participants to share information about where they lived, including shared images from Birmingham and Queensland. Kear

(2012) suggests that online environments can be impersonal, resulting in low levels of engagement, but by inviting students to share a little about themselves and upload images for context we could overlay a sense of realism to proceedings, giving participants a sense that they were communicating with "real" people. Kear (2012), citing Gunawardena & Zittle (1997) acknowledges this sense of authenticity to be an important factor for establishing a social presence. Uploaded images included photos of family life, recreational and work-based activities helped to establish individual profiles. From the text-based discourse within the week 1 discussion, 51 markers of interpersonal interactions were identified which is suggestive of socialisation. Some examples of these markers were terms such as, "Welcome, I'm excited…, I look forward to…,*cry face*…, a great experience…, I love to travel…, Yippee!" The socialisation during week 1 offered a solid foundation to scaffold future engagement; however, such markers of social presence declined as the discussions progressed over subsequent weeks. The changing nature of the discussion themes influenced this, of course, but Salmon (2011) warns against the "rush to get on with the learning" that could be detrimental to cultivating an online community. Nevertheless, collaborative markers such as replying to peers, offering opinions, and seeking agreement (Bartholomew, 2015) should also be viewed as inclusive, interpersonal interactions contributing to the development of this learning community. Such markers of collaboration were clearly evident in many of the posts, as participants offered their opinions to discussion themes, demonstrated agreement with colleagues and prompted further discussions, e.g., "I was wondering about others' views on this…, I completely agree with…, As xxxx mentioned…, could you elaborate a little more…?"

Participating students responded well to discussion themes (except during week 4) and exchanged information about health and social care from their regional perspectives that were evidence-informed. Many students attached resources/articles and links to web pages to establish context and promote deeper understanding as a collaborative activity. A key affordance of an online learning environment is that it better enables information exchange, and student-centred pedagogies encourage information exchange, collaboration between students and problem solving, which is fundamental in a globalised society. Derrick (2002), on behalf of the Global Information Infrastructure Commission, acknowledges the changing shape of education to meet the demands of the rapidly increasing world store of knowledge and promote the empowerment of students to learn for themselves:

> *"The globalization of the economy and its concomitant demands on the workforce requires a different education that enhances the ability of learners to access, assess, adopt, and apply knowledge, to think independently to exercise appropriate judgment and to collaborate with others to make sense of new situations."*

Forum discussions revealed commonalities relating to the impact of an ageing population on healthcare systems across both the UK and Australia. Heart disease, obesity and diabetes were common issues, with students promoting public health and wellbeing campaigns targeted at young people to reduce the healthcare burden. Unsurprising perhaps for two first world countries however, further discussions focused on urban-rural issues, and this demonstrated that students from both countries were well aware of the wide range of factors contributing to health outcomes and the impact of healthcare. Students demonstrated evidence of reflection, drawing from their own experiences to reinforce healthcare issues.

While the forum themes encouraged the sharing of both information and opinions, there could have been scope to adopt a more problem-based approach to further encourage collaboration and sustained engagement. Again, student feedback suggests that goal-orientated "tasks" would have been welcomed. However, it could also be argued that the more open-ended discussion themes would prompt the consideration of abstract concepts. Derrick (2002) also acknowledges this to be fundamental to globalisation as problems emerging within a "rapid fire global economy" are not clearly defined. One student offered an interesting observation about healthcare in the time of Florence Nightingale and speculated how the heightened levels of education and advanced practice for modern nurses would be perceived back in the 1850's. Was advanced practice appropriate? She argues both ways to acknowledge the benefits of empowering nurses whilst acknowledging the potentially negative impact on basic levels of care, clear evidence of abstract and critical thinking. Perhaps a staged approach would be beneficial, with close-ended problems discussed early on to reinforce collaboration, leading on to open-ended questions to promote more abstract thinking as the project progresses.

Overall, student feedback indicates that students generally enjoyed and appreciated this transnational learning experience.

> *"How amazing that two countries so many miles apart can get together because of the world-wide web."*

> *"it has been extremely helpful to find out how other services and professions work."*

> *"I enjoyed participating from this forum. I have learnt a lot which is out of my profession field."*

Key issues perceived to impact negatively on student engagement reflect the perceived extra workload, student motivation, time-management issues and the need for more focused discussions (to meet the needs of different disciplines). Some student respondents would have preferred the project to be more of a social network site, a support mechanism for asking questions and seeking viewpoints. Reminders to post would also have been welcomed. Greater alignment of discussion themes with the courses being studied was a further consideration as some students felt the topics did not relate to their own course and thus found it difficult to contribute. There were also suggestions for this transnational discussion activity to be woven into curriculum design (rather than be left an extracurricular activity) and assessed accordingly, awarding credit for engagement and boosting motivation (albeit extrinsic). An interesting viewpoint, which reinforces the view of students as strategic learners perhaps? One of the aims of this extracurricular project was to develop further the transferable skills and graduate attributes sought after by future employers. Students would receive a certificate of participation on completion of the project, which would provide evidence of "going the extra mile" to future employers. There was scope to reinforce this principle as a motivating factor for engagement. However, there is also scope to include this activity within a curriculum design as the activity itself could be a robust assessment task that can foster deeper learning, irrespective of student motivations for engagement.

Following an extensive review of the literature, Wilson *et al.* (2016) identify some concepts related to the definitions of global health, which could be used to frame curriculum design and offer themes for discussion as an assessed item. These include planetary health, transnational collaboration, equity/social justice, health promotion and disease prevention, population and public health, determinants of health, international health, global health improvement, interdependence across nations, individual-level healthcare and 'glocal', which describes the interdependence of global and local health. A virtual exchange forum could easily be deployed as an assessment item shared by two (or more) courses from different disciplines, thus promoting interdisciplinary learning. Taking this concept one step further, the assessed item could be shared across institutions from different countries to offer a more authentic global learning experience. Collaboration on course content, learning activities and assessment across institutions would ensure that knowledge exchange is reciprocal and that global concerns and cross-disciplinary issues are addressed.

Conclusion

This project has demonstrated that international virtual exchange offers a potential solution to enable all students to engage in a global learning experience. There is certainly scope to develop this project further by setting up similar schemes with institutions from other countries with varied economies and different models of healthcare provision. However, through this model of knowledge transfer, we must be mindful of the potential effects of cultural imperialism. While we have the potential to cross national boundaries easily through the use of information communication systems, we must not overstep the mark and impose Western values to the detriment of local culture. Furthermore, developing countries may lack the infrastructure and funding for such projects. Nevertheless, an alternative view is that knowledge transfer projects can be used to further develop a global workforce and standards of education whilst offering opportunities for comparative medical research.

In the late 1980s, the World Health Organization recognised that if health professionals were taught together within a multi-professional educational setting and learned to collaborate as a team during their student years they were far more likely to work effectively together in their professional lives within a clinical setting (WHO, 1988). Jones & Sherwood (2014) acknowledge the increasing mobility of healthcare professionals working within and across countries in a globalised healthcare system and they promote the need to simulate intra- and inter-professional conversations to shape the workforce of the future. Such conversations spanning international boundaries can be supported through different media and communication technologies, offering heightened access to knowledge and personal development. Since undergraduate health profession students can typically face practical and financial barriers to physical overseas experiences, a virtual exchange experience, using a VLE asynchronous discussion forum offered us a simple method of connecting students across the globe to share ideas and learn collaboratively. Participating students found that the UK and Australia shared similar care systems, structures and processes, and they were able to discuss some healthcare challenges in detail. For example, students considered the determinants of health and social care delivery to be a major policy issue for both countries. They discussed issues around funding and access to health, including their responsibilities as healthcare professionals to improve the health and access of the population to services. Grootjans and Newman (2012) identified social justice as an important aspect of nursing care in a global context where inequalities are all too common. It was clear from the forum discussion that students from all professional backgrounds see this is an important part of their role but had also identified that the professional groups they belong to need to work together to improve the population needs.

Although the forum generated some fruitful discussions and evidenced the development of 21st-century competencies, such as collaborative, cognitive and interpersonal skills, participant engagement could be sporadic at times. Extra workload, student motivation and time management issues were identified as factors that impacted on engagement. Perhaps there is scope to consider weaving a virtual exchange project as an assessed item into curriculum design, as a low-cost model to develop cross-border higher education. The key lesson, therefore, is that transnational virtual exchange must be designed to maximise stakeholder engagement from the outset in order to reduce these potential barriers to participation.

Recommendations

Having completed this project, we have identified some pedagogical and operational recommendations, which we believe should be considered in the establishment of any virtual exchange opportunity.

We believe that the integration of the virtual exchange within the core curricula would be advantageous as this would demonstrate the relevance of the global context of health to all students and would also maximise student engagement. We do recognise, however, that this can be challenging, especially given the inter-professional and inter-university nature of the programme and consequently it may be necessary to re-imagine modules to fully embed this (see Parkes & Hayes, in this volume). There are a number of key learning outcomes which could form the focus of this programme and, therefore, it is important for the academic team to define and agree this at the programme design stage; for example, the focus could be based on technical aspects of care. However, our experience showed that the greatest exchange of experiences is related to living, working and studying in the specific cultural setting. Therefore, we plan to review our discussion themes to streamline discussion topics and offer more emergent personalised learning themes and believe that this would also encourage deeper discussions.

The organisation and management of the project are crucial to its success and, therefore, there are a number of operational considerations when establishing such an exchange. We would advise that a detailed memorandum of understanding be developed between the collaborating organisations, which addresses the issues related to intellectual property, level of contribution and governance considerations. Each individual organisation will then need to operationalise this within its own working policies and particularly academic workload allocation. It is important that training requirements for staff are considered, both in the use of the software and in facilitating an online forum. We would suggest that it would be best practice for the facilitation team(s) to have at least one online meeting beforehand to agree on key principles and a further mid-point review so that the team can adapt accordingly. This will maximise academic stakeholder engagement and interprofessional working, which we believe is fundamental to the success of the project and provides a role model to students.

About the Authors

Nicola Bartholomew is an Associate Professor (Learning & Teaching), Faculty of Health, Education and Life Sciences, Birmingham City University. She can be contacted through this email: nicola.bartholomew@bcu.ac.uk

Geraldine Nevin is an Associate Professor (Curriculum Lead, Nursing), Faculty of Health, Education and Life Science, Birmingham City University. She can be contacted through this email: gerri.nevin@bcu.ac.uk

Hannah Abbott is an Associate Professor and Associate Head of School, Allied and Public Health Professions, Faculty of Health, Education and Life Sciences, Birmingham City University. She can be contacted through this email: Hannah.Abbott@bcu.ac.uk

Deborah Pittaway is an Independent Education Consultant. She can be contacted through this email: d.pittaway@alliedhealtheducation.co.uk

Robyn Nash is a Professor of Health, Faculty of Health, Queensland University of Technology. She was formerly the Assistant Dean (Learning and Teaching) for the Faculty of Health. She can be contacted through this email: r.nash@qut.edu.au

Bibliography

Australian Bureau of Statistics (2013). Australian Social Trends, April 2013: Doctors and Nurses Online Resource: www.abs.giv.au [Accessed 08 November 2016].

Australian Health Practitioners Regulating Authority (2014) Code of conduct for registered health practitioners. AHPRA. Australia.

Bartholomew, P. (2015). Enhancing academic practice through the use of video: A longitudinal case study of professional development in higher education. PhD Thesis. University of Birmingham.

Birmingham City University (2013). Birmingham City University Moodle Code of Conduct. Birmingham UK.

Birmingham City University (2014). Birmingham City University Strategic Plan 2020. BCU. Birmingham UK.

Bradbury-Jones, C. (2009). Globalisation and its implications for health care and nursing practice. *Nursing Standard.* 23, 25, 43–47.

Brownie, S.; J. Thomas; L. McAllister & M. Groves (2014). Australian Health Reforms: Enhancing interprofessional competency within the health workforce. *Journal of Interprofessional Care,* Vol. 28, No. 3, pp. 252–253.

Claman, F. L. (2015). The impact of multiuser virtual environments on student engagement. *Nurse Education Practice.* Vol. 1, pp. 13–16.

Connor, C. (2003). Virtual learning and inter-professional education: Developing computer mediated communication for learning about collaboration, *Innovations in Education and Teaching International,* Vol. 40, No. 4, pp. 341–347.

Cornali, F. & Tirocchi, S. (2012). Globalization, education, information and communication technologies: What relationships and reciprocal influences? *Procedia – Social and Behavioural Sciences.* Vol. 47, pp. 2060–2069.

Derrick, L. (2002). Globalisation, knowledge, education and training in the information age. Online Resource: http://www.unesco.org/webworld/infoethics_2/eng/papers/paper_23.htm [Accessed 08 November 2016].

Doerry, E.; R. Klempous; J. Nikodem & W. Paetzold (2004). Virtual Student Exchange: Lessons Learned in Virtual International Teaming in *Interdisciplinary Design Education.*

Edwards, H.; R. Nash; S. Sacre; M. Courtney & J. Abbey (2008). Development of a virtual learning environment to enhance undergraduate nursing students' effectiveness and interest in working with older people. *Nurse Education Today.* Vol. 28, pp. 672–679.

Gerard, S. & J. Billington (2014). The perceived benefits of belonging to an extra-curricular group within a pre-registration nursing course. *Nurse Education in Practice,* Vol. 14, pp. 253–258.

Grootjans, J. & S. Newman (2013). The relevance of globalisation to nursing: A concept analysis. *International Nursing Review.* Vol. 60, pp. 78–85.

Gunawardena, C. N, & F. J. Zittle (1997) Social presence as a predictor of satisfaction within a computer-mediated conferencing environment. *American Journal of Distance Education.* Vol 11, No. 3, pp. 8–26.

Haugen, S.; J. LaBarre & J. Melrose (2001). Online Course Delivery: Issues and Challenges. IACIS. Online Resource: http://iacis.org/iis/2001/Haugen127.PDF [Accessed 15 November 2016].

Health and Care Professions Council (2016). Standards of conduct performance and ethics. HCPC. London.

Hutt R. & J. Buchan (2005). Trends in London's NHS Workforce. An updated analysis of key data. London: The Kings Fund.

Jisc (2004). Effective practice with e-learning. Online Resource: http://www. elearning.ac.uk/effprac/ [Accessed 07 November 2016].

Jisc (2015). *Developing student's digital literacy.* Online Resource: https:// www.jisc.ac.uk/guides/developing-students-digital-literacy [Accessed 15 November 2016].

Jisc (2016). *Using digital media in new learning models (flipped and blended learning).* Online Resource: http://www.jiscdigitalmedia.ac.uk/infokit/ models-of-learning/consider-the-students [Accessed 15 November 2016].

Jones, C. & G. Sherwood (2014). The globalization of the nursing workforce: Pulling the pieces together. *Nursing Outlook,* Vol. 65, pp. 59–63.

Kear, K. (2010). *Social presence in online learning communities.* Proceedings of the 7th International Conference on Networked Learning, 3–4 May, Aalborg, Denmark.

Milne, A. & J. Cowie (2013). Promoting culturally competent care: The Erasmus exchange programme. *Nursing Standard.* Vol. 27, No. 30, pp. 42–46.

Pellegrino, J. W. & M. L. Hilton (2012). *Education for life and work: Developing transferable knowledge and skills for the 21st Century.* The National Academies Press.

Nursing Midwifery Council (2010). *Standards for pre-registration nursing education.* NMC. London.

Nursing Midwifery Council (2015). *The Code Professional Standards of practice and behaviour for nurses and midwives.* NMC. London.

Queensland University of Technology (2014). *QUT Blueprint 4.* Brisbane QLD 4001 Australia.

Parker, V. & M. McMillan (2007). Challenges facing internationalisation of nursing practice, nurse education and nursing workforce in Australia. *Contemporary Nurse.* Vol. 24, pp. 128–136.

Quality Assurance Agency (2015). *The UK Quality Code for Higher Education Overview and the Expectations.* Gloucester UK.

Saade, R. J. & Q. Huang (2009). Meaningful learning in discussion forums: Towards discourse analysis. *Issues in Informing Science and Information Technology.* Vol 6., pp. 87–96.

Schrire, S. (2006). Knowledge building in asynchronous discussion groups: Going beyond quantitative analysis. *Computers and Education,* No. 46, pp. 49–70.

Thistlewaite, J. (2012). Interprofessional education: A review of context learning and the research agenda. *Medical Education,* Vol. 46, No. 8, pp. 62–-70.

Tirado, R.; I. Aguaded & A. Hernando (2011). Collaborative learning processes in an asynchronous environment: An analysis through discourse and social networks. *Journal of Latin American Communication Research*. Vol 2., No. 1, pp. 123–134.

Tjadens F.; C. Weilandt & J. Eckert (2013). *Mobility of Health Professionals: Health Systems, Work Conditions, Patterns of Health Workers' Mobility and Implications for Policy Makers*. Berlin: Springer.

Todhunter, F.; L. Hallawell & D. Pittaway (2013). Implementing a Virtual Exchange Project for student nurses in Queensland and Nottingham. *Nurse Education in Practice*, Vol. 13, pp. 371–376.

Upvall, M. & J. Leffers (2014). Global Health Nursing: Building and Sustaining Partnerships. Springer.

Wakely, L.; L. Brown & J. Burrows (2013). Evaluating interprofessional learning modules: Health students' attitudes to interprofessional practice. *Journal of Interprofessional Care*, Vol. 27., No. 5, pp. 424–425.

World Health Organization (1988). *Learning Together to Work Together for Health*. Geneva: WHO.

World Health Organization (2016). *Globalization of Health*. Geneva: WHO.

Wilson, L.; C. Mendes; H. Klopper; C. Carambone; R. Al-Maaitah; M. Norton & M. Hill (2016). Global Health and Global Nursing: proposed definitions from the Global Advisory Panel on the future of Nursing. Informing Practice and Policy Work.

Xia, J.; J. Fielder & L. Siragusa (2013). Achieving better peer interaction in online discussion forums: A reflective practitioner case study. *Issues in Educational Research*, Vol. 23, No. 1.

Xiao, L. D.; E. Willis & L. Jeffers (2014). Factors affecting the integration of immigrant nurses into the nursing workforce: A double hermeneutic study. *International Journal of Nursing Studies*, Vol. 51, pp. 640–653.

Chapter 9

The Mikkeli Programme: International Education and Flagship Response to Globalisation

Joan Lofgren & Elyssebeth Leigh

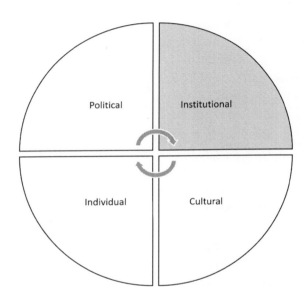

Introduction

This chapter is an important contribution to this book on the globalisation of higher education as it presents lessons learned from the experiences of an international 3-year, 180 ECTS undergraduate business programme conducted on the Mikkeli campus of Aalto University in Finland. The international nature of the approach, enshrined in the original design, has created opportunities and challenges on the programme's path to becoming a flagship response to globalisation. Now in its 29th year, the Mikkeli BScBA has much to share about its well-earned global reputation.

The lessons learned are discussed in relation to the literature on globalisation in higher education, drawing on the strengths and experiences of students and staff involved in creating its unique approach to international education. Administrative staff, based in the regional Finnish city of Mikkeli, are full-time employees of Aalto University. Academic staff are contract employees who come to Mikkeli from all over the globe to teach intensive three-week courses using English as the common language. The student community is similarly international in nature, including Finnish, Vietnamese and as many as ten other nationalities in any one cohort. Its longevity as a tertiary education programme, whose format has not changed markedly in 28 years, is a testament to both the original design and the commitment of several generations of staff and graduates.

The landscape for higher education in business studies has changed dramatically in recent decades, reflecting an internationalising trend in higher education as a whole. For example, the number and proportion of university programmes taught in a language other than the local language have grown significantly; often such programmes are delivered in English, the new lingua franca (Anglia) of education. Europe and the Nordic region provide many examples of English-medium instruction (EMI), from the humanities to the technical fields. This trend is attributed to such factors as the increasing need for English-speaking graduates and their improved employment prospects, especially in international trade. University league tables (regardless of their questionable objectivity) are another influence as also is the increasing use of English in research contexts. (ICEF Monitor, 2012)

Business curricula in the Nordic countries reflect these dynamics since preparing students for working in multicultural contexts is now a key goal in most business curricula in the region. For example, it is becoming common practice to offer Master's degree programmes entirely in English alongside study abroad programmes and joint and networked degrees (e.g. the Global Alliance in Management Education, CEMS).

The Bachelor's programme (BScBA) in International Business studied at the Mikkeli campus of the Aalto University School of Business is an undergraduate programme that pioneered this trend and since 1989 has promoted a multicultural, international approach to undergraduate business education that has withstood the challenges of globalisation. This chapter explores the unique characteristics of the BScBA Programme in the context of evolving discussions of internationalisation and globalisation and provides insights into the work required to maintain an intentionally globalised undergraduate degree on a regional campus. Students and staff have learned together to build and reinforce this global approach to learning about effective business management in times of stability— especially in times of disruptive change and discontinuous development. Reading this chapter, you will gain the following three insights:

1. insight into the Mikkeli Model of international higher education, which may inspire in its own rights;

2. reflections on the European, Nordic and Finnish higher education models;

3. specific knowledge of the role of key stakeholders in the creation and delivery of the international higher education program.

The Mikkeli Model

The Mikkeli programme was designed around a "flying faculty" model, which has remained the same since its inception. It is an intensive study programme with a comparatively small intake each year, where only four to six parallel study modules are in operation at any one time. Students spend two years on the Mikkeli Campus and are also required to study abroad for one full semester. The model includes these key elements:

+ the Programme Director invites academic staff (visiting instructors) to join/return to the programme, each teaching within their own research and teaching specialisation;

+ visiting instructors are hired on contract to usually teach three-week courses, providing 45 contact teaching hours and daily open office hours;

+ students take courses year-round, completing up to 15 (6 point) modules of study each year. Each module involves students being in the classroom three hours a day, five days a week, for three weeks plus additional study time, for a total of 160 hours every three weeks;

+ students complete most of the mandated courses in the first year and the beginning of the second year and take electives starting at the end of the first year;

+ electives vary from year to year, depending on faculty availability and student interest and include pre-requisites for Master's programmes;

+ there are several short breaks in the schedule, a longer one during the winter and two short ones during the summer;

+ a Bachelor's thesis is completed during the second year of study. This is mentored by thesis supervisors recruited separately from the course instructors. Each supervisor works with a small group of students either in Finland or virtually;

+ all students are required to study abroad and take advantage of at least one of the 50 partnerships the Programme maintains around the world;

+ the programme does not currently charge tuition fees, but recent changes in Finnish law mean that non-EU/EA students entering the programme starting in 2017–18 will be charged tuition;

+ The Helsinki School of Economics—now known as the Aalto School of Business—had established the programme, and gradually incorporated it into the School and the new Aalto University, while allowing it to maintain significant autonomy due to its special structure.

The Mikkeli model was designed with three purposes in mind. First, it exposes students to a wide variety of academic styles and a broad range of international knowledge through working with visiting faculty who offer a variety of intensively concentrated learning experiences. Second, the focus on one subject at a time helps students stay on track. In this regard, it is worth noting that the BScBA has a good record for on-time completion with the average time to graduation remaining steady at just over 3 years. Third, it makes the programme an attractive option for exchange students who are able to focus their energies on a sequence of subjects, completing as many as four subjects in twelve weeks. This is especially relevant to its global nature as international students bring to the programme a further variety of experiences and insights that contribute to the global nature of the classroom experience. While class profiles differ widely, one recent group had eight different nationalities and seven different languages. At times, non-Finnish students outnumber Finnish students in particular courses, making the experience of learning together truly international in nature. In recent years, the number of foreign degree students from Asia has grown, especially from Vietnam.

History of the Mikkeli programme

In 1989 Veikko Jääskeläinen, Professor of International Corporate Finance at the Helsinki School of Economics (HSE), recognised the importance of providing Finnish students with a degree offered entirely in English. He acquired extensive experience observing American MBA programmes as a visiting faculty member in the US. At the time he began the work of establishing the BScBA, Jääskeläinen held leadership positions, including Director of the International Centre and Dean of an MBA programme. He had proposed introducing an MBA programme to the Finnish market well before the concept was considered important enough to receive formal support. Once the MBA was established, although not yet a formal degree programme, it opened the door to the proposal for a Bachelor's programme (BBA) using a similar design.

HSE decision makers later recognised the need to provide some undergraduate teaching in English, while initially requiring separate funding and not allocating any permanent teaching staff to the proposed programme. Any degree offered in this format had to charge tuition fees—a challenging prospect in a country where state-sponsored education was free of fees—and would be without the benefit of having a permanent teaching faculty. Whatever the reasons for these restrictions, the eventual agreement to proceed meant the programme could be comparatively autonomous while remaining affiliated with HSE.

Mikkeli became the chosen campus through a combination of Finnish regional development policies, and the fact that HSE already had the Small Business Center in the town. In its own way the remoteness has contributed to the mystique of the course while allowing it to develop and maintain itself as a having a format very different from other types of Finnish tertiary education. One aspect of the mystique is the way it has become known as "the Mikkeli programme" among staff and students. Only on formal occasions is it called a BScBA.

Despite having the precedent of an MBA programme delivered entirely in English, the concept of developing an undergraduate programme entirely international in its structure and focus was novel. The programme was deliberately designed to attract students from other countries with the goal of providing Finnish undergraduates with first-hand experience of working with students from other cultures. The way Veikko Jääskeläinen realised his vision for a truly international programme was recently described by a veteran Mikkeli faculty member as an "intelligent conversation about an unknowable future" (Fodness, 2016). From 1989 onwards, the programme has been able to attract well-qualified students, acquiring a strong alumni presence around the world as well as a loyal and highly diverse teaching faculty. The present Program Director is the fourth since Jääskeläinen established the programme. Since its inception 28 years ago, the Mikkeli programme has grown in stature and recognition while remaining quite a small programme with around 200–250 students enrolled at any one time.

From the beginning, the design anticipated that both international and intercultural factors would be important elements for preparing students to work in the business world, both as it was at the time of conception and as it has been evolving since the end of the 1980's. To an interesting extent, the initial design of the degree programme has accentuated contact with, and the exploration of, broader processes occurring in society. The programme reflected a deep awareness of the importance of recognising the diversity of cultures and the complexity of working within, and with, different social contexts. The experience of exploring forces tending towards increasing globalisation is enhanced as students address relevant global and international issues in the context of their immediate learning environment rather than at a distance or as an abstract concept. While the initial motivation for establishing the programme may have been internationalisation, its structure and practices have become de facto global. The longevity of the original design is evidence of the foresight of its designers and supporters in anticipating the current extent of globalisation.

The comparatively long history of the BScBA as an internationally and globally focused programme gives it a special position in regard to reflecting on issues of globalising learning. There have been five directors—including the present one—and their shared learning experiences have emphasised that globalisation cannot be taken for granted. Clearly, given the programme structure and intent, individual participants will encounter students and faculty from many different cultures and gain some insights into the differences among them. However, creating a continuing series of constructive learning experiences that encourage students to think more broadly and reflect on their own cultural identities takes a special effort and intentionality. While this is still a challenge for all involved, graduates' comments indicate this is a valued aspect of their study experience.

Admission to the Mikkeli programme occurs on several tracks. An incoming class of about 80 would comprise about 60 Finns, some of whom have lived abroad, and 20–25 foreign degree students from both Eastern and Western Europe as well as Southeast Asia and South America. In addition, 50–70 exchange students may be studying in Mikkeli in any given academic year. The diversity of student experiences provides a different view of the world, a more powerful process of internationalisation than is achievable in programmes where the focus is on "received/transmitted" abstract knowledge. In Mikkeli, the goal is to encourage students to look inwards to their immediate experience of working collaboratively in an international cohort. Given that students regularly work in teams, with students from other countries, they are likely to frequently encounter the direct results of cultural differences, such as those between collectivism/ individualism-oriented cultures (Hofstede, 2016).

For the Helsinki School of Economics, 2010 was a momentous year; it merged with two other Helsinki-area universities to form the large Aalto University. In the years since then, there have been many adjustments to the study programmes previously offered by the three institutions. Despite making many changes, the Aalto leadership acknowledged the unique nature of the Mikkeli programme and its special role in the unified university and recently confirmed that the Mikkeli programme will stay on its regional campus and retain its unique format.

The European Context

How unique is the Mikkeli Model in the European context? The internationalisation of education in Europe has intensified in recent years, following initiatives such as ERASMUS and the Bologna reform. The number of "English as a Medium of Instruction" (EMI) degree programmes has increased significantly in recent years (see Airey *et al.*, 2015; Wächter & Maiworm, 2014) and Coleman (2006) emphasises the accelerating globalisation and marketisation of forces driving the adoption of English while highlighting problems created by this Anglicisation of European Higher Education.

"Norden" at the forefront

In this regard, Finland's position in the broader European context is worth noting. The Nordic countries ("Norden" in Scandinavia) are at the forefront of the internationalising and globalising trends in higher education. Indeed, a recent study reports that the highest share of institutions (out of all higher education institutions) that offer English-Taught Programmes (ETPs) could be found in Finland (83%) and Sweden (81%) while Denmark is at the top with respect to the proportion of programmes taught in English (38%) and the number of students enrolled (12%). (Wächter & Maiworm 2014).

In addition, expectations concerning language acquisition play a large role in the development of new courses. Finnish is difficult to acquire as a second language, hampering the rapid transition to studying alongside local students and giving rise to English-language instruction for exchange students and foreign degree students. Wächter & Maiworm (2014:27) describe it as a response to perceptions of "linguistic disadvantage", explaining it thus: *"How could Iceland, Finland, Hungary or even the Netherlands ever hope of attracting considerable number[s] of foreign students (credit and degree mobile students alike) if they continued to exclusively teach in their own language? One obvious strategy to overcome the "linguistic disadvantage" was to revert to the most widely taught language in secondary education world-wide, i.e. English."*

Seen from a broader perspective, multilingualism is a clearly stated public value and policy in Finland (for an overview, see Tallroth, 2012).

High literacy rates and a tradition of reading and informal education have combined to strengthen the position of Finnish as the first language in society while making capability in multiple languages commonplace. Finns are avid readers, book buyers, and library visitors. While the use of English alongside Finnish and Swedish is sometimes viewed as a threat, it is mostly seen as a sign of Finland's identification with Western (rather than Eastern) Europe. It has also enhanced the national ability to compete more effectively in international business. An indicative comment on acceptance of the current state of affairs is found in a website on life in Finland, "This is Finland", which asserts that "Finland makes multilingualism easy" and refers to polyglots as "an asset for Finnish society". ("This is Finland", 2016).

In this regard, it is useful to note that the Finnish education system is dominated by the public sector, although there has always been room for private and semi-private initiatives, such as the process whereby the Mikkeli programme was begun in 1989. The 2010 Law on Universities opened up the possibility of "foundation", or public-private, universities, of which Aalto University is one. However, the Finnish education landscape is still state-dominated.

Due to Finland's strong emphasis on multiculturalism, international students enrolling in the Mikkeli programme are assured that English will be widely available throughout the country. Conversely, Finnish students opting for an English-language programme in their own country are assured of a linguistic and cultural experience of broad international proportions without having to leave home.

English as a Medium of Instruction (EMI)

The use of English in higher education in Finland is supported by a school system that introduces foreign language instruction by the third grade with English as the most popular foreign language today. The Finnish Ministry of Education (2015) data shows that over 90% of Finnish third-graders have started studying English. So, they are well-prepared for studying in English once they reach university.

A recent study by the Finnish Higher Education Evaluation Council (Airey et al., 2015, citing Välimaa et al., 2013) of EMI programmes in Finland documented 399 International Degree Programmes across the two types of Finnish higher education institutions — "Universities" and "Universities of Applied Sciences" (UAS). Universities provide academic education based on research, while UAS provide higher-level vocational education and promote applied research emphasising close contacts with business, industry and the service sector, especially at the regional level. Of the university-level EMI programmes, 98% were at the Master's level, whereas 75% of the UAS (Universities of Applied Sciences) programmes were at the Bachelor's level. Some 13,000 students were studying in these programmes; 22% of the students at the university programmes were Finns, compared to 40% at the universities of applied sciences. The Mikkeli program is offered at the university level of study—so is part of the 2% of courses offered in English at that level.

The increasing trend towards EMI has been documented also more generally in Europe by Wächter & Maiworm (2014) across a wide spectrum of disciplines. However, as the figures above show, it is still unusual to find university undergraduate programmes offered in a language other than the national language. In the Mikkeli programme, English has been the language used from the beginning although the programme (excluding the exchange) is run entirely in Finland. While the number of Master's programmes offered in English in non-English language countries (Dearden, 2014) is growing rapidly, undergraduate programmes are still far from common. One reason may be that the proportion of high school/upper secondary education that provides sufficient instruction in English is still small. Another may be national goals of competency in national languages.

Finland is indeed an excellent testing ground for foreign language programmes. Finnish students are exposed to English not only in primary and secondary education but also in popular culture. The tradition of multilingualism is rooted deeply in Finnish culture. For example, in Finland, TV and films are rarely dubbed; dubbing is usually only for preschool audiences and the common mode is the use of Finnish subtitles. Finnish students must also learn Swedish, which is the second official language of Finland. Thus learning a Germanic language early on helps prepare students for studying English and studying in English. In short, young Finnish young students are enculturated into a multilingual society.

The trend towards offering instruction in English is clear in Finnish business schools, and it "seems to work", as Lavelle (2008:137) explains: *"...business schools outside native English-speaking countries are offering some or all of their instruction in English. This too is a trend that is intensifying, and again there is no reason to believe the graduates of these institutions have failed to learn in these settings or failed to succeed professionally. In other words, business education in English works."*

As a small, open economy, Finland has apparently felt compelled to introduce English to many areas of society, while maintaining a close focus on the uniqueness of being Finnish. Thus, the initial decision to offer the course in English could be seen as predicting, even heralding, a trend towards the use of English as a medium of instruction. This has been a causal factor in its continuing success, regardless of whether it was a clearly understood component of the impetus to begin.

Internationalisation and Globalisation in Higher Education

The internationalisation of higher education has been defined as the *"process of integrating an international, intercultural or global dimension into the purpose, functions or delivery of higher education"* (Knight, 2009, cited in Bernini, 2015). Globalisation can be characterised by the compression of time and geographical distance, or *"a set of processes that tend to de-territorialize important economic, social, and cultural practices from their traditional boundaries in nation-states."* (Suárez-Orozco & Qin-Hilliard, 2004:14). Coleman (2006) also suggests (citing Hüppauf, 2004) that the spread of English is inseparable from globalisation.

In contrast to internationalisation, which is often linked to policy actions, globalisation is often referred to as a force beyond policy-makers' control, one to which educators must react. Knight & Altbach (2007:290) describe it as *"the economic, political and societal forces pushing 21st century higher education toward greater international involvement."*

Johnson (2014) outlines four sets of indicators of globalisation in education, one of which is the social and cultural rationale. All of the dimensions of that rationale apply to the Mikkeli programme: global consciousness, global programmes and activities, meaningful interaction/ integration on campus and a student exchange/study abroad. Interestingly, the Mikkeli programme also fits all the dimensions within the stakeholder perspective, as it promotes a global consciousness through a global programme, fosters meaningful interaction on a satellite campus, and includes a study abroad.

The literature on globalisation in education more generally underscores integration as the core of what it means to be "global". However, some scholars still also focus on the free trade context: *"The contemporary emphasis on free trade stimulates international academic mobility. Current thinking sees international higher education as a commodity to be freely traded and sees higher education as a private good, not a public responsibility."* (Altbach & Knight 2007:291).

As the founder of the innovative and unprecedented Mikkeli programme, Veikko Jääskeläinen had the foresight and vision to recognise the need for an internationally competitive programme to prepare Finnish and foreign students for the global marketplace. He saw that it would not be enough to study English, students would also need to study *in* English. By offering the curriculum in English, his programme de facto entered the global education market almost before such a concept was recognised. Thus, the Mikkeli programme illustrates what it means to be intentionally global—not simply integrating an international dimension into a national programme, but rather bringing the global marketplace for education into a local Finnish context. It demonstrates that globalisation can be intentional and proactive, rather than just conceived of as mega-level forces to which programme designers should react. Overall, the distinction between internationalisation and globalisation is less relevant for the Mikkeli case since although it was not *intentionally global* from its inception, it is indeed today.

Perspectives from Key Stakeholders

The key stakeholder groups of students, faculty, and staff at Mikkeli each have their own perspective on the way in which the programme highlights and contributes to the globalisation of higher education—and each is different. The first stakeholder group—the students—appreciate the need to function in various cultures other than their own, using at least English and to some extent other languages. Qiang (2003:248) explains the need for global competences in this way: *"Academic and professional requirements for graduates increasingly reflect the demands of the globalization of societies, economy and labour markets and thus higher education must provide an adequate preparation for that. These requirements include not only academic and professional knowledge, but also multilingualism, and social and intercultural skills and attitudes."* Undergraduate study in English also stimulates interest in English-language Master's programmes, further promoting a global view (see Altbach & Knight 2007). Today's graduates of the Mikkeli programme consider a wide range of options for graduate studies; for example, in Copenhagen, Rotterdam, London, Frankfurt and various Asian destinations.

The second stakeholder group, the "flying" or "fly-in" international academic staff, see teaching abroad as an enrichment of their careers, providing them with opportunities to benchmark teaching practices and bring lessons learned back to their home universities. Academic staff in business schools are increasingly mobile, seeking chances to teach abroad for short periods. MBA programmes organised on the basis of using short-term intensive study modules taught by short-term academic staff from abroad are becoming widespread. While full-time researchers may have more flexibility in arranging stints abroad (Kim & Locke, 2010), the teaching staff committed to teaching at Mikkeli are also able to arrange their teaching and advising schedules at home more easily today, thanks to online teaching and Skype. The experiences of the visiting instructors in Mikkeli have helped to build lifelong relationships and created personal memories that influence their "at home" activity, and this network of current and former instructors is a key part of the "Mikkeli Spirit" (see Powell, 2010).

Members of the third group of stakeholders are the dedicated, locally based administrative staff. Their capacity to manage the diversity of tasks involved in recruiting, supporting and enabling the international students and staff has been a vital component in sustaining the complex web of functions that go to make up each new programme. For them, the requirement to operate in English across all the nationalities they encounter opens up international employment opportunities as well as ensuring their skills are highly marketable within Finland.

The student community

Finnish students comprise the majority of students, but Finnish versus foreign origin is a distinction that is increasingly blurring—as quite a few

Finns in the programme have lived abroad and studied in English before arriving to begin their studies in Mikkeli. Students do face a special challenge in transitioning to a learning community of the type that Mikkeli offers in Finland. This is especially true for students who have been socialised in learning communities in the US, Asia, or elsewhere in Europe. Increasingly students are enrolling with a hyphenated identity, e.g. Finnish-Italian, Finnish-South African and this is adding to the complexity of the teaching/learning environment. Students are oriented to the unique approach in Mikkeli in an intensive weeklong "on-boarding" experience before starting their first course. Students are frequently on a first name basis with academic staff and are all well known to the administrative staff. Third, an array of student groups support and sustain new and continuing students. As a new first-year student remarked recently: "We became a tight-knit group in two days".

Foreign degree students are also a key part of the design. There is deliberate and substantial attention paid to ensuring that each new intake of students meet and mix right from the start of the programme. The stated goal is to ensure that English will be used in daily life throughout the Mikkeli campus, which in turn ensures a more global experience. The Programme Director sometimes faces a balancing act in allowing the faculty the freedom to organise students to work in teams while ensuring that teams do not comprise students all from the same language group. In a high-pressure environment, it is natural that students will revert to their mother tongue if the opportunity presents itself. Creating the context for using English is essential.

All students enrolled full time in the programme are required to go on exchange, so incoming students from partner universities also contribute to the globalising nature of the campus. The mandatory exchange for Mikkeli degree students is a selling point—the exchange partner network offers the opportunity to study abroad with no additional tuition.

Probba—student engagement in design and evaluation

Student engagement in shaping the learning community is very strong on the Mikkeli campus. Once every three weeks, at the start of the module, the board of Probba, the student organisation, meets with the Programme Director, manager of academic operations, and IT systems administrator to go over upcoming events and issues and generally to share information. In addition, the Probba academic affairs coordinator serves on the Mikkeli programme committee, undertaking such tasks as reviewing the curriculum proposal for the following year. The student quality committee, mentioned above, comprises class representatives and the Probba academic affairs coordinator. In addition, several students work part-time for the programme in marketing and in business and community development, as well as in admissions.

The fast pace of the programme—and a deliberate focus on addressing the "storming" component of group development (Tuckman 1990)—also builds community. One alumna, who later studied at Copenhagen business school, said that she didn't feel stressed meeting tight deadlines, compared to her fellow students, because she had studied in Mikkeli and "if you survive Mikkeli, you can survive anything". So, the idea of accomplishing the impossible creates a kind of personal pride coupled with loyalty to peers. It creates a tight-knit community that is maintained many years after leaving campus; the Mikkeli alumni network is strong and professional referrals are common. The "baptism of fire" helps students to cope in a globalising world.

Student satisfaction with the programme

Students enrolling in the Mikkeli programme are particularly interested in studying in English as a key qualification for their career aspirations in international business (cf "global consciousness" and "brand image"). Rogerson-Revell (2007) points out that within Europe there is growing evidence that English has become the most used business "lingua franca". Among other reasons for studying at Mikkeli, they cite its demonstrated academic quality since the Aalto School of Business has triple-crown accreditation, meaning that the business school is acknowledged as excellent by all three of the world's leading business school accreditation bodies: AACSB, AMBA, and EQUIS.

Another factor attracting students is the style of teaching. While Finnish undergraduate business degrees offered by universities (collectively known as BScBA programmes) can be considered more theoretical than their American counterparts, given that, for example, they require a Bachelor's thesis, the Mikkeli programme is known for promoting communication skills and simulating business life. The Finnish Business School Graduates annual survey consistently rates the Mikkeli programme at the top of the scale for communication and interaction in the classroom. Mikkeli graduates are the business graduates in Finland that are most satisfied with their education (Finnish Business School Graduates, 2014).

Quality standards in a Global Faculty Network

The current academic staff on the Mikkeli programme are from more than 15 different countries and all are visiting academics, except the Programme Director. Diversity of cultural background is valued highly as a criterion in recruitment plans, while selection criteria include demonstrated excellence in teaching and research currency as well as availability for short-term appointments. All academic staff are required to demonstrate high standards of achievement in regard to teaching standards. The academic staff advise the Programme Director on various development issues, and cohesion is promoted in their network via regular communication and social events in Mikkeli.

During the past 28 years, the programme has had a large number of North American academic staff perhaps because of the initial influence of Veikko Jääskeläinen's experiences there. However, the recent trend is towards a more European faculty, as it is anticipated that graduates will work mainly in Europe. Quite a few faculty members are from India, although most are currently teaching at universities in countries other than India.

The Mikkeli programme benefits from the continuing support of a core of veteran visiting academics returning from year to year, complemented by instructors visiting while on sabbatical or when their teaching schedule at home allows. The academic staff contribute to various development projects, offer additional seminars and workshops, and serve as Bachelor's thesis supervisors. All faculty members are categorised according to the AACSB (Association for the Advancement of Colleges and Schools of Business) standards for accreditation.

Flexibility and close attention to quality are both built into the recruitment of faculty members for the Mikkeli programme. The Programme Director begins with a "blank slate"—that is, an empty curriculum schedule—for each academic year. The task is then to match up mandated and elective subjects with the list of academic staff who have indicated—well ahead of time—that they are willing and able to contribute. To remain on the list, a faculty member must perform well in the classroom as measured on each and every occasion via a five-step Mikkeli quality assurance system.

The primary element in this process is the student course evaluations [completed electronically and administered by the local staff in the third week of each module (data from this survey is released after grades are submitted)]. The second component in the five-step process is completion, by each faculty member, of a feedback survey collecting data about their own teaching experience as well as the quality of services provided by the local staff. At the third, a programme quality committee reviews both sets of evaluations and identifies any necessary follow-up steps, which are usually implemented by the Programme Director. Once this is on track, the fourth step involves a programme committee reviewing the programme curriculum and the teaching performance of all faculty in an annual cycle. This committee includes representatives from various Master's programmes at what is now known as the Aalto School of Business main campus and other academic staff. Finally, at several points in the annual cycle, a Student Quality Committee advises the Programme Director and Manager of Academic Operations on various development issues emerging within the programme.

Academic staff who have performed well in Mikkeli demonstrate qualities such as the ability to cope with a fast-paced, intensive learning environment, responsiveness to student needs, creativity in teaching methods, and a willingness to change direction if necessary. As one veteran instructor comments, Mikkeli "keeps you on your toes". Academic staff are oriented by the Programme Director in several stages before coming to Mikkeli and are advised to provide as much personalised help as possible.

Over the years, the Mikkeli programme has traded some of its original independence to assure acceptance and sufficient integration into the Aalto School of Business to continue operating on its own campus and with its own unique structure. When the initial BBA degree became a BScBA degree in 2001, the curriculum structure was amended to ensure that it met School-level objectives for the degree. Since it became an official Finnish degree, fees were no longer charged. More recently, Key Performance Indicators (KPIs) for the programme are being more closely monitored and some changes are observable. For example, in regard to the recruitment and accreditation of the faculty, their research and publishing achievements are considered more closely than in earlier times, while teaching quality and relevance of knowledge are still at the core of the selection process. Productivity measures remain excellent. For example, approximately 80% of Mikkeli students complete more than 55 ECTS credits each year, compared to the norm of 20–30% in other Finnish university programmes.

The Mikkeli Experience—Lessons Learned

The history of the Mikkeli BScBA programme reveals a program that was designed to be international but has withstood the challenge of globalisation. It brings cultural encounters into the daily life of the students. Students are already aware of the diversity of cultures awaiting them in their future workplaces or in Master's programmes because they are confronting that diversity each day. Working in teams, carrying out thesis research, dealing with faculty and their thesis supervisors are all inevitably multi-cultural experiences. For these student's globalisation is a process that de-territorialises the educational experience, rendering redundant the more familiar constraints of nation-state boundaries.

Learning needs community

While rooted in the South Savo region of Finland, the Mikkeli experience is about the mix of cultures and identities brought together under the programme's umbrella. While it might be argued that such an experience could be created anywhere, there is a strong consensus among stakeholders that being located in a small city that is three hours from both the capital and the main university campus and School of Business is essential to the programme's success. This challenges notions of virtual learning environments, suggesting that the physical space for intercultural learning is very important. Being clearly local in a small city in the region of South Savo allows the freedom to explore what it means to be global.

The programme also serves as a reminder that culture is bound up with "ways of doing things" and skills. For example, Finnish students, who are typically task-oriented, may perceive long discussions as "wasting time", while Asian students perceive them as a necessary part of the team-work. The programme has faced a challenge in enabling both groups of students to find their own way to common ways of working that are effective for learning while acknowledging that their enculturation causes them to value very different approaches.

The phrase "the Mikkeli experience" or "Mikkeli Spirit" is the way students reference the unique nature of studying in Mikkeli. A young woman from a farm in central Finland might work on a team project with students from Vietnam, Nigeria, and Ukraine in a course taught by a professor originally from India. That same young woman could go on exchange to Tokyo. However, just placing such a young woman in those contexts is not enough—the interaction and opportunities for reflection must be sufficient to create a more global mindset. The context and setting for developing such a mindset can be provided by a programme, but inevitably building one is always the work of the individual. This is one of the challenges which the Mikkeli students find they must address. While many do enter the programme with a burgeoning global mindset, the programme continues to face the problem of how to deepen that mindset so that each individual student can, over time, demonstrate his growing awareness of his own ways of thinking and working and the capability for adapting that when encountering fellow students from another culture.

Success through agility and diversity

A second major challenge is also a great opportunity—mirroring the fast pace of business life by expecting students to perform well on short notice. This is a strength of the programme—embedding employability skills. The usual time pressures and other factors that are external to the programme, yet are impinging on the drive to succeed, can breed conflict rather than cooperation. This makes it vital that the programme provide sufficient, but not too much, guidance to academic staff and students. The orientation activities organised for new students addresses this factor from the beginning, with attention being paid to ways of enabling the normal process of "forming, storming, and norming" (Tuckman 1990) to unfold and achieve a sufficient balance within each three-week cycle of study. Similarly, academic staff all receive an orientation session on the day of their arrival and are provided with highly structured support that begins well before their arrival for each new teaching cycle.

The contribution made by the mix of faculty nationalities and cultures is a factor not encountered in other, more conventional, undergraduate programmes. Every three weeks, students must assess how to relate to a new faculty member they will be working with. While an Indian student may understand that a Brahmin Indian professor will expect to be addressed more formally than the Finnish communications professor, an Italian student may initially be as unaware of this as are her Finnish peers who are used to more informality. While students have opportunities to reflect on these experiences in various courses, the programme faces a challenge in promoting other opportunities for reflection. Over time students learn that culture is relative in the sense that there is no absolutely right or wrong strategy. Every three weeks a new context is entered, new expectations are encountered, and new methods of managing in the emerging context must be devised as a class and individually. Exercising appropriately respectful behaviour requires attention to both the moment and the context at all times.

In a recent course on leadership, students collaborated to build a single 3-dimensional image of their learning. That they could do so without reference to any academic assistance indicated how much the student group could work together and see the intersections and connections among their individual learning journeys. The instructor provided the opportunity, but they did the work of making the connections. It was a striking example of the capacity of the students to work across cultures and languages.

In a capstone course run for the first time, students were asked to play a global strategy simulation/game in teams; due to the short time period and experimental nature of the course, the students had to deal with many uncertainties. It proved a good learning experience because the students demonstrated a collective capability to adapt and deal with new information as it came along. The second time the simulation was used the students could benefit from the faculty learning from the students in the first year; so the co-creation of the learning in a way stretched back to the previous year. The faculty learn with and from the students.

Power distance practices vary among the students, and the programme staff try to create a welcoming environment for a range of practices. The modes of address, for example, are particular to the staff member's expectations, and the students learn to greet the programme director by her first name (in the Finnish manner) while using the title of professor when addressing the visiting (Indian) academic.

Student traditions in Finland are sometimes linked to the drinking culture, which has posed challenges to foreign students, both in the degree programme and on exchange. The student organisation and staff are constantly seeking ways to bridge the cultural gap and create social settings that are comfortable for students coming from a variety of cultures. This is not amenable to a single solution as each cohort brings its own membership profiles and particular national issues with it. What Mikkeli staff and students do learn quickly is to identify the root cause of differences and unease, and seek solutions that are particular to the current moment. There is less concern for "global solutions". But dealing with these issues at the micro level in a diverse cultural context can promote a global mindset.

Finally, the opportunities for networking in such a tight-knit programme abound. For example, a South Korean degree student who had grown up in the US is now working for a social media company founded by Mikkeli students while still on campus and the student may eventually take up work in their UK office. The very strong network of the Mikkeli alumni—affectionately referred to as the "Mikkeli mafia"—not only provides opportunities for referrals and recommendations, but the alumni themselves are a resource for the programme, returning to be guest speakers, hosting students on field trips, etc. Mikkeli alumni are a source and evidence of globalisation in themselves.

Why language is not enough

Using English as the language of instruction may ensure that the BScBA programme is international, but it does not guarantee that it is global. As Lavelle (2008:137) points out, *"some of our subjects frequently involve group projects and thus social interaction both within teams and with external stakeholders such as host companies. This interaction can be difficult even when everyone speaks the same language, and even worse when we add a foreign language to the mix, most pointedly if there are doubts about either 'learners or teachers' proficiency in that language."* (Lavelle 2008:137)

Starting several years ago, the majority of the foreign degree students in the Mikkeli programme come from Vietnam. This created two distinct groups, Finns and Vietnamese, with different approaches to their studies, how they work in teams, and socialise, etc. For example, Finnish culture rates highly on individualism according to Hofstede's model (rating of 63), whereas Vietnamese culture is much less so (20). Power distance is very low in Finland (33) whereas it is high in Vietnam (70). Interestingly, uncertainty avoidance is shown as high in Finland (59) compared to Vietnam (30), whereas anecdotal evidence of learning styles in Mikkeli suggest that Vietnamese students would tend towards more uncertainty avoidance than would Finnish students. (Hofstede Centre, 2016)

This distinction can be seen in the way students approach their project work. Finnish students will be prone to quickly divide up tasks and only meet again after individuals have completed their work, whereas Vietnamese students would like to discuss it in more detail first. In more lengthy projects, such as in the project management course, exceptionally stretching over several months, or the very team-based simulation capstone course, these distinctions become more nuanced. In the recent team-based capstone course based on a business simulation, students pointed out cultural and personality differences in decision-making, reflecting an awareness that will serve them well in the international workplace and multicultural graduate programmes.

The Mikkeli programme leadership faces a challenge, however, to provide the students with a good forum in which to explore their differences constructively, not just going through the same frustrating experiences again and again. Methods used to address this challenge include reflection reports, learning diaries, and town hall meetings. Language can make the learning community international but not necessarily lead to a global mindset—our hardwiring about how we work in teams persists, so the question becomes what kind of change the programme can inculcate that might lead to further growth in the future.

Fast pace prepares for working life

Graduates of the programme report that they become used to thinking on their feet and have plenty of experience in dealing with different cultures—so their ability to simply take things as they come is well developed by the time they graduate. Bloom discusses the ways in which globalisation affects education and points to the increasing speed of change. "*New skills are required if people are to respond to new threats and new opportunities.*" (Bloom, 2004:69).

The VUCA construct developed in the 1990's (volatility, uncertainty, complexity, and ambiguity) is helpful when considering how the Mikkeli Programme prepares students for a fast-paced, globalising world (see Bennett & Lemoine, 2014). For example, volatility demands taking action and probing changes. The curricular structure allows experimentation, such as running a large capstone course around a business game. Second, uncertainty demands wider understanding from different perspectives. Mikkeli students encounter faculty from various cultures and change courses every three weeks. So they deal with uncertainty with regularity. Third, complexity demands clarity of focus, flexibility, and creativity. Teaching in Mikkeli involves meeting students for 3 hours a day for 3 weeks, allowing more space to test new teaching methods and a closer collaborative learning environment than in traditional undergraduate courses. Finally, ambiguity calls for agility in decision-making. Recruiting academic staff on an annual basis ensures that more agile decisions are made based on recent performance. As Suárez-Orozco & Qin-Hilliard (2004:6) state: "*The skills needed for analyzing and mobilizing to solve problems from multiple perspectives will require individuals who are cognitively flexible, culturally sophisticated, and able to work collaboratively in groups made up of diverse individuals.*"

Intensity may breed stress

One factor not anticipated in this design is the reality that the stress of such an intensive programme can take its toll on students such that some show signs of failing to cope with the regularity of new settings and goals. A joint initiative of staff and students to provide for student well-being is the provision of a time management/stress workshop offered to first-year students. Students in the Mikkeli programme also provide a lot of peer support. The question then becomes, when does healthy stress—mimicking the fast pace of the workplace—become unhealthy stress that then becomes a concern for the leadership of the programme and has implications for the overall design? This question is the focus of regular monitoring, and programme leadership has focused intently on ensuring Mikkeli students have access to study-oriented psychology services at the university level.

On the other hand, some may argue that this approach may actually create barriers to learning by creating too stressful an environment. Here the peer student support seems to mitigate the inherent stress in the program, also as witnessed by the very strong alumni networks that persist after Mikkeli.

Conclusion

The Mikkeli Experience has been 28 years in the making. In its first years, it was considered more of an oddity and an experiment than a long-lasting degree programme. The commitment and energy of the five Programme Directors have created a programme with a well-earned global recognition, providing students with an amazing range of international and globalised experiences. In addition, it provides faculty with the same kinds of experiences, giving them insights and perspectives they are unlikely to encounter at more traditional and conventionally structured undergraduate programmes. As the earlier discussion of globalisation indicators suggests, the Mikkeli programme is intentionally global while also preparing students to deal with a volatile and uncertain world.

Aalto University recently made a decision to integrate all of its campuses into the Otaniemi campus outside Helsinki—all except the Mikkeli Campus. The Aalto University and Business School leadership recognises the importance of continuing to offer the programme on a satellite campus and acknowledge that integrating it into regular Bachelor's teaching would destroy the original intent of the programme. Moreover, the programme remains unique because the model is difficult to adopt in part—it is a programme to be offered in its entirety.

The lessons learned through the years of the Mikkeli programme are shared in this chapter in the hope that this rich and varied programme can assist other academics and universities who are presently designing globally focused programmes around the world. It offers up an example of a tight-knit community as a "safe" place to encounter an intensive learning experience.

About the Authors

Joan Lofgren is Director of the Bachelor's Program in International Business at the Aalto University School of Businesss in Mikkeli, Finland. She can be contacted at this e-mail: joan.lofgren@aalto.fi

Elyssebeth Leigh is Director at FutureSearch. She can be contacted at this e-mail: Elyssebeth.Leigh@uts.edu.au

Bibliography

Airey, J.; K. Lauridsen; A. Räsänen; L. Salö; V. Schwach (2015). The expansion of English-medium instruction in the Nordic countries: Can top-down university language policies encourage bottom-up disciplinary literacy goals? *Higher Education*, Vol. 14, No. 3, pp. 227–239.

Altbach, P. G. & J. Knight (2007). The Internationalization of Higher Education: Motivations and Realities. *Journal of Studies in International Education*, Vol. 11, No. 3/4, pp. 290–305.

Bennett, N. & G. J. Lemoine (2014). What VUCA Really Means for You, *Harvard Business Review*, January-February.

Bloom, D. E. (2004). Globalization and Education: An Economic Perspective. In M. Suárez-Orozco & D. B. Qin-Hilliard (Eds.), *Globalization*. Berkeley, US: University of California Press, pp. 58–77.

Coleman, J. A. (2006). English-medium teaching in European higher education. *Language Teaching*, Vol. 39, No. 1, pp 1 – 14.

Dearden, J. (2014). *English as a medium of instruction—a growing global phenomenon. British Council*. Online Resource: www.teachingenglish.org.uk [Accessed 17 November 2016].

Finnish Business School Graduates (2014). *Annual surveys of business school graduates.* https://www.ekonomit.fi [Accessed 17 November 2016].

Finnish National Board of Education (2015). *Statistics of the month: Most basic education pupils in Finland learn two languages.* N.A. April 29.

Fodness, D. (2016). Informal interview of veteran Mikkeli faculty member Dale Fodness of the University of Dallas. *Mikkeli*, No. 8, May 2016.

Hofstede Centre (2016). Online Resource: https://geert-hofstede.com/finland.html [Accessed 17 November 2016].

Hüppauf, B. (2004). Globalization: Threats and opportunities. In Gardt, A. & B. Hüppauf (Eds.), *Globalization and the future of German*. Berlin & New York: Mouton de Gruyter, pp. 3–24.

ICEF Monitor (2012). *Trend Alert: English spreads as teaching language in universities worldwide*. Online Resource: http://monitor.icef.com/2012/07/trend-alert-english-spreads-as-teaching-language-in-universities-worldwide/ [Accessed 7 November 2016].

Johnson, L. (2014). *Indicators of Globalization: Measuring and Assessing Global Impact and Engagement in Education*. Slide presentation prepared for Higher Education Teaching and Learning Conference (HETL) in Anchorage, AK, delivered on June 1, 2014.

Kambhammettu, V. (2014). *Startups in the VUCA World*. Article posted on LinkedIn.com/pulse on July 21, 2014 [Accessed on 9 November 2016].

Kim, T. & W. Locke (2010). Transnational academic mobility and the academic profession. Centre for Higher Education Research and Information. The Open University, London.

Knight, J. (2009). Internationalisation: Key Concepts and Elements, In: M. Gaebel; L. Purse; B. Wächter & L. Wilson (Eds.), *Internationalisation of European Higher Education*. An EUA/ACA Handbook, Stuttgart, Raabe, A. 1.1.

Lavelle, T. (2008). English in the Classroom: Meeting the Challenge of English-Medium Instruction in International Business Schools. In P. Mårtenson; M. Bild & K. Nilsson (Eds.), *Teaching and Learning at Business Schools: Transforming Business Education*. Gower: Farnham, UK, pp. 137–163.

Powell, C. R. (2010). The Traveling Professor. In E. Pöykkö & V. Åberg (Eds.), *Tulkintoja, tosiasioita, tarinoita: Helsingin kauppakorkeakoulun historiaa* (Interpretations, facts and stories: The history of the Helsinki School of Economics). Aalto-yliopisto kauppakorkeakoulu: Helsinki.

Qiang, Z. (2003). Internationalization of Higher Education: Towards a conceptual framework. *Policy Futures in Education*, Vol. 1, No. 2, pp. 248–270.

Rogerson-Revell, P. (2007). Using English for International Business: A European case study. *English for Specific Purposes*, Vol. 26, pp. 103–120.

Suárez-Orozco, M. M. & D. B. Qin-Hilliard (2004). Globalization: Culture and Education in the New Millenium. In Suárez-Orozco and Qin-Hilliard (Eds.), *Globalization*. Berkeley, US: University of California Press, pp. 1–37.

This is Finland (2016). Online Resource:
http://finland.fi/life-society/finland-makes-multilingualism-easy/ [Accessed on
18 November 2016].

Tallroth P. (2012). Multilingualism in Finland: A Legal Perspective. *Language
& Law*, Vol. 1.

Tuckman, B. W. (1990). Development sequence in small groups. *Psychological
Bulletin*, No. 63, pp. 384–999.

Wächter, B. & F. Maiworm (Eds.) (2014). *English-taught programmes in European
higher education. The state of play in 2014.* Bonn: Lemmens.

Chapter 10

Transnational Academic Staff Development: Cultural, Practical and Policy Challenges of Globalisation in Higher Education

Julian Lamb, Paul Bartholomew & Sarah Hayes

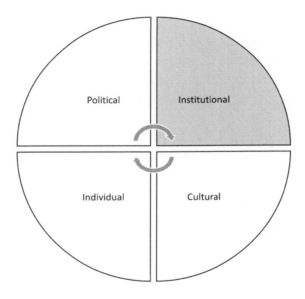

Introduction

This chapter is an important contribution to this book on the globalisation of higher education because it addresses the practice-facing challenge of supporting collaborative partners across diverse geographical, cultural and economic settings. By "collaborative partners" we mean universities (and occasionally commercial higher education providers) who have entered into formal contractual arrangements with our university to co-deliver credit-bearing programmes of study. In the chapter, we explore the challenge of requiring overseas partners to embrace UK quality values for teaching in HE but using a methodology for support that encourages emancipation, critical reflection, and choice. The chapter begins by explaining the national and institutional framework for quality assurance and enhancement that drives the requirement to support overseas collaborative partners. It then explains the philosophy of Aston University's approach to taught programmes, which lead to HEA fellowship: these are rooted in emancipation, critical reflection and choice (in pedagogy) and underpins the provision of support for overseas partners. The chapter continues by unweaving the complex themes that run through three recent trips to support collaborative partners in Italy, Vietnam, and India. Finally, it draws recommendations for those who seek to enhance the quality of teaching for overseas collaborative partners. The key lesson from the chapter is that when supporting overseas collaborative partners it is not a matter of simple training or declarative instruction but rather about revealing the ideologies embedded in the raft of approaches to learning and teaching, including that within the UK.

Reading the chapter, you will gain the following three insights:

1. insight into how the Aston University in Birmingham, UK, has organised academic staff development offerings to professionalise its globalisation.

2. insight into how we work with an emancipatory agenda in an international context to help globalisation of our offerings;

3. insight into three specific cases of transnational academic staff development projects, which has been part of our globalisation endeavour.

In our writing of this chapter, we draw upon our experience during three recent transnational staff development events (in Italy, Vietnam, and India) to explore the real-life demands of running such a provision. We explore the key emergent themes from our work in Italy and Vietnam and then provide a vignette of the work in India to give a rich description of the experience. We advocate the need to remain agile to the emergent needs of overseas partners while ensuring that certain non-negotiable tenets of quality and institutional (and personal) identities are upheld. We also offer a conclusion that such provision is as much a development opportunity for the development staff themselves as it is for the overseas participants.

Although United Kingdom (UK) higher education institutions (HEIs) have a long history of teaching international students, there is a need to ensure that teaching within collaborative arrangements in an international setting meets the quality expectations of a range of stakeholders, with particular reference to what a UK higher education qualification means to the global marketplace.

This chapter contextualises globalisation in terms of the expansion of UK-centric approaches to teaching quality in the context of collaborative provision. This is not to be mistaken for anything that could be seen as imperialistic: there are clear cautions about this in Ilonya and Mathew's chapter in this anthology about the historic context of Britain's colonial impact on overseas HE provision. Instead, our aim is focused on ensuring that, where teaching is under the "brand" or "flag" of a UK HEI, the core principles encompassed in the UK's academic quality infrastructure are adopted and even embraced.

A significant part of this chapter shares our (the authors') recent experiences supporting teachers as part of collaborative partnerships in three different international settings: Italy, Vietnam, and India. Each of these visits lasted approximately one week and was intended to provide support for overseas higher education teachers in order to address a range of quality expectations. Broadly, these quality expectations reflect the UK's Quality Assurance Agency's Quality Code, specifically Chapter B10: Managing higher education provision with others (QAA, 2012); the United Kingdom Professional Standards Framework (UKPSF) for teaching and supporting learning in higher education (Higher Education Academy, 2011); and the University's own policy framework relating to collaborative provision. Each one of these frameworks is expanded upon in the next section.

Together, the three transnational collaborations mentioned above and described in detail in the latter part of this chapter provide a comparative framework for the exploration of issues such as teaching identity, the relationship of teachers with students, attitudes towards assessment, and approaches to quality enhancement and assurance. Additionally, the chapter offers a model that describes our approaches to designing and delivering academic staff development in a transnational context.

The chapter commences by exploring the policy position (national and institutional) and concomitant philosophy for supporting our transnational collaborative partners. The chapter then moves on to explore the real-life challenges of our "first contact" with these partners (in relation to academic staff development) and then concludes with a design-approach to effect meaningful support for overseas collaboration within the context of the demands and expectations of UK Higher Education.

The aim of this chapter then is to provide a general insight into the challenges faced when supporting collaborative partners in their specific and different settings and to share our modelled, experience-based response to the transnational academic staff development challenge.

The Policy Context Underpinning Collaborative Provision

Nationally, within the UK, Chapter B10 of the QAA Quality Code sets out the clear responsibility of degree-awarding bodies for academic standards and the quality of learning opportunities irrespective of where they are delivered and who provides them. Whilst Chapter B10 is heavily orientated towards risk management and procedural quality assurance, it also encompasses the support of international partners in assuring and enhancing the quality of learning. The consequence of this is that a student's experience should reflect the same learning and teaching quality standards, whether they study through a university's "native" provision (delivered by a university's own staff, perhaps on the university's "home" campus) or via a university's collaborative provision delivered through that university's partner's staff.

At Aston University, we have developed a "sliding scale" of academic staff development support to address the needs of any transnational collaborative provision partnership. All of the academic staff development on this "sliding-scale" is delivered through the University's Centre for Learning Innovation and Professional Practice. This "sliding scale" is shown below in Table 1.

Delivery model	Minimum requirement for the development of overseas academic staff	Contact time	Costs to be met
1. Aston Faculty delivering an Aston programme overseas.	N/A	N/A	N/A
2. Overseas partner staff delivering Aston-designed programmes using Aston-designed materials and session plans.	Unaccredited multi-day CPD programme that broadly maps to the content delivered on the Level 6 course: An Introduction to Learning and Teaching Practice.	Twenty hours of taught content.	Travel and accommodation for two individuals from CLIPP.
3. Overseas partner staff delivering Aston-designed (or collaboratively designed) programmes using their own materials, session plans, and curriculum plans.	Postgraduate Certificate: Learning and Teaching in Higher Education.	Sixty hours of taught content plus online activities.	Applicable student fees.

Table 1: Aston University's "sliding-scale" of academic staff development.

The Centre for Learning Innovation and Professional Practice (CLIPP) is a central department of the University; it is responsible for academic staff development, curriculum design, academic quality enhancement and assurance, student academic support, and central support for student retention and progression. It is relatively unusual, in the UK, for the department responsible for academic staff development to also be the department responsible for academic quality assurance and enhancement. That close articulation of functions and responsibilities has led to academic staff development being enacted as a distinct facet of the University's quality arrangements. This is as true for our native campus-based provision, as it is for our transnational collaborative provision.

CLIPP Academic Staff Development Offerings

CLIPP offers four "levels" of academic staff development to its "native" academic (and academic-related) population:

1. Ad-hoc non-accredited continuous professional development provision—normally enacted through half-day or full-day workshops.

2. The Introduction to Learning and Teaching Practice course—a three-day credit-bearing programme. This is a Level 6 course [according to the UK Framework for Higher Education Qualifications (FHEQ)] and is thus equivalent, in academic level, to a module/course within the final year of an undergraduate degree programme. Successful participants are awarded 10 (UK) credits—this is equivalent to 5 (ECTS) credits, where ECTS = European Credit Transfer System.

3. The Postgraduate Certificate: Learning and Teaching in Higher Education (PGCertLTHE). This is a Level 7 (FHEQ) programme, which is Master's Degree level (a PGCert is 1/3 of a Master's Degree). Successful participants are thus awarded 60 (UK) credits, the equivalent of 30 (ECTS) credits.

4. The Master's in Education: Learning and Teaching in Higher Education. Successful participants are awarded 180 (UK) credits, the equivalent of 90 (ECTS) credits.

The second and third entries on the list above are particularly noteworthy since the UK Higher Education Academy (HEA) accredits them. This national (and increasingly international) organisation is the custodian of the UKPSF (the United Kingdom Professional Standards Framework). The UKPSF is a set of competencies and descriptors that set the expectations for professional practice for teaching in higher education. The full set of competences (dimensions) is shown below as Figure 1:

Dimensions of the Framework

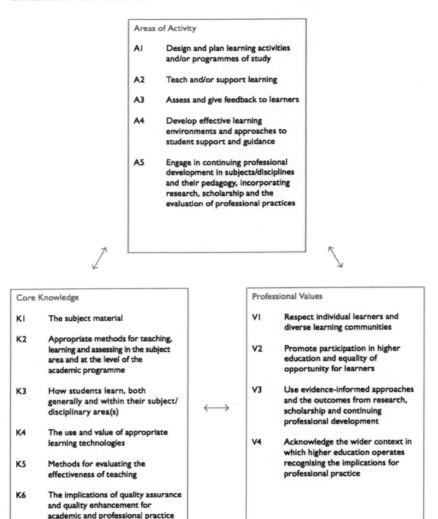

Figure 1: The dimensions of the UKPSF.

Our ILTP programme (Item 2 on the provision list) is accredited at Descriptor 1 of UKPSF. People who successfully complete that programme can be awarded Associate Fellowship of the HEA. This is recognition that they have demonstrated an understanding of specific aspects of effective teaching, learning support methods, and student learning. Individuals should be able to provide evidence of:

+ successful engagement with at least two of the five Areas of Activity;

+ successful engagement in appropriate teaching and practices related to these Areas of Activity;

+ appropriate Core Knowledge and understanding of at least K1 and K2;

+ a commitment to appropriate Professional Values in facilitating others' learning;

+ relevant professional practices, subject and pedagogic research and/or scholarship within the above activities;

+ successful engagement, where appropriate, in professional development activity related to teaching, learning, and assessment responsibilities.

Our PGCertLTHE programme (Item 3 on the provision list) is accredited at Descriptor 2 of UKPSF. People who successfully complete that programme can be awarded Fellowship of the HEA. Individuals should be able to provide evidence of:

+ successful engagement across all five Areas of Activity;

+ appropriate knowledge and understanding across all aspects of core knowledge;

+ a commitment to all the Professional Values;

+ successful engagement in appropriate teaching practices related to Areas of Activity;

+ successful incorporation of subject and pedagogic research and/or scholarship within the above activities as part of an integrated approach to academic practice;

+ successful engagement in continuing professional development in relation to teaching, learning, assessment and, where appropriate, related professional practices.

It is this articulation with the UKPSF that underpins our claim that we assure the quality of our teaching staff. As a consequence, if we are to extend the quality assurance of teaching into transnational collaborative provision (as implied within Chapter B10 of the QAA Quality Code), we are compelled to support the staff of overseas partners in some way. Table 1 above demonstrates how we enact that commitment for a range of transnational contexts.

The purpose of the academic staff (faculty) development provision delivered by CLIPP is to support the quality enhancement and assurance needs (as it relates to teaching) of the five Schools at Aston University (Aston Business School, Life and Health Sciences, Engineering and Applied Sciences, and Aston Medical School). In relation to transnational collaborative provision, CLIPP's role is to support the *schools'* transnational provision, not to develop programmes for CLIPP's own sake or to develop an autonomous income stream separate from the business of the schools. As a consequence, there is a level of support we are able and willing to commit on an "expenses-only" basis since such activity is part of the core function of the department. The Academic Team (one of four teams within CLIPP) is small though (3.8 whole time equivalent staff) and already runs an extensive provision for campus-based staff— we currently have around 180 members of staff per year enrolled on our academic staff (faculty) development programmes.

Of the three models of transnational provisions the schools might enact (Table 1), there are staff/faculty development models for just two of them. Where "flying faculty" travels overseas and delivers Aston's programmes (Delivery Model 1), no staff development is required—as those staff will already have been supported/developed. Aston's PGCertLTHE is mandatory for all new academic staff at Aston and procedures are in place to ensure equivalence for all academic staff. For Delivery Model 2, where the programme to be delivered has been designed down to the teaching session level by Aston staff/faculty, there is a (self-imposed) requirement for the overseas staff to be developed through 20 hours of teaching. This teaching aims to support overseas staff in their understanding of UK

Higher Education and the broad philosophies that underpin the design choices relating to programme structure and pedagogic practice, including assessment practice. This level of support is not credit bearing and does not carry any recognition against UKPSF; rather, it uses UKPSF as a common reference point between UK campus and overseas teaching. It is this model of support that is described within the Italian and Vietnamese contexts later in this chapter.

Unlike support for Delivery Model 2, which has little resource commitment beyond face-to-face delivery of the programme, Delivery Model 3 requires a step-change in the support for transnational partnerships. Here, overseas staff are collaborating on overall programme design and are exclusively responsible for the design and delivery of session materials and for the enactment of assessment. Although Aston's quality infrastructure continues to take responsibility for such things as advice and decisions on regulatory matters, the delivery of teaching and assessment is enacted at the partner's institution and their ability to do so relatively autonomously needs to be supported. As a consequence, Delivery Model 3 requires partner staff/faculty to study and pass the PGCertLTHE. This is a resource-intensive programme (from CLIPP's perspective) and requires the levy of tuition fees to make it viable within current funding structures (the provision of academic staff development, including the full MEd, incurs no fees to Aston University staff of their schools). As a broad guide the following outline resource requirements were estimated in initial discussions with a potential transnational partner (Table 2):

Activity	Required person hours
Management and preparation of the programme	168
Delivery of the programme (teaching—two staff members), including travel to and from the country	240
Mentoring and tutorial support	38
Assessment, marking and moderation	136
Examination Board administration and annual monitoring/ reporting	68
Total	650

Table 2: Outline of resource requirements in a transnational program.

In addition to funding this level of academic commitment, there remains the need to cover expenses for travel and accommodation for the teaching staff. The overall package of costs is thus quite expensive and really only becomes viable for cohorts of 15 students or more. Even then, especially for developing countries, the cost-base for this model is prohibitive. Indeed, we have yet to be commissioned to run this model despite protracted negotiations taking place with potential partners.

There may be potential in developing online models but this would compromise some of the teaching approaches, are expensive to develop (initially), and still require ongoing input through web-based tutorials, marking, and examination board facilitation. Thus, it has been Model 2—the overseas teaching workshops—that has been attractive to the schools we support and their transnational collaborative partners.

The Philosophical DNA of the Overseas Teaching Workshops

As seen above, the UKPSF is taken as the central framework for defining competence in teaching within collaborative partnerships, and it was decided that Aston's 20-credit, Descriptor 1 (D1 of UKPSF) accredited ILTP would be used as the starting-point for the design of the "Supporting Overseas Teachers" workshop.

The ILTP provides a firm platform from which to enhance workshop delegates' appreciation of the centrality of the UKPSF in the UK Higher Education context; it also provides systematic and tested coverage of the UKPSF in a manner that is appropriate to Descriptor 1. The curriculum covers three broad areas:

- teaching identity, which includes pedagogy as an expression of relationships with students;

- module (and programme) design, including assessment design;

- working with others, including diversity, inclusivity, and conflict resolution.

Whilst overseas delegates are not required or expected to submit any form of assessment that could lead to the award of Associate Fellow of the HEA, nothing precludes the possibility that this could be implemented in some sort of follow-up project with those delegates.

Cross-cutting the UKPSF D1 centric curriculum of the ILTP, our pedagogy is informed by our published CLIPP team philosophy:

> "This work-based learning programme is designed from the perspective that learning is a social activity, best undertaken within a multi-disciplinary community. We see learning as a product of discussion and debate. Using conceptual modules and theoretical perspectives of learning and teaching to underpin debate we intend to be provocative and so enhance critical reflection upon tacit assumptions about professionalism and 'power' within higher education. We uphold diversity of identities and approaches to teaching within an anti-oppressive and anti-discriminatory context. We support the development of creative academic practice and innovation." (published teaching philosophy, CLIPP, Aston University).

The DNA of our teaching is emancipation through critical reflection on the dominant ideologies within HE teaching practice. We provide a clear practice-base focus and proceed on the premise that delegates should "unlearn" their taken-for-granted assumptions about learning and teaching in order to teach in a truly authentic manner: where authenticity mirrors the UKPSF "Professional Values" of respect, equality, emancipation, reflection, personal development, and scholarship. We believe that this approach has much in common with the general praxis of secular Buddhism, in which enlightenment can only be achieved through "rejecting" received wisdom in order to better understand one's own authentic views (Suzuki, 2004). This approach also embraces the spirit of the humanistic school of psychotherapies and the Rogerian Person-Centred approach in particular where the agenda is to "tune into" a sense of self (Rogers, 2004). The Rogerian perspective also leads into the essential relationship between the workshop delegate and teacher (as facilitator) in which each person's perception of the other is crucially important and the teacher deeply involves him or herself: we are not "acting" as teachers—we draw on our own experiences (self-disclosure) and personality to facilitate the relationship with our overseas delegates (Munson, 2013).

There is an often-quoted truism that compares two fundamental models of teaching: "The sage on the stage or the guide by their side." Whilst, philosophically, we can critique such a bivalent view of teaching, our teaching on the overseas workshops is aligned to the latter position: one where as teachers we "are a guide by a delegate's side". This should not be mistaken for a passive role: the "teacher as guide" is one of action, decision, expertise, and even provocative opinion when required. However, all such efforts are directed towards a delegate's engagement with, and embracement of, the UKPSF.

We have nothing invested in persuading participants to adopt our views or assimilate an approach that they might be perceived as "institutionally-specific", although we do have a commitment to the UKPSF, which could lead to seemingly paradoxical situations and even a dilemma between promoting both "emancipation from ideologies" and UKPSF at the same time. We could be mistaken for promoting equality of ideologies, where our ideologies (UKPSF) are a little more "equal" than others (cf George Orwell's *Animal Farm*). In reality, however, there is a clear parallel in this respect with Dawson's findings (in this anthology) about the co-creation of a new global identity between ourselves (Aston staff) and our overseas partners: our encounters with overseas colleagues leaves us all enriched and, indeed, changed by the experience.

The bivalent model of teaching identity as "guide or sage" does not adequately encompass the real-life fuzzy blend of instruction and emancipation that we have to maintain as a teacher (Kosko, 1993). For example, when we deliver the topic of "inclusivity and equality", it is incumbent on us to provide clear instructions about the purpose and requirements of the Equality Act 2010 in the UK setting. There is no room for compromise or personal view regarding the intent of, and compliance with, this legislation in the setting of UK HE. Furthermore, our personal and professional (UKPSF) values would suffer injury if we compromised on equality. For example, when we explore anti-discriminatory practice, we have to maintain a fine balance between facilitating participant's open and authentic reflection on their personal values (related to gender, race, and disability, for example); in doing so, however, we cannot teach in any way that might be perceived as condoning views that we believe are discriminatory or oppressive. As such, in these contexts, we are prepared to voice a personal view in a manner that is one-step beyond "sage on the stage" to become a "political activist" (Thompson, 2012). In this respect, the Rogerian proposition of "Unconditional Positive Regard" (UPR) can be challenging in our practice; that is to say, we do not find it challenging to achieve, but the role requires us to challenge the views of those we teach so that they may gain a better awareness of the impact of their views.

The Trans-National Workshop's Relationship with Theory (and Literature): Authority and Emancipation Revisited

It is, perhaps, unsurprising that our philosophical relationship with delegates crosscuts and parallels our relationship with theory (and literature). In this respect, we have nothing invested in providing a definitive, authoritative body of theory or literature that participants must acquire and assimilate. Having said this, we have everything invested in participants taking a rational, conceptual, evidence-based approach to their reflective practice.

During the overseas workshops our pedagogical intention in relation to theory is two-fold.

First, delegates choose for themselves which theoretical perspectives suit their setting and are most useful to them. This parallels the emancipatory agenda: workshop delegates are on their own personal journeys of learning in which they are encouraged to "tune into" themselves; they are not on a journey to become a replica of ourselves (as the workshop teachers), Aston University, or indeed the prevailing culture of UK HE pedagogy. This approach accords with Robinson's (2013) frank critique of dominant ideologies in HE teaching that lead to student intellects being "strip-mined" of all but the required knowledge a teacher identifies for a particular profession. Rather than strip-mining, we urge students towards innovation and creativity in their thinking about teaching.

Our relationship with theory (and literature) also listens to the voice of Freire (1996) who issues a warning about the political imprinting that is often embedded in a teacher's attempt to define an approved body of literature. Above all, we want students to make informed honest decisions about their view of effective teaching; this agenda enhances their journey towards becoming a reflective practitioner.

Our second intention is that theory and conceptual approaches are treated as maps, rather than blueprints, of the social world in which teaching exists. The epistemological nature of the material we teach is aligned to the "social construction" of reality (Berger & Luckmann, 1967) and as such it is the practice-based sense-making of teaching that is the focus rather than presenting "the classroom" as a topic for sociological scrutiny and analysis in itself. We do not see the overseas workshops as a course in the sociology of teaching; rather, they are a work-based learning programme intended to facilitate a participant's own reflection on, and evaluation of, their teaching. It is fundamentally embedded in workplace practice and not isolated abstract ideas.

Agile Intervention

Readers of this chapter are probably thinking: *"This is all very nice but how will an emancipatory agenda work in an international context?"* Based on our prior experience working overseas, we were alive to the need to implement an approach of "agile intervention" in the delivery of the overseas workshops. These workshops would be as much about us learning from our international colleagues and their world-view of teaching in HE as it is about enhancing their UKPSF-centric competence to teach on programmes in association with Aston University.

For the three countries explored in this chapter, we anticipated cultural, social, and political challenges. We were alive to the single-party socialist republic framework that exists in Vietnam and the implications for promoting free thought and critical pedagogy. We understood that whilst India is a secular, federal parliamentary democratic republic, there are differences related to religion, caste, and language that lead to differing ideologies about social practice and pedagogy in Indian Higher Education. We appreciated that whilst Italy is a multi-party democracy, the culture of intra-institutional quality assurance within Italian higher education is unlike that in the UK.

Our intention in these workshop interventions was to remain alive and agile to the emergent themes and issues. This is not to say that we would compromise our philosophy or the centrality of the UKPSF but that we would seek work with our overseas partners in a way that is most appropriate to their local needs, priorities, and institutional settings, and not to appear imperialistic in the promotion of our UK-centric views.

The Italian Context

The "Italian Job" was our first experience supporting teachers on an overseas collaborative teaching partnership. The host organization was a private school of optometry in Bologna that had recently been approved under a franchise agreement with Aston University to run an undergraduate programme in optometry. We were able to ascertain a simple brief from Aston's School of Optometry prior to the workshop that included an appraisal of the Italian team's ability to teach in English and their views on assessment and marking.

The workshop was designed to run over two and a half days with a core curriculum to include:

+ teaching identity (expectations about the nature of the student-teacher relationship);

+ module design and assessment (constructive alignment, and quality assurance in assessment);

+ enhancing inclusivity (the social module of disability and the Equality Act).

We very quickly found our Italian colleagues to be fluent in English and skilled reflective practitioners. Moreover, whilst they had contracted to work with the private college, they there all experienced teachers from a range of state universities across Italy.

Our warm-up exercise, a simple line-up activity intended to explore the relationship between teachers and students, was met with enthusiastic engagement to the point at which we often found the need to actively facilitate closure in order to proceed. By the first coffee break, our Italian colleagues reported great surprise that we (representatives of the franchise-granting institution) were interested in their views: they had assumed the workshop would be two days of one-way instruction about "how to teach Aston-style".

We found that their understanding of equality and inclusivity matched our expectations within a UK setting. Their concept of the student-teacher relationship was one characterised by coaching, mentoring, and the sharing of the learning experience; it was not one characterised as predominantly declarative or transmissive (Sterling, 2001; Bransford & Donovan, 2005).

Moving onto module and assessment design, however, revealed interesting differences between the UK and Italian contexts. Whilst the idea of "constructive alignment" was unfamiliar to them, they accepted the concept as being sensible and reasonable but continued to reveal that the creation of new modules and programmes never followed a design approach in their experience and would not involve stakeholders beyond the immediate teaching team. Additionally, they were astonished to learn that every assessment in the UK was subject to the independent scrutiny and verification of an external examiner from another institution. They questioned if there was a culture of corruption in the UK that required such heavy-handed inspection. One Italian teacher abruptly retorted, *"Don't they trust you to mark correctly and fairly in the UK?!"* There was a genuine sense of surprise that UK academics do not have full independent unscrutinised authority in the marking of their students.

At this point in the workshop, it became apparent that an agile response was required to extend a 30-minute session to a 3-hour exploration of the national and institutional context of quality assurance in the UK HE sector. Whilst the different approach to quality assurance in Italy could have been revealed through extensive desk research prior to the visit, the strength of personal feeling about the UK approach would have been difficult to ascertain at a distance. The agile response to the emergent issue ensured that this issue did not cause a great problem (of misunderstanding) at a later stage in the collaboration between the two institutions.

The Vietnamese Context

Our work in Vietnam was provided in the context of pre-sessional support for a new collaborative project for teaching between a consortium of UK and Vietnamese universities.

A trip of one week to Vietnam included two days for a learning and teaching workshop and a day in which delegates from both the workshop and across the Vietnamese HE sector contributed short presentations to a conference on Quality in Higher Education.

Upon entry to the teaching room, it was clear that the expectation for our session was one of the transmission of knowledge from us to them. The room has been arranged in tight rows and at the front had been placed a "top table" dressed in red velvet fabric and facing the audience. A single beam projector was provided but no other teaching resource. This was despite prior correspondence where we had specified a "cafe-style" room layout.

After a short preamble and introduction, we set our first activity in motion: the same line-up exercise we had used in Italy. The front rows of tables were set aside and the delegates, most of whom were early career academics in their middle to late twenties, grasped the activity with a similar degree of enthusiasm as our Italian colleagues. At the end of the activity, the participants returned to their seats and awaited instructions. During the first coffee break, several of the delegates said they enjoyed Karaoke very much and were pleased to start the day in this fashion. Returning from the coffee break, it was apparent that during our absence the teaching room had been rearranged back into neat rows, the velvet fabric on the top table straightened, and order returned.

The second activity required table-based discussions and feedback from groups using whiteboards or flip charts. The neat rows of tables were rearranged into café-style, but no flip charts or white boards were available: it was some surprise to our hosts that we needed such resources. Luckily, we had brought a supply of "Magic White Boards": static-cling vinyl sheets that can be used as temporary white boards on any smooth vertical surface, and the activity could be resumed—albeit by moving into the corridor to find the space for people to gather around their makeshift whiteboards.

One of the distinguishing features of this overseas teaching workshop was the degree to which what we came to deliver was at variance with what we had planned to deliver. That is not to say we compromised in relation to the tenets of UKPSF, but we had been asked to prepare additional materials in relation to conducting surveys in higher education—for the purposes of research and collaboration. In fact, that session (a full half-day) had to be abandoned to accommodate emergent additional materials around assessment.

Delivering the programme with multiple teachers (three in this case) meant that while one person delivered content the others could plan sessions to address emergent needs. Indeed, at one point one teacher constructed an entire presentation on the topic of assessment while the other two were presenting. Additional support in relation to assessment practice became quite detailed as the concept of rubric construction became a target for discussion and a rubric (for a notional assessment) was constructed collaboratively by the session leader and the participants. This agility of delivery, coupled with a commitment to deliver key tenets of UKPSF, is what has come to characterise this sort of workshop for us.

The Indian Context

This example of a transnational overseas teaching is presented as a vignette in order to provide a richer description of one author's experience (Sarah Hayes). Rather than directly supporting an existing Aston University collaboration, this trip was a commissioned workshop funded by the British Council. The expertise of UK scholars is valued and sought out. Coincidentally, India is a key priority country in our University's International Strategy, with successful interactions with India, including student recruitment, exchange, and research partnerships. However, the opportunity to teach academic staff at the Administrative Staff College of India (ASCI), Hyderabad, in India, in January 2016, funded by British Council (BC), was independently brought to our attention, via a colleague from another UK university. Through BC and the Government of India, her team members were working with Vice Chancellors and the Ministry to help them build a national professional network and digital capabilities in universities across the State of Andhra Pradesh (AP). Within a larger vision, to position the State as an Educational Hub and Knowledge Society, the Higher Education Department, Government of Andhra Pradesh (GoAP), had designed "Entry Point Projects" (EPPs 4 and 5). This place-special emphasis on faculty development and training programmes for academic staff served to build their competencies so they could acquire leadership positions in their respective domains.

In taking up the invitation to design and facilitate a 3-day workshop for 36 senior academic staff from across AP, around online programme design and blended learning techniques, I was aware this was one of a series, requested by the government, and that representatives from the various authorities would be present. I invited a former colleague to co-deliver the teaching. David Pollard is Learning Technology Manager in Aston's School of Languages and Social Sciences (LSS). He teaches and has a strong background in design and support of online learning.

The Dean of LSS, the Director of CLIPP, and our Deputy Vice Chancellor were supportive of us undertaking the initiative, and so preparation began. Between the point of agreeing to design the workshop and the flying to India to deliver sessions, there was less than one month (with the Christmas break in between)! This was not ideal, given strict visa requirements. It raises a question for UK university academic development teams concerning readiness to respond to challenging and potentially transformational international work at a short notice. Fortunately, institutional letters of support, as well as visas, were approved quickly. We were given a formal email introduction to the Assistant Director, Internationalising HE (India), who facilitates internationalisation activities on behalf of the BC in India, and to our hosts at ASCI, and details of the programme of our workshop were to be delivered within. Day 1 would be a conference, where government officials would lay out expectations, and a local e-learning expert would be present. In Vietnam, we participated in a local quality conference, which followed our taught programme. In Hyderabad, we could absorb the unfamiliar context on Day 1, tweak our approach to support *local* aspirations, and notice cultural nuances not visible through email.

Globally, competing trends exert pressure on institutions and their internationalisation efforts (de Wit *et al.*, 2015). These may require a rethinking of roles and responsibilities in universities, within national borders and beyond, to define missions and operational strategies (Guri-Rosenblit, 2015). Rushed, ill-conceived shared programmes may threaten international relationships, but bringing competing agendas under a blanket of "quality" has mutual benefits. Global value is placed on UK quality and host countries can demonstrate progressive behaviour (Lea & Purcell, 2015:8) in applying quality frameworks. This shifts focus away from programmes constructed on consumerism and economic gain towards shared social and academic aims, diversity of cohorts, opportunities for collaborative global research, promotion of equality, and cross-cultural understanding (Lea & Purcell, 2015:18). Including e-learning and decisions related to learning technologies under the quality blanket facilitates richer conversations based on frameworks like UKPSF and structured curriculum design choices, e.g. learning outcomes, and combinations of technology to best support these.

With such ideas in mind, David and I designed an active, flexible three days. We talked with our hosts over Skype about our plan and the equipment available. We learned that technology is currently very limited in our participants' universities, and Moodle, Google classroom, and MOOCs are in use in some universities, as well as Visual Interactive E-Learning World (AVIEW) and NPTel. This was valuable to know to avoid assumptions on our part. David drew up a list of software to install, including a stand-alone Moodle installation as a "Plan B" should we encounter problems using a cloud-based version, Screencast-o-matic, Audacity, Paint.NET, and VideoPad. We requested headsets and webcams too. As the visit grew close, our hosts emailed our plan to participants with the message: "We wish you and your family a very Happy Sankranthi!"

On arrival, although tired, we checked that the teaching room had display facilities. Our hosts had hired a laptop for each participant, and a PG student and two technical support assistants for us.

Day 1 consisted of formal presentations, communicating India's digital strategy and setting the AP context. We asked the local e-learning expert for permission to integrate some of her instructional design models with those we planned to show. Although an informative day for us, it was clear the group, who were formally dressed as befits the local culture in AP, were expecting a week of listening in this way. On Day 2 we immediately intervened to disrupt this... We gave them answers relating to topics about ourselves and challenged them to guess the questions... After the initial surprise, our new colleagues swiftly participated in our humorous opening. As in Italy and Vietnam, a lively, fun cultural exchange accompanied the challenges. We provided them with their learning outcomes for the 3 days, which were to: 1) *Analyse their personal and institutional needs;* 2) *Evaluate the suitability of e-learning tools and models;* 3) *Create and present their own e-lessons, assessments, and media.* We included our own too. *Throughout the workshop, David and Sarah will: seek to learn more about your own systems, techniques, and challenges.*

We asked them to form groups and draw a concept map of e-learning on whiteboard sheets, first creating a whole group mind map together, where (conveniently for us) they told us about Hyderabad and where we should go sightseeing! Their e-learning maps enabled us to share theory and models and link these to their own identities and create a further link between students, assessment, and quality. E-Learning is often regarded as a "macro-tool" (one big thing) rather than a collection of "micro-tools"—each with its own set of "affordances" to apply as part of a well-designed, aligned curriculum. We discussed constructive alignment (Biggs, 2003) and "affordances" as properties of a system, which encourage *specific types of learning behaviour* (Salmon, 2002). They were asked to consider how ubiquity, accessibility, rapid feedback and ease of use are all features of a learners' daily experience with digital technologies that can raise their expectations of education (Beetham *et al.*, 2009). We used a continuum to demonstrate approaches between face-to-face and/or online activities and discussed how a "flipped classroom" approach might work in their contexts, emphasising that such choices are more effective when structured within a clear rationale. Following a sociable and authentic local lunch, we moved into practical sessions and discussions that set the pattern for Days 3 and 4. We had asked them to bring their own teaching materials, course design documents and assessments, and what their department or institution would like to develop. In groups, they reviewed their own courses, learning outcomes, reasons to introduce technology, and the tools they wished to trial. They planned a course title and approach and we asked them to undertake a skills review. In the hands-on sessions, they set up discussion forums and quizzes in Moodle, practiced creating screencasts and worked on group projects to present on Day 5.

The final presentations were a real reward and I have videos to remind me of how far the group progressed and how much David and I learned. They created a Google group and added us to continue to exchange practice after the event. After anticipating as much as is possible, there is a need for an ongoing reflexivity within a UK teaching team abroad to integrate, *local*, culturally important aspects and political agendas that it would be hard to be aware of before teaching in the host institution begins. Developing a shared understanding of the institutional prerequisites and conditions needed to support the design and engaging digital learning environments for students have challenged UK universities over two decades. However, an integration of these considerations into quality frameworks provides a way forward. The design of workshops to support academics who are required to lead on choices concerning learning technologies then becomes a sub-section to quality frameworks, such as QAA and UKPSF guidelines.

Exploring significant practice-based cross-cuts between the three transnational experiences— modelling academic staff development in transnational contexts

The three settings can be seen as diverse and different; however, there are clear themes and issues that cross-cut each experience. One significant cross-cut is the crucial ability to embrace uncertainty in the planning of overseas support: this is not to suggest that tutors should "wing-it" but that support is planned as a "menu of possibilities" rather than a rigid curriculum. Notwithstanding the above, the experience of each setting highlighted the need for core or minimum content that would need to be addressed by the end of the intervention. In our experience, core content included an exploration of teaching identity and the design of modules (to include the centrality of constructive alignment).

Another significant crosscut in the three settings is an awareness, agility, and reflexivity towards local culture, politics, and legislation. A clear illustration of this comes from our work in Vietnam where, immediately prior to a workshop on equality and diversity, we realised that we had not fully researched the legal position regarding the promotion of sex, gender, and transgender rights. In fact, after half an hour research on the internet, we found Vietnam to be quite liberal in this respect, and it had hosted various gay-pride events in recent years. We could have got this wrong and it raised the importance of detailed desk research prior to travel to ensure that topics or viewpoints that we, in the UK, consider unproblematic, are acceptable and indeed legal topics for discussion in the partner country. There is an interesting parallel in emancipatory agenda to a chapter in this anthology by Rasmussen *et al.*, where they use the "CRASS" model to explore the quality dimensions of Bologna. It is clear that the view of our students (who are also teachers) is one of autonomy, cooperation, empowerment, flexibility, and transparency.

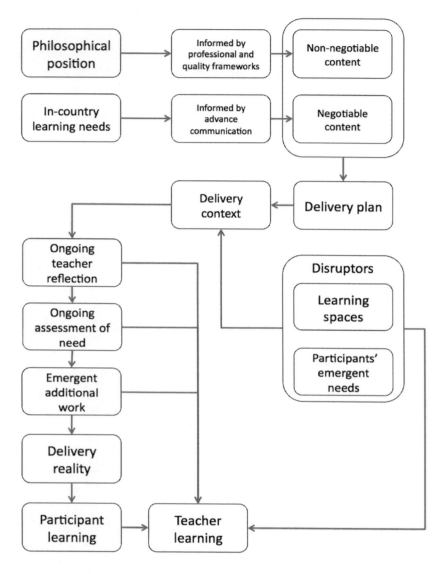

Figure 2: The evolution of academic staff development provision—from initial planning to delivered reality.

From our experience it is also apparent that transnational academic staff development serves two masters—the two collaborating institutions. This means that some of the intended learning outcomes for the participants will be defined by the lead institution (i.e. the partner who owns the degree) and others by the partner institution. The lead institution, as was/ is the case in our context, will have particular quality parameters that will frame the provision. These parameters can be grouped into those that relate to professionalism and those that relate to professionality. Bartholomew (2015:xx) defines this distinction like this: *"[P]rofessionalisim [is] subscribing to, and working within, the 'service' and practice parameters that have been negotiated between 'professionals', an associated professional body and (often) wider society through the proxy of authoritative agencies. 'Professionality', Evans (2002:6–7) contends, is different from this socio-political construct of 'professionalism' and relates to the ideological and attitudinal disposition of the 'professional'."*

Therefore, we have sought to deliver content that reflects the tenets of UKPSF, the requirements of Chapter B10 of the QAA Quality Code and our overall values as encapsulated in the CLIPP team philosophy statement shared earlier in this chapter. This relates to the "non-negotiable content" shown in Figure 2 below. It is non-negotiable because the raison d'être for such programmes is to inculcate the participants in the ways and thinking of UK Higher Education, as interpreted through the agents of the lead institution.

Broadly, transnational academic staff development is characterised by predictable unpredictability! That is to say, it is dangerous to assume that the plans and learning designs constructed prior to delivery will survive "first contact", they will not and those undertaking such a provision should make advance preparations for how they will adapt. These demands and the pattern of evolution of the provision once delivery begins is summarised below as Figure 2:

Conclusion

This chapter has described the purpose of transnational higher education academic staff development as it relates to the UK context through the sharing of the first-hand experiences of three recent transnational staff development events. Drawing on this experience we have modelled the evolution of such provision as summarised in Figure 2. There are some clear pragmatic ramifications that cascade from our experiences and these are summarised as advisory learning points below:

+ Transnational academic staff development can be expensive. There needs to be a clear position in terms of what is achievable. Savings can be made through deploying non-credit bearing, not accredited provision. Avoiding the need for assessment eliminates a significant proportion of the potential costs.

+ Transnational academic staff development requires team effort. Aside from ensuring that (in-country) illness can be covered, you should *expect* to have to generate new teaching materials "on the fly"—this may require one person to deliver/facilitate while another authors new bespoke materials.

+ Related to the above points, the staff concerned will need the capacity to generate new materials/sessions. They will need laptops with access to all of their teaching materials. All of the CLIPP team use laptops as their main computer—this offers great access to materials when overseas.

+ Assume the worst when planning for a variety of learning spaces. Academic staff development provision is characterised by collaborative pedagogies. You will need ways to repurpose learning spaces that are broadly inadequate—such materials as the "Magic Whiteboards", marker pens, white paper tablecloths, flipchart paper and Post-it notes are all simply and readily-sourced items that can literally save the day.

+ Academic staff development personnel develop as a consequence too, not just the participants! Figure 2 shows that although the participants learn as a consequence of the "delivered reality", the teaching staff learn from the participants (cultural exchange) and from the adaptive process of continually flexing the programme as to emergent needs. Although this is a feature of any academic staff development provision (not just those situated in transnational contexts), the degree of unpredictability and particularly poor control of learning spaces create a rich learning opportunity/challenge for academic development staff. In addition to the *professional* development for those staff who deliver the support, we also feel that there is a significant *personal* development perspective. For example, spending time with colleagues who work within a one-party communist society was deeply insightful and provided new perspectives from which to understand the power and hierarchy of our own work setting.

Finally, we see that the recent political context in the UK has been characterised by more robust border controls. This had led to real challenges in relation to the UK continuing to attract overseas students. This is particularly acute within the postgraduate-taught market space. As a consequence, many institutions, including Aston University, are developing increasing numbers of collaborations with overseas partners. These collaborations allow for the continuance of the offering of UK higher education awards while avoiding the difficulties associated with robust border control. The need to support this provision within established quality parameters has been one of the foci of this chapter. Through having strategies to deploy an institution's academic staff development team overseas, an institution can ensure that it can "project" its provision transnationally while safeguarding its learning and teaching philosophies—not only those that cascade from notions of professionalism but those that cascade from notions of professionality too.

About the authors

Dr Julian Lamb has an eclectic background that includes a degree in Accountancy, a PhD in Construction Management, and Master's degrees in Archaeology and Social Work. Julian leads the HEA accredited PGCert Learning and Teaching in Higher Education at Aston University. He can be contacted at this e-mail: j.lamb1@aston.ac.uk

Professor Paul Bartholomew is former Director of Learning Innovation and Professional Practice at Aston University, Birmingham, England. He is now Pro-Vice-Chancellor for Education at Ulster University, Northern Ireland. He can be contacted at this e-mail: paul.bartholomew@ulster.ac.uk

Dr Sarah Hayes is a Senior Lecturer in Technology-Enhanced and Flexible Learning in the Centre for Learning Innovation and Profession Practice at Aston University in Birmingham, UK. Sarah is Director of the PG Diploma and Masters in Education. She can be contacted at this e-mail: s.hayes@aston.ac.uk

Bibliography

Bartholomew, P. (2015). Learning Through Auto-enthnographic Case Study Research. In C. Guerin; P. Bartholomew & C. Nygaard (Eds.), *Learning to Research—Researching to Learn*. Oxfordshire, UK: Libri Publishing Ltd.

Beetham, H.; L. McGill & A. Littlejohn (2009). Thriving in the 21st Century: Learning Literacies in the Digital Age (LLIDA). *JISC Project*.

Berger, P. & T. Luckmann (1967). *The Social Construction of Reality: Treatise in the Sociology of Knowledge*. Allen Lane.

Biggs, J. B. (2003). *Teaching for Quality Learning at University*. Buckingham: Open University Press/Society for Research into Higher Education.

De Wit, H.; L Deca & F. Hunter (2015). Internationalization of Higher Education—What Can Research Add to the Policy Debate? *The European Higher Education Area*, Vol. 3, No. 12. Springer International Publishing.

Freire, P. (1996). *Pedagogy of the Oppressed*. Penguin Education. Oxford

Kolb, D. A. (2014). *Experiential Learning: Experience as the Source of Learning and Development*. Person Press. London.

Kosko, B. (1994). *Fuzzy Thinking: The New Science of Fuzzy Logic*. Harper Adams. London.

Lea, J. (Ed.) (2015). *Enhancing Learning and Teaching in Higher Education: Engaging with the Dimensions of Practice*. Berkshire: Open University Press.

Robinson, K. (2013). *TED talk: How to Escape Education's Death Valley*. www.ted.com [Accessed 12 November 2016].

Rogers, C. (2004). *On Becoming a Person—New Edition*. Robinson. London.

Rosenblit, G. (2015). Internationalization of Higher Education: Navigating Between Contrasting Trends. *The European Higher Education Area*, pp. 13–26.

Salmon, G. (2002). *E-tivities: The key to online learning. Educational Technology & Society*. London, United Kingdom: Kogan Page.

Schön, D. S. (1984). *The Reflective Practitioner*. Basic Books. London

Suzuki D. T. (2011). *Essays in Zen Buddhism*. Kindle Edition. Souvenir Books.

Thompson, N. (2012). *Anti-Discriminatory Practice: Equity, Diversity and Social Justice*. Palgrave Macmillan, London.

Chapter 11

The Emergence of a Global Culture: Are We Part of the Solution?

Chris Dawson

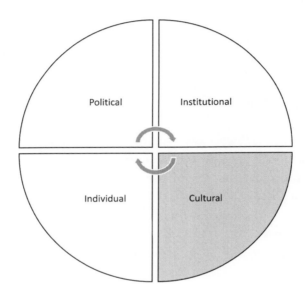

Introduction

This chapter is an important contribution to the book on the globalisation of higher education as I look into the notion of a global culture, which has been mooted and disputed. I argue that something new is beginning to emerge which may be more deserving of that name and that a new global intellectual tradition may be founded on it and in it. My conclusion is based partly on findings in the literature from psychology, sociology, political theory, theory of education, and philosophy, and partly on survey-based research into student attitudes conducted in Switzerland. Our perception of global culture has clear consequences for how we should think about our activities in university administration and in teaching. Reading this chapter, you will gain the following three insights:

1. insight into the particularities of the cultural diversity of the Swiss Higher Education system;

2. reflections on culture, national culture, and global culture and their implications for the globalisation of higher education;

3. a thorough discussion of how cultural diversities affect the globalisation of higher education.

The Swiss Model of Cultural Diversity

Switzerland is an unusual country in several ways. Its political system is the nearest thing to direct democracy the world has to offer. It has four official languages, one of which has only about 50,000 speakers (but 6 distinct dialects), and English is also used in some contexts. It has remained a stable political entity for 800 years and succeeded in staying neutral as war tore Europe apart on several occasions. Bewes (2012) claims that there is such a thing as a Swiss identity and even a Swiss culture, albeit a highly paradoxical one based on contradictions and on compromise, but with strong shared values centred around trust and privacy. That feeling is strong where I work, in Lugano, Switzerland's ninth largest city, which is more than three times larger than Bellinzona, the capital of its Italian-speaking canton (Ticino), and which contains three very different higher education institutions (USI, SUPSI and Franklin). It is right in the heart of Europe, at the crossroads of the continent's major cultures, yet it feels provincial and homely, even insular and inward-looking. Of course, its banks have enriched it, and not always to the social benefit of nearby Italy.

If Switzerland can be so socially—and culturally—diverse, and yet maintain both political stability and national identity down the ages, we might think that the global community, in this new age of instant communication, might have some hope of pulling off the same kind of trick. But, in many ways, that appears to be far from happening, and there are good reasons to think that we are actually moving in the opposite direction, with cultural differences and divisions becoming more, rather than less, important. Even within universities, in many parts of the world, there can often be the same kind of insular, inward-looking traditionalism that may be felt in Lugano. Nevertheless, nobody is in any doubt that we live in a time of immense and complicated changes, and if the effort to understand and take control is to be successful, then the world's universities will have to be in the forefront of it. Universities are both scientific and cultural institutions: the successes of their scientific initiatives have led to the communication technology that now makes the cultural issues much more urgent.

So, what might it mean for a global culture to emerge? What might that culture look like, and what form should we want it to take? In order to tackle these questions, we need to understand, as best we can, the ongoing process of globalisation, and to be clear about what a culture is and what it takes for one to emerge. Having done that, this chapter will go on to examine the digital possibilities and the geopolitical realities that confront the current generation, and students' actual perceptions of them. I will argue that biculturalism is widespread and that a global cultural identity can, therefore, be held alongside a local cultural identity without necessarily weakening either of them. Once we have seen how students might be expecting to find, and so might be helping to create, a global culture, we will be able to see what the role of higher education institutions might be in the formation of such a culture and, in turn, what impact the process might have on universities.

A Global Culture?

The academic discussion of "globalisation", to be found principally in the sociology literature, has been lively and varied. Axford (2013) aligns two outline summaries from Holton (2005) and Held & McGrew (2007) of how the debate has progressed. Initially, a number of "hyper-globalist" commentators laid out theories which saw globalisation as a monolithic all-embracing sea change in world affairs; this was generally seen in politico-economic terms, organised around the question of whether or not the world was in the process of being "Americanised". Later, sceptical voices pointed out that this was far from being a uniform process and introduced more sophisticated historical readings of actual events and processes around the world, often emphasising the differences between them. In the most recent phase—"post-sceptical" or "deconstructive"—commentators have recognised that important changes are taking place, but they have refrained from trying to over-generalise in their theorizing. Cerny (2010), for example, describes "neo-pluralist transnational" processes that involve a variety of interest groups across borders and lays out how non-governmental organisations and parts of government institutions themselves are "imbricated" internationally in a similar way. Harrison (2006) insists that the world is a complex system operating on many levels with many feedback loops between them, which makes it inherently unpredictable. Axford (2013) also distinguishes globalisation from "globalism"—the ideological attempt to spread neoliberal "democratic" capitalism around the world—and "globality", which refers to the factual conditions of converging practices and systems in various fields without presupposing a privileged narrative or a uniform politics of domination.

This globality is generally thought of as being, to at least some extent, new. Complex and imbricated as they undoubtedly are, it is useful to distinguish two separate (if intertwined) kinds of processes here. On the one hand, there is an ongoing politico-economic globalisation that began in the age of trading empires or before, which spread with the technologies that stemmed from the industrial revolution and led to the establishment of a worldwide system of nation states which are now ever more closely drawn together into a single global system. On the other hand, we have the novelty of the last twenty years—the Internet, and all of the new communication technologies associated with it—which has, almost overnight, brought all parts of the world into instant contact, thrusting previously much more isolated cultures up against each other. It may not always be possible to separate the symptoms or the effects of these two kinds of change, but each of them can affect universities in a different way, and it might be possible for us to influence one trend more directly and thereby also have an impact on the other. Additionally, if we are looking to see whether any kind of global culture is emerging, we ought to distinguish the potential contribution of the long-term gradual process from responses to the sudden challenge that has been presented by the Internet.

The Concept of Culture

To understand what "culture" really amounts to, we need to look at how the concept is put to use in practice, and then also at its history. Cultural differences are a major issue in the business literature, of course, and in that practical context Trompenaars & Hampden-Turner (2012:14) define culture as *"the way in which a group of people solves problems and reconciles dilemmas."* They draw on the work of Hofstede *et al.* (2010:26) whose general definition of culture is *"the unwritten rules of the social game that is passed on to newcomers by its members, nesting itself in their minds."* On the account of Hofstede *et al.* (2010), culture consists of symbols, heroes, rituals, and values (they give a detailed account of how the latter can vary). Each individual has a personal life story about how his character and goals have together led to his learning experiences; in parallel to all of these personal stories runs a collective story of how a society's roles, values, and structures have together led to learning experiences that add up to the society's cultural history.

On this collective social picture of culture, what matters are the differences between cultures. As Thornton (1987:7) says, these can be very easy to perceive and define because *"That is what culture does. But the boundaries that are created,"* that is, the differing values and practices that distinguish one society from another, *"are at the centre of culture, not its edges."*

This leaves us with something of a paradox for the notion of global culture. If cultures consist centrally in their distinguishing themselves deliberately from other cultures, how could there possibly be a single culture that is globally valid? If each group solves its dilemmas in accordance with a set of symbols, heroes, and rituals that explicitly excludes alternatives, where is the possibility for cosmopolitan cultural communication?

Sartori's (2016) review of the history of the concept is of help here. The idea goes back to Cicero's metaphor of the agricultural cultivation of the mind (*cultura animi philosophia est*) but came during the Enlightenment to be (first) equivalent to and (later) distinguished from "civilization". Where the latter term stood for material, rationalized progress, "culture" came to signify the individual's self-determined freedom from the rigidities of such progress. For Matthew Arnold, individuals could seek a perfection of mind and spirit in cultivating themselves into the best selves they could be. This is the central idea of culture, according to Sartori (2016:44): *"the gradual emancipation of human life from the despotism of nature"*—and it also lies behind the first usages of the word in a collective sense. So, the culture of a group would consist in all of them trying to become the best people they can be together, rather than just being driven by their natures (or even their customs) or making cold, dehumanized, purely rational material progress.

From this idea we can see how TS Eliot (1948) came to "defend" the notion of culture as something inherently elitist, inextricably bound up with religion. Eliot separated culture from individuals completely, locating it in societies—and only in the productions of the privileged classes of those societies that produce "what makes life worth living"; or, perhaps more importantly for Eliot, what makes the society admirable to rival and to later societies. This elitist view can be sensibly challenged, but it perhaps produced a worthwhile insight when it prompted Eliot to observe that rivalries are central to a culture, which must, therefore, contain not only similar people but also people who are different enough to be problematic. Culture, for Eliot, is not something individuals can deliberately aim to acquire—he thinks of it as the preserve of a privileged, creative class. But even on his account, it is clearly connected with education and with the development of the social values of the group.

What Eliot missed is what Dawkins (1976) captured in his concept of a meme. Eliot's own poetry, for example, is a part of our culture—of the literary heritage of the English-speaking world—not because it makes life worth living in itself, nor because other cultures envy and admire it, nor yet because it makes us intellectually rich or aristocratic, but because it has been popular. People continue to read his poems and perform his plays. What matters for the cultural status of those works is not their conception or their content but the fact that they caught on and continue to get passed around, quoted, and taught in schools. That requires the participation, not of an elite, but of everyone acting individually and collectively.

To summarise, then, if anything is to qualify as a "world culture", it must involve the parallel efforts of many individuals, who will be—and must be—diverse to make the most of themselves (through education or by other means), referring in the process to a common set of symbols, heroes, and rituals, and so coming to espouse a similar set of values.

World culture has been seen as an already well-established reality. Lechner & Boli (2005) locate it not just in international law, economics, medical collaboration, etc., but above all in such institutions such as the Olympic Games, the conventions that underlie international aviation, or even the standard ways in which one can, say, set up a chess club in any town in the world under the auspices of the World Chess Federation. Here we certainly have some common rituals and some symbols everyone shares. But this "culture" seems incomplete according to our definition. It is not clear that institutions of this kind embody any shared values, and they are "global" precisely insofar as they apply to everybody, no matter what people's attitude to them may be. If culture is built on individuals' aspirations to make the most of themselves, then such institutions as universities must be centrally involved. For cultural heroes to emerge there must be enemies against whom the adherents of the culture can identify themselves.

Universities

One element of a culture, which contributes to its choice of heroes and symbols, is its intellectual and artistic tradition. Such a tradition is not a necessary part of any culture—there can be cultures that contain no such element (yet?)—but where such a tradition exists, and where it is studied, perpetuated, and built upon, anyone who aspires to build themselves an identity within the culture—to become the best person they can be, to become cultivated—will inevitably draw on that tradition. This makes it a central element of the culture in question, along with the actual practice of artists of all kinds, and of academics, who both study the tradition and add to it.

Universities around the world have changed and adapted to the long-term processes of globalisation whilst remaining places that uphold, enshrine, and develop the cultural traditions of the societies of which they are a part. They usually combine the two functions of research and teaching. There is now a well-established and genuinely global community of scientific researchers, collaborating in, replicating, and critiquing one another's experiments (Marginson & van der Wende, 2007). Some of this scientific research is conducted outside of universities and is often funded by the commercial interests that intend to profit from the technologies the research may lead to. At the same time, many academic disciplines remain within the channels of thought that they have been following for years without looking at what the literature from other disciplines has to say on related topics. These "academic silos" [a term adopted from the literature on business process re-engineering, perhaps most influentially by Neely (2002)] arise partly from the institutional structure of universities: departments and chairs are devoted to particular subjects, with the professors also teaching courses in those subjects to students who study those subjects, and publish their research in journals that also specialise in the same way. Interdisciplinary research has existed for many years, but only in the last few years has it gained much traction (Rylance, 2015). As Appelbaum (2013) describes, universities are now setting up "Global Studies" departments with a view to achieving a higher degree of inter-disciplinarity, even if their actual concerns still depend to a large extent on the academic interests of the scholars who happen to be available to participate in such departments. It may be that some more radical restructuring may soon come to be seen as necessary.

The people who are most obviously becoming cultivated, however, and thus driving the world's cultures on into the future are not the researchers or the lecturers but the students. Many students, of course, still study in their home town, but since the UNESCO report on globalisation in higher education was published (Varghese, 2008), the number of students travelling abroad to study has doubled from 2.6 million to over 5 million, as that report foresaw. Students are no longer heading overwhelmingly to highly developed or to English-speaking countries, either (ICEF Monitor, 2015); the global distribution of this phenomenon is starting to level out. Teichler (2004) observed that the higher education reforms that were taking place in Europe with the establishment of the European Higher Education Area (see Rasmussen et al., this volume) had led to universities moving together with more of an emphasis on such practical or economic concepts as "marketization, competition and management" (Teichler, 2004:23) than on more high-minded ideals like the establishment of a "global village" or "knowledge society". Branch (this volume) sheds further light on this tension between economic and pedagogical issues in transnational education. Nevertheless, these students are clearly moving abroad or joining international programmes because they see their future careers potentially unfolding, at least to some extent, in an international context (Findlay *et al.*, 2012), so that an international hierarchy of universities with reputations for a world-class education is emerging. As this volume clearly demonstrates, existing models of projects linking universities in different countries (see Bartholomew *et al.*; Li & Wang; and Lamb *et al.*, all in this volume), explicitly international study programmes (see Lofgren & Leigh, in this volume), and even institutions that straddle national boundaries (see Pauna & Branch, in this volume) have all been growing in popularity and influence. Whether they study internationally or not, students' friendship circles now frequently include many countries or many continents (Bilecen, 2014). Rather than merely catering to more foreign students, universities now increasingly aim to prepare all of their students for a globally connected future (Robson, 2011).

Today's Students and their World

Lugano is a small city, but in some ways its universities can be seen as a microcosm of the global intercultural situation. SUPSI, the vocational university, has about 4,000 students who are mostly aiming to pursue professional careers in Ticino. At USI there are 2,500 students of either economics, computer science, communication science, Italian literature or architecture; its plurilingual and multicultural situation has recently been the object of a very interesting study by Sabine Christopher (2015). And there is also Franklin University, an American university with about 400 students, half of whom come from North America and the others from all around the world. I teach at Franklin and at USI, and I actually live across the border in Italy, where my own children are at school, so I am continually confronted with all sorts of cultural and generational issues and conflicts.

I asked all of the students from USI and Franklin to say to what extent they agreed with fifteen statements about culture and education, such as "Learning works differently in different cultures" and "Students socialise only in groups with a shared cultural background and rarely mix." I had a good response rate, with 10–15% of the entire student body replying. The survey generated a lot of rich data, which there is no space to explore in full detail here. Perhaps the most remarkable finding of this survey was the extent to which students disagree about these kinds of questions. Of the fifteen very different statements I chose, none could boast either that nobody disagreed strongly with it or that nobody agreed strongly with it. The two institutions showed quite similar patterns, although there was interesting divergence over the statement "I behave very differently depending on the national background of the people I'm with"—something Franklin students apparently do much more than USI students.

More interesting than the actual proportions of agreements and disagreements, however, were some of the correlations between particular answers. Among the Franklin students, there were just three pairs of answers that moved together with an extremely strong correlation (>99.9%). Those who saw Franklin as a model of intercultural integration were also particularly keen to be educated in a global cultural context—given their choice of Franklin, this is scarcely surprising, although the same pattern came out at USI. Those who were keen to be educated in a global cultural context were also more likely to be in the habit of going out of their way to find people who disagreed with their views, a habit which, overall, was more prevalent still at USI. But, interestingly, there was a similarly strong correlation between responses to "I expect the world to be more sharply culturally divided in future" and "All approaches to teaching at university can be equally valid when used appropriately". This would suggest that pessimists about future cultural integration are more prepared to allow for a wide range of teaching methodologies, while cultural integration optimists tend to have some specific range of ideal methodologies in mind. Maybe there are simply some teaching styles that the optimists object to more than the pessimists do.

Learning and Culture Outside of Academia

At both USI and Franklin, 77% of students agreed that "I consider skills that I learn from my non-academic Internet use to be valuable to me." Only three Franklin students said they disagreed with that and none strongly (although a few USI students did strongly disagree). So, nobody should assume that all valuable global learning experiences take place in universities or in classrooms. Freedman *et al.* (2013) examined the spontaneous emergence of learning groups of like-minded video producers, computer demosceners, and conceptual artists, who set up strict rules and use their peer interaction to learn and push their art forward. They also traced similar groups—generally locally based and meeting in person as well as virtually—of cosplayers, fan-fiction writers, manga artists, and even gamers and graffiti writers, sharing tips and hanging out for the sake of collaborative learning and creativity. All these people are seeking and finding a creative and technical stimulus and also social support, validation, and artistic challenges, that their schools are unable to offer them. All of this creative activity is plainly cultural but, equally plainly, it is not elitist in the way that Eliot might have expected, nor does it have a local focus based on a long-standing tradition—everyone is potentially included.

The Internet has made a huge difference in this regard, enabling the emergence of many new such activities whilst removing the need for face-to-face interaction so that people with minority hobbies can engage in them together with like-minded enthusiasts anywhere in the world. Lankshear & Knobel (2011:53) identify a *"knowledge society paradigm"* of *"new literacies"*. They claim that entirely new forms of *writing* now exist so that for computer literate "insiders" (anyone born after 1970 can be partly such, and anyone born after 1990 is said to be completely such) traditional writing is only a less interesting alternative to a richer version of writing that involves embedded edited videos, hyperlinks, mashups and remixed memes.

Furthermore, Dawkins' notion of a meme has become one itself; it has caught on and moved on. Teenagers all over the world with no conception of genetics or sociology know exactly what a meme is (see Figure 1). In the context of the Internet it has been re-defined as a *group of digital items "(a) a group of digital items sharing common characteristics of content, form, or stance; (b) that were created with awareness of each other; and (c) that were circulated, imitated, or transformed via the Internet by many users."* (Shifman, 2014).

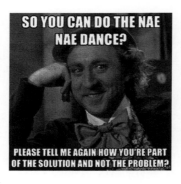

Figure 1: a typical "meme".

Although their importance can be overstated, as Milner (2012) cautions, these Internet memes do constitute a new way in which people habitually interact creatively around the whole world in order to communicate. While that communication may often seem extremely flippant, the mere fact that, for these things to survive, many different people have to engage with them enough to want to pass them on or adapt them means that established memes must embody something universally recognised as useful for human expression over and above people's individual cultural differences.

So, while the parallel efforts of individuals around the world to make the most of themselves certainly push some of them to seek out world-class universities where they hope to find an education within a global context and to become part of a worldwide academic tradition, similar forces are pushing people together entirely outside of education and without reference to any academic tradition at all. University students are anything but isolated from these external interactions, and we should expect whatever culture today's students share around the world to include and to draw on influences from outside academia as much as from what may be learned in the lecture hall. By the same token, as more of the generation of "digital natives" become lecturers, we ought to expect and embrace moves to integrate the techniques, the interaction patterns, and the concerns of creative people across the Internet into the content and the methodology of university teaching.

Real Divisions

At this point we have some grounds to assert that the interactions of students from around the world and their peers outside the universities may, given their aspirations and the possibilities opened up by the Internet, be giving rise to a new, global culture. There are a number of ways in which this claim might be misunderstood, which I shall address in turn. Divisions remain in terms of politics, religion, wealth, and access to technology. The situation is highly complex and the claim that a single culture is emerging might seem an over-simplification. There are already global institutions and there are already cultural traditions, but the claim here is that a global cultural tradition is in its infancy, not that it is already established. There further remains the worry that the very idea of a global culture might be incoherent, either because such a culture would seemingly lack outsiders or because it might be confused with the idea of a blending of existing cultures, which does not seem to capture what is happening.

Norris & Inglehart (2009) caution that the process of globalisation is extremely uneven—they develop an index for the extent to which different countries' citizens are exposed to, or have access to, global ideas—and also claim that many cultures have "firewalls" that protect their values and attitudes from contamination by, say, American popular culture. Just because someone is exposed to a practice from elsewhere does not mean that they will take any notice of it at all, let al.one assimilate it, reject it, or adopt it. They will, presumably, engage with it only if it captures their interest because of their prior concerns, and often then only insofar as they need to. Furthermore, as Sinno (this volume) points out, there is much justified ambivalence about the dominance of the English language internationally, and the mere existence of that global phenomenon is enough to alter people's feelings about their own cultural identity, instilling a sense of insecurity or inadequacy even in those who teach the language.

Of course, in any part of the world, people who pursue neither academics not creative hobbies may still acquire all of their cultural values from the tradition that physically surrounds them, even if their Facebook feed contains a non-stop stream of entertaining and potentially useful views from elsewhere. Those who make no effort to inquire or expand their horizons tend to be hostile to outsiders—and perhaps much more so now that so many outsiders are so visible so much of the time. To speak of a global culture, then, is certainly not to speak of a move towards global governance; for as Beck (2008) points out, democratic attempts to increase international integration in that sense would require the support of large sections of most societies which, in fact, react strongly against outsiders, immigrants and other perceived threats to their cultural identity.

Nor is there any congruence of political worldviews on the horizon. It is now clear that however actively China may be seeking influence from other countries' universities (see Li & Wang, this volume), its one-party "communist" system is a robust alternative that is here to stay. Putin's Russia clearly demonstrates that the need to be seen to be throwing one's political and military weight around can still be viewed as decisive in international *realpolitik*. Events in Egypt, Palestine, Syria and Libya reveal how electoral democracy is a meaningless alternative in the absence of the cultural presuppositions and other conditions on which its success depends (West, 2015). The popularity of extreme right politics in the USA suggests how little has been learned from the violence of the 1940s and how undesirable it would be to roll out an American system across the world. Extremist Islamic groups have an avowedly global agenda based on bigotry, hatred, and the caricature of the religion they profess to adhere to. Notwithstanding the progress made with the UN's sustainable development goals, extreme poverty and hunger are still the only issues of any importance for millions of people. The Internet may have brought great changes, but as of 2015 only 46.4% of the world's inhabitants are able to use it at all (Miniwatts, 2016), which means that more than half of them are being rapidly left behind.

Faced with this situation, it seems laughably naïve to talk about a global culture. In fact, once we look at things on a truly global scale the problems are worse still, to the extent that most of us prefer to look elsewhere. The global system of nation states with their often highly corrupt governments unscrupulously clinging onto power is now up against the economic domination of the much larger economies of corporations and financial speculators beyond the jurisdiction of any kind of regulator. And the real elephant in the room remains Malthus' simple observation that the human population increases exponentially while our technological progress is merely linear. (In fact, the population situation is worse than Malthus foresaw. When he made his prediction in 1798, the world population was around 905 million, double what it had been in 1521, 277 years earlier. It then took the world population 116 years to double from its 1798 level, a mere 55 years to double again, and a further 50 years to double again from there (which brings us to the figure of 7,244,000,000 in 2014) (World Population History). This makes the suggestion that we may only reach 10 billion by the end of this century look wildly over-optimistic: by then we could easily be over 20 billion, even with vast numbers of extra deaths.) Whether or not we overrun the planet and use up its resources, it is clear that we face very great danger from climate change, that we may be completely powerless to prevent such change, and that there are political barriers, which may be insurmountable, to even trying in any serious way to prevent it.

In addition to growing up with digital technologies, students of the current generation have had to come to terms with these realities. They respond in different ways. Some become cynical or fatalist, a few become politically active—as, perhaps, there seems to be little point in that. Many cling to such values as they find to be shared in the hope of working together to solve the problems we face. After all, even if the problems may actually turn out to be insoluble, it is clear that no other approach holds out a comparable hope for the current generation. The hope is that a worldwide culture of open co-operation might move us towards a situation where people can work together, especially in universities, much more closely, much more quickly and much more interactively. Maybe, then, human innovation can also increase its speed exponentially (as perhaps it may seem to some it has already begun to do) and so keep up with the population explosion, pulling the world gradually together rather than apart. The claim at issue here, then, is not that a global culture is already established but rather that the aspirations of people now in their late teens and early twenties are bringing them together in this perhaps forlorn hope of building a new kind of cultural identity that is explicitly global in reach and in intent.

Cultures Side by Side

Will this new culture lack outsiders? In a sense it clearly will, as the whole point is to include everyone's viewpoint. At the same time, in practice, there are certain viewpoints that are explicitly against such openness. Popular resistance to any form of bigotry, prejudice or discrimination has been noticeably on the increase in recent years. If the new global culture has outsiders and enemies, they are the world's outspoken bigots.

But it is not possible to be straightforwardly antagonistic to all forms of prejudice, as that in itself is a prejudiced and discriminatory outlook. There are a number of lessons to be drawn here from Gadamer (1960). The first is that we must acknowledge that we are all prejudiced, since it is not possible to grow up and learn a human language without doing so within a tradition that also includes a lot of partisan beliefs; and while it is possible to question any one belief, it is not possible to escape from them all at the same time. No group, culture, language, or tradition has a better claim than any other to understand truth or reality. Even scientific methodology is rooted in human practices and human societies. There is no special or privileged situation in which truths are revealed, so we can only try to put our own prejudices into play and move towards others' viewpoints. Since there is no firm ground on which to stand in order to criticise anyone else, it is important that we take others' views as valid, and presuppose not that they can be conveniently labelled, categorised, answered, and forgotten, but that they each have a valid claim to make that could or, potentially, ought to shift our own perspective. Thus we are "always on the way", always trying to improve our understanding on the basis of an imperfect pre-understanding, and we can never arrive at truth, certainty, or a correct characterisation of reality. The best we can do is seek out different viewpoints and, in a real conversation where both parties put their prejudices into play, move towards a fusion of horizons in which both might see further than either could otherwise.

Different viewpoints may be sought in two ways: we can talk to people from elsewhere, and we can look at texts from the past. Anything from our own time and our own culture will likely share too many of our own prejudices to be particularly enlightening. This hermeneutic engagement with people from other places is, at least, made possible for many people by the existence of the Internet. As it is so difficult, though, it does not happen terribly much. Where these real conversations certainly can and must happen, both with people from elsewhere and with texts from the past, is in universities, which exist to research, preserve traditions, bring people into contact, and make them think and work together.

Pretending to know, then, is the arch epistemological crime of which most people (including many university lecturers) are guilty: what real knowledge is available comes at the price of humility. Only if we accept that we need to go looking for different viewpoints, and to continue to allow them to modify what we have already learned, can we maximise the extent to which we can in any genuine way be authoritative. David Deutsch made this point in his wide-ranging philosophical treatise *The Beginning of Infinity* (2011). Deutsch takes the term "meme" in its most general sense, looking back across all of history and distinguishing between "rational" memes and "anti-rational" memes (387). Anti-rational memes, generally bound up with religion, have held whole societies static for centuries, with everyone's creativity channelled only into the rein-forcement and perpetuation of cultural presuppositions. But these static societies always turn out to fare poorly when confronted with a range of other similar but incompatible anti-rational memes from elsewhere. By contrast, we have now been able to attain sufficient scientific certainty to develop a sophisticated technology because of the emergence of a culture of criticism in which rational memes survived across many different times and places just because they persisted in the face of that criticism. On Deutsch's account, this means that a meme that adapts and survives enough to be replicated around the world embodies a truth, and the discovery of such a truth is "a beginning of infinity" in the sense that it is not made necessary by anything that came before it but has an impact on everything that comes after it.

Objectivity can arise only from moving beyond parochial viewpoints and seeing what survives confrontation between radically different ideas. There is no need to suggest that everyone who interacts on a global scale might be aware of this. The ongoing public juxtaposition of conflicting ideas will of itself lead to ideas being passed around more if more people find them interesting or funny. When people find ideas offensive, the easiest and most effective way to respond is now to mock those ideas publicly on the Internet. Many of the internet memes that go viral do precisely this, changing frequently until a version is established that upsets few and entertains many. That humour should be central to this process is no more than we ought to expect if we accept Hurley et al.'s (2011) thesis that humour evolved to smooth the resolution of epistemic conflict and that that is still the thread that links together the things we find funny.

Humour needs a target, just as a culture needs to distinguish itself from enemies. The above considerations suggest that the juxtaposition of cultures in the age of the Internet might be expected to produce a new culture with four kinds of enemies who can safely be laughed at without prejudice:

1. those who insist on ideas without subjecting them to criticism—who think they know or have the answers;

2. those who take themselves too seriously and are unable to laugh at themselves;

3. those who remain closed off, clinging to one tradition, and refuse to put their ideas into play and work together with others;

4. those who exclude or attack people in groups without the justification of their individually falling into any of these categories.

I leave the reader with the task of observing the extent to which real world interactions now take these kinds of people as targets.

Biculturalism

Discussions of how cultural differences relate to globalisation have often remained with the rather limiting assumption that each individual can have (or belong to, or be a part of) only one culture, which makes the view we have been considering of an emergent global culture look impossible. If cultures come together, on the standard view, individuals must either choose one of them or mix them somehow. Consequently, the cultures will either remain separate (one will dominate), or they will converge. Nederveen Pieterse (2015:46), for example, expresses the position this way: "*The first view, according to which cultural difference is immutable, may be the oldest perspective on cultural difference. The second, the thesis of cultural convergence, is as old as the earliest forms of universalism, as in the world religions. Both have been revived and renewed as varieties of modernism, respectively in its romantic and Enlightenment versions, while the third perspective, hybridization, refers to a postmodern sensibility of traveling culture.... Arguably there may be other takes on cultural difference, such as indifference, but none have the scope and depth of the three perspectives outlined here.*"

Even this "postmodern" view of hybridization, however, misses the crucial possibility that individuals might belong simultaneously to more than one culture and might be able to keep their two (or more) cultures separate, even while allowing them to influence one another.

But psychological research into how second generation immigrants deal with the two cultures they grow up with reveals that biculturalism is a complex and varied phenomenon. Huynh *et al.* (2011) identify two independent continua along which biculturals may vary: they can be more or less "blended", which is mostly a matter of their behaviour, and more or less "harmonized", which is mostly a question of affect, of how they feel about being bicultural. Less blended individuals keep their two cultures separate in their own behaviour, which means in practice that they describe them more richly—they analyse them more—and they have a tendency, according to Huynh *et al.*, to respond obstinately to cues of one cultural type with behaviour from their other culture. Individuals who perceive greater harmony between their two cultures (which can happen equally well when the cultures themselves are objectively extremely different and can still happen when the same individuals choose to keep their cultural behaviours separate) draw great psychological benefits from being bicultural, becoming more creative and experiencing less depression (Huynh *et al.*: 833). In their review of what they see as an underdeveloped literature on this issue and their suggestions for further research, Huynh *et al.* suggest that these same scales may be applied to other kinds of subcultures—professional, racial, gender, etc.—and to people with more than two cultures. We could certainly posit that those of us who live in a global culture may do so as biculturals, and that global culture emerges from the efforts of people all over the world to interact in a global way *alongside* their existing cultures. This would potentially mean that instead of our replacing or adapting the local cultures with which we start out, entering into a global culture could provide a forum within which to reassess, validate, and reinforce those cultures.

This idea gets some confirmation from the finding of Chiu and Cheng (2007) that creativity is heightened when two cultural stereotypes are activated together in a context that does not threaten identity. Only when the juxtaposition occurs in a context that is essential to the identity of one of the cultures—as when a Starbucks opened in the Forbidden City in Beijing—do we find a resistance to the cultural juxtaposition. This would tend to suggest that a global culture that emerged in the way I have been sketching would ultimately evolve towards the reinforcement of values that are shared across all cultures and the avoidance of symbols that clash directly with the identity of anybody's culture.

Systematic work on how cultures and subcultures emerge and divide over time appears to be only just beginning. Fischer's (1995) sociological work on the emergence of and influences between urban subcultures focused specifically on cities, and the analogies between living together in cities and interacting on the Internet are far from perfect. More recently, Gelman *et al.* (2016) have started to look at how subcultures emerge within a community in a specific Internet environment. But what we are considering here is not really a sub-culture; it is rather more a super-culture, and while its emergence may well have a certain amount in common with subcultures and it may well, to a large extent, emerge from and across subcultures, it will be defined by its openness to new voices. Its boundaries will, therefore, exclude only those who reject that openness.

Better evidence comes from works in linguistics about how languages change and how new languages are born. In discussing how pidgins develop where no language is shared, how they evolve into creoles and eventually become established as languages in their own right (Lightfoot, 2006), it is not presupposed that individuals will mix their language competences or that one repertoire will dominate. A range of individual responses to bilingualism allows for the emergence of highly complex shared linguistic codes in which competing existing languages are each preserved and enriched as new hybrid forms develop. It seems reasonable to suppose that the wider cultural picture might be broadly similar. Where people must negotiate clashes and shocks from many other cultures, they may both cling to their own values and, separately, embrace new shared ones. Once sufficient common ground has been established, each individual tradition then becomes a rich resource for the wider converging community and may, therefore, be preserved and celebrated, at least insofar as it surrenders its most prejudiced intolerances.

Intellectual Tradition and Higher Education

Before we look at the implications of this for practice in higher education, let us retrace our steps for a moment to take stock of what we have said. Since belonging to a culture is not an all-or-nothing matter and many people have a range of different cognitive, behavioural, and affective responses to their relationships to more than one cultural group, there is no reason individuals should not aspire to participate in a global culture as well as whatever local cultures they may have grown up with. Students who travel to study abroad and other young people who create and share various kinds of art, both on the Internet and in their local area, seem to be aspiring to participate in just such a global culture. Given the availability of instantaneous global communication through the Internet, that is all it will take for a global culture to begin to emerge, establishing new symbols, rituals, and heroes. These are likely to reinforce core notions of inclusiveness, acceptance, and collaboration, and to differentiate global culture from all that is bigoted, narrow-minded, or shallow since all such ideas will be mocked, adapted, and twisted into memes that everyone will want to pass on. Indeed, the only kind of objectivity that we can in principle achieve depends on our efforts to embrace these values, seeking out views different to our own, rather than just classifying them, allowing them to contribute to our own ideas by calling our beliefs into question.

One thing that is reasonably clear about new cultures is that they emerge independently of any intellectual or artistic design but simply from people's interactions. Artists capture, and academics analyse, the worlds people already inhabit; in doing so they enrich and extend those worlds, allowing their inhabitants to dwell in them in more deliberate and self-aware ways. Universities are institutions that facilitate, embody, and celebrate this process, handing down and updating cultures from one generation to the next. We must not allow their role in scientific critique and development to blind us to their equally important role in cultural critique and development.

If there is any hope to be drawn from the emergence of a global culture, cultural diversity must be preserved. I have argued that that can happen and is happening, with globally shared values representing a second, separate culture for many open-minded individuals along-side the tradition within which they grew up and whose practices, and many of whose values, they will want to hand on to future generations. In the same way, universities must be right to resist too much pressure for structural institutional change in response to the long-term forces of globalisation. Each university must maintain and enrich its own traditions, even as it invites a broader range of students and prepares them for global interactions more than for local ones; otherwise, we will lose the very possibilities of objectivity that come with diversity. As Tierney & Lanford (2016) point out, many university teachers are rightly sceptical about altering what traditionally takes place in institutions that depend on their established procedures to produce complex results over a great deal of time. Universities have generally managed both to resist pressures to become just another product in the marketplace defined by consumer desires and to uphold academic standards. So, university teachers must continue to propagate cultural traditions completely and richly, whilst also calling them into question by deliberately including as wide a range of alternatives and other voices as possible.

The cultural shift I have outlined, then, will have a twofold impact on universities, making a difference both to research and to teaching. And if collaborative work is our best hope in facing and dealing with the problems we continue to create, action at these two levels in universities is both necessary and urgent.

Since the open incorporation of as many different viewpoints as possible is fundamental to improving our understanding, research must be restructured so as to be systematically interdisciplinary at all levels and across all disciplines. But that is not to say that the existing disciplines are simply to be abandoned or merged into one another, or that it is better to organise research universities with no reference to existing academic traditions. Jacobs (2013) cautions that this interdisciplinary restructuring has in some cases already gone too far. But just as a new global culture can promote and reinforce individual existing cultures in bringing them together, academic disciplines can retain their identity and continue their work independently, whilst also profiting from conversations that cross disciplinary boundaries, from the habit of researching both within the discipline and outside of it. It is those conversations that need to be institutionally stimulated and, perhaps, required.

At the same time, as regards teaching, we need to continue to explore a full range of classroom innovations in response to the new mindset of our "digital native" students. This is not just a matter of making use of new technologies, or even of making good use of them. The pace of change is now such that lecturers may never again have the ICT skills of many of their students, so we can and must continually learn from them, in addition to stimulating critical dialogue around each new development.

The gulf between what most lecturers are willing or able to provide in terms of innovative teaching and what students would expect as a minimum given what they see available every day on the Internet is currently very wide. Certainly, a number of useful innovations have been introduced. The idea of the "inverted" or "flipped" classroom (Lage *et al.*, 2000) is now increasingly put into practice, with materials and presentations being made available electronically and class time being devoted to discussion and interaction. An international forum on education and technology in 2014 produced recommendations about taking learning beyond the classroom and integrating the use of multimodal input and "top of mind" practices, including gamification and edutainment (Yáñez *et al.*, 2015), but some of these innovations are more challenging for most lecturers to put into practice. Nevertheless, as McLaughlin & Lee (2008) point out, many learners now are, and expect to be seen as, *"active participants, creators of knowledge, and seekers of engaging, personal experiences."*

In my experience, it is perfectly possible, in many contexts, to involve our learners more directly, to get them engaged, and to awaken their creativity through collaborative interaction. This need not be entirely a matter of using ICT. As students become more absorbed in their electronically-mediated lives, student engagement in the classroom has become both more difficult and more important to achieve. When they are engaged together interactively in tasks where the level of challenge is appropriate and they have a large degree of freedom in selecting the focus of their energies (providing the teacher is able to structure this activity so as to provide the necessary scaffolding), students often become highly creative, proactive learners. The teaching values labelled by McLaughlin & Lee (2008) as "Pedagogy 2.0" can make good use of, but do not depend on, lecturers' ability to integrate new technologies into their teaching. If teachers are humble enough to move away from centre stage, interested enough to involve and to learn from their students, and creative enough to design structures within which students can really engage, then students will be able to bring their new global culture into the university and collaborate effectively.

I have been lucky enough to work in contexts that have given me enough freedom to experiment with this to some extent. At USI, for example, I teach "sectorial English" to classes of 100–150 students of communication or of literature, who have a B2 level in English. After initially grouping them according to their professed interests, I give the group the opportunity to debate, alter, and vote on a constitution for the rotation of power in their classroom interactions through the semester, under which control for the entire course rests in the hands of the students. They develop their own projects, which end up highly varied and wonderfully rich and impressive. Films have been made, books and magazines written, websites developed, charitable initiatives undertaken in the community, and much more. At Franklin, my advanced academic writing course draws on some of the same methods. Under the umbrella topic of business ethics, groups of students co-author academic books, taking them from the first idea to finished printed book in the course of a single semester, reviewing, supporting, and editing one another's work, in addition to writing introductory and concluding text together.

The difficulties which are presented by these new approaches have to do with assessment. When students work creatively together, we need to find new ways of following individuals' progress, and of examining them and grading their final performance in ways that are transparent and fair. In many higher education contexts, this will mean some reform of the exam system and some imaginative work on the assessment problem within the faculties. If there is too much control from above of instructors' assessment procedures, it can be impossible to allow students the freedom to bring their creativity into play. But students still need to know that their efforts will result in a grade that reflects their learning achievements and that the same standards are being applied to everybody. Different learning styles also need to be systematically accommodated within the structure of these courses so that alternatives are provided for those students who can contribute more richly within their own private textual work. On my courses I have sometimes had to invent grading structures whereby equivalences between very different kinds of work are captured in a rubric transparent enough to demonstrate to students which practical choices the course really presents them with.

Above and beyond the specifics of course design and assessment, however, the broader cultural shift I have outlined is progressing whether or not universities change and adapt themselves to be a central part of it. The change required of them is significant, but easily achievable. It is merely a matter of institutionalising two new attitudes and designing the bureaucratic structure of universities—and of national and international higher education systems and standards—around those attitudes. First, interdisciplinary interaction needs to be maximised—without weakening the disciplines themselves—so that all researchers and commentators are in regular contact with everyone else's findings and ideas, and, secondly, teaching and assessment need to be set up in such a way that students are involved fully and creatively in their courses and may be learned from and listened to.

About the author

Chris Dawson is a Lecturer in English Language at Lugano University (*Università della Svizzera italiana*) and Adjunct Professor of Philosophy at Franklin University Switzerland. He can be contacted at this e-mail: dawsonc@usi.ch

Bibliography

Appelbaum, R. P. (2013). Comments on Jan Nederveen Pieterse's Essay, "What is Global Studies?" *Globalizations*, Vol. 10, No. 4, pp. 545–550.

Axford, B. (2013). *Theories of Globalization*. Cambridge: Polity Press.

Beck, U. (2008). *Die Neuvermessung der Ungleichheit unter den Menschen*. Frankfurt am Main: Suhrkamp.

Bewes, D. (2012). *Swiss Watching: Inside the land of milk & money (2nd edition)*. London: Nicholas Brealey.

Bilecen, B. (2014). *International Student Mobility and Transnational Friendships*. Basingstoke: Palgrave Macmillan.

Cerny, P. G. (2010). *Rethinking World Politics: A Theory of Transnational Neopluralism*. Oxford: OUP.

Chiu, C-Y. & S. Y. Y. Cheng (2007). Toward a Social Psychology of Culture and Globalization: Some Social Cognitive Consequences of Activating Two Cultures Simultaneously. *Social and Personality Psychology Compass* Vol. 1, No. 1, pp. 84–100.

Christopher, S. (2015). *I flussi comunicativi in un contesto istituzionale universitario plurilingue*. Bellinzona: Osservatorio linguistico della Svizzera italiana.

Dawkins, R. (1976). *The Selfish Gene*. Oxford: OUP.

Deutsch, D. (2011). *The Beginning of Infinity: Explanations that Transform the World*. London: Penguin.

Eliot, T. S. (1948). *Notes towards the Definition of Culture*. London: Faber & Faber.

Findlay, A. M.; R. King; F. M. Smith; A. Geddes & R. Skeldon (2012). World Class? An investigation of globalisation, difference and international student mobility. *Transactions of the Institute of British Geographers*, Vol. 37, No. 1, pp. 118–131.

Fischer, C. S. (1995). The Subcultural Theory of Urbanism: A Twentieth-Year Assessment. *American Journal of Sociology*, Vol. 101, No. 3, pp. 543–577.

Freedman, K.; E. Heijnen; M. Kallio-Tavin; A. Kárpáti & L. Papp (2013). Visual Culture Learning Communities: How and What Students Come to Know in Informal Art Groups. *Studies in Art Education*, Vol. 54, No. 2, pp. 103–115.

Gadamer, H-G. (1960). *Wahrheit und Methode: Grundzüge einer philosophischen Hermeneutik*. Tübingen, J.C.B.Mohr (Paul Siebeck).

Gelman, B. U.; C. Beckley; A. Johri; C. Domeniconi & S. Yang (2016). *Online Urbanism: Interest-based Subcultures as Drivers of Informal Learning in an Online Community*. Online resource: https://cs.gmu.edu/~carlotta/publications/LAS16.pdf [Accessed on 8 November 2016].

Harrison, N. E. (Ed.) (2006). *Complexity in World Politics: Concepts and Methods of a New Paradigm*. New York: SUNY Press.

Held, D. & A. McGrew (2007). *Globalization / Anti-Globalization: Beyond the Great Divide*. Cambridge: Polity Press.

Hofstede, G.; G. J. Hofstede & M. Minkov (2010). *Cultures and Organizations: Software of the Mind* (3rd edition). New York: McGraw Hill.

Holton, R. J. (2005). *Making Globalization*. Basingstoke: Palgrave Macmillan.

Hurley, M. M.; D. C. Dennett & R. B. Adams, Jr (2011). *Inside Jokes: Using Humor to Reverse-Engineer the Mind*. Cambridge, Mass.: MIT Press.

Huynh, Q-L.; A-M. D. Nguyen & V. Benet-Martínez (2011). Bicultural Identity Integration. In S. J. Schwartz, K. Luyckx and V. L. Vignoles (Eds.) *Handbook of Identity Theory and Research*, New York: Springer, pp. 827–842.

ICEF Monitor (2015). Online resource: http://monitor.icef.com/2015/11/the-state-of-international-student-mobility-in-2015/ [accessed on 18 March 2016].

Jacobs, J. A. (2013). *In Defense of Disciplines*. Chicago: University of Chicago Press.

Lage, M. J.; G. J. Platt & M. Treglia (2000). Inverting the Classroom: A Gateway to Creating an Inclusive Learning Environment. *The Journal of Economic Education*, Vol. 31, No. 1, pp. 30–43.

Lankshear, C. & M. Knobel (2011). *New Literacies: Everyday Practices and Social Learning* (3rd edition). Maidenhead: Open University Press.

Lechner, F. J. & J. Boli (2005). *World Culture: Origins and Consequences*. Oxford: Blackwell.

Lightfoot, D. (2006). *How New Languages Emerge*. Cambridge: CUP.

Malthus, T. (1798). *An Essay on the Principle of Population*. London: J. Johnson.

Marginson, S. & M. van der Wende (2007). Globalisation and Higher Education. *OECD Education Working Papers*, No. 8.

McLaughlin, C. & M. J. W. Lee (2008). The Three P's of Pedagogy for the Networked Society: Personalization, Participation and Productivity. *International Journal of Teaching and Learning in Higher Education*, Vol. 20, No. 1, pp. 10–27

Milner, R. M. (2012). *The World Made Meme: Discourse and Identity in Participatory Media*. Ph.D. thesis, University of Kansas. Online resource: https://kuscholarworks.ku.edu/handle/1808/10256 [accessed on 19 November 2016].

Miniwatts Marketing Group (2016). Online resource: www.internetworldstats. com [Accessed on 3 April 2016].

Nederveen Pieterse, J. (2015). *Globalization and Culture: Global Mélange* (3rd edition). Lanham, Maryland/London: Rowman & Littlefield.

Neely, A. (ed) (2002). *Business Performance Measurement: Theory and Practice*. Cambridge: CUP.

Norris, P. & R. Inglehart (2009). *Cosmopolitan Communications: Cultural Diversity in a Globalized World*. Cambridge: CUP.

Robson, S. (2011). Internationalization: A transformative agenda for higher education? *Teachers and teaching*, Vol. 17, No. 6, pp. 619–630.

Rylance, R. (2015). Grant Giving: Global funders to focus on interdisciplinarity. *Nature*, Vol. 525, pp. 313–315.

Sartori, A. (2016). The Resonance of *Culture*: Framing a problem in Global Concept-History. In M. Pernau & D. Sachsenmaier (Eds.), *Global Conceptual History: A Reader*, London: Bloomsbury.

Shifman, L. (2014). *Memes in Digital Culture*. Cambridge, Mass./London: The MIT Press.

Teichler, U. (2004). The changing debate on internationalism of higher education. *Higher Education*, Vol. 48, pp. 5–26.

Thornton, R. J. (1987). Culture: A contemporary definition. Online resource: https://www.academia.edu/686188/Culture_A_contemporary_definition [accessed on 19 March 2016].

Tierney, W.G. & M. Lanford (2016). Creativity and innovation in the twenty-first century university. In J. M. Case and J. Huisman (Eds.) *Researching Higher Education: International Perspectives on Theory, Policy and Practice*. Abingdon: Routledge.

Trompenaars, F. & C. Hampden-Turner (2012). *Riding the Waves of Culture: Understanding Diversity in Global Business*. London/Boston: Nicholas Brealey.

Varghese, N. V. (2008). *Globalization of Higher Education and Cross-Border Student Mobility*. IIEP/UNESCO.

West, E. (2015). *Asabiyyah: What Ibn Khaldun, the Islamic father of social science, can teach us about the world today* [Kindle Single e-book]. Retrieved from Amazon.co.uk.

World Population History (2016). Online resource: worldpopulationhistory. org [accessed on 5 April 2016].

Yáñez, C.; A. Okada & R. Palau (2015). New learning scenarios for the 21ˢᵗ century related to Education, Culture and Technology. *RUSC. Universities and Knowledge Society Journal*, Vol. 12, No. 2, pp. 87–102.

Chapter 12

Bridging the Transnational Education Challenge

Geoff Parkes & Sarah Hayes

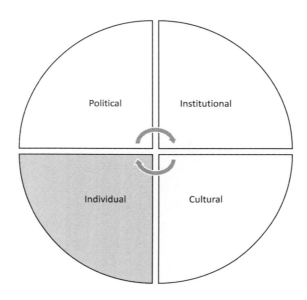

Introduction

This chapter is an important contribution to the book on globalisation of higher education, as it focuses on the challenges facing universities engaged in transnational education (TNE). TNE refers to the provision of educational qualifications from institutions in one country to students in another. This is distinct from both international student mobility and international research collaboration (Lawton & Jensen, 2015). In 2013 HM Government in the UK identified "supporting transnational education" as one of five key policy strands in the education component of a broader industrial strategy (BIS, 2013). This report estimated the size of TNE activities at £496m, of which just over half came from masters' programmes. Distance learning, including online provision, is the most common TNE activity and "delivers strong revenues". In the higher education sector, generally, Transnational Education (TNE) has grown since 2010 as a new phenomenon within the internationalisation of higher education (see Branch, this volume).

For UK institutions, China (42,475 students), Singapore (50,025) and Malaysia (68,020) are the largest TNE markets (Hesa, 2010) and the majority are delivered through partnership arrangements across different institutions. This activity is forecast to grow. The British Council (2013) suggests that demand for higher education globally will continue increasing over the next decade but at a slower rate (1.4% annually). There will be differences, however, at the country level—China, for example, will increase domestic capacity, and India is estimated to grow its student population from 28 million in 2014 to 70 million in twenty years. There was a 5% growth (24,500) in the number of students on TNE programmes in 2012–13. The highest concentration of TNE students is in South-East Asia, which alone accounts for 23% of the total TNE population. This growth contrasts with changes in the market for UK delivery models (HEFCE, 2014):

+ overseas entrants to higher education in England declined in 2012–13—the first fall in numbers in 29 years;

+ EU full time undergraduates fell by 25% (probably due to tuition fees);

+ UK full time masters' courses are increasingly reliant on international students—74% of students in 2012–13 were from outside of the UK, and 23% of these are from China;

+ more English higher education is now delivered through TNE.

In addition to the trend towards TNE, over the last two decades UK university strategies have increasingly emphasised the importance of building an international reputation and visibility, developing students and staff as "global citizens". This development has been facilitated via placements and exchanges, and building collaborative partnership programmes of study. Enabled by a liberalisation of international trade, via the General Agreement on Trade in Services (GATS) (WTO, 1995), the international elements of a university's offerings have moved from being simply interesting and appealing, as they were at the start of the 21st century, to becoming core components to the Higher Education (HE) enterprise. It is simply *"not possible for higher education to opt out of the global environment, since its effects are unavoidable"* (Altbach *et al.*, 2009:7). The internationalisation of HE not only remains a key agenda, it has significance too for the sustainability of each HE institution, for example, in terms of building relationships globally and developing its people in order to be able to do so. It raises questions of a university's *"social and curricular relevance, institutional quality and prestige, national competitiveness and innovation potential"*, not to mention the additional sources of potential revenue (Rumbley *et al.*, 2012:3).

Our Approach

Against this background, we focus, in particular, on the aspect of developing people and building relationships for the many challenges that global TNE partnerships present in a digital age. Within this anthology on the *globalisation of higher education*, this chapter focuses on the individual academic and their involvement in new programme introduction. We emphasise the importance of sensitive and critical cultural exchanges, at home and abroad, as central in our response to the TNE agenda in HE. More particularly, we discuss our approach to developing the MSc in Global Strategic Marketing Management (GSMM) programme in Aston University's Business School in central Birmingham. For the GSMM master's degree, we have been challenged to explore both an intercultural adaptation of existing modules, but also to plan for the reconstruction of these campus-focused materials, design and style of teaching, for active student participation in an online blended learning environment. In both of these considerations, we have sought to place our colleagues and those who will study the GSMM programme at the centre of our philosophy, which also promotes a global outlook, flexible forms of delivery and experiential learning as part of a professional community.

We provide, firstly, some context around TNE and globalisation theory, describing relevant models and then proceeding to explain the Aston response and approach. We discuss how as academics we have each drawn on our own diverse HE backgrounds, knowledge and experience from teaching in the UK and abroad. This has supported our shared emphasis on building relationships of trust with our colleagues, at the home university and at partner institutions, and on learning from each other in the development of programmes of mutual benefit. Rather than adopting a *"deficit view"* (Weller, 2016:171) of international students and partner staff where a one-way acculturation into the UK system is assumed, we have approached the GSMM programme and indeed each of our new TNE collaborations as vehicles for learning. We have noticed that these intercultural developments, though necessarily economically-driven, also provide new ways to critically reflect on our on-campus teaching. This "de-familiarisation" is potentially transformative (Smith, 2009) in a number of ways. For example, it can cause us to re-think how we interact with international students in our own campus. We can learn new ideas and perspectives from the colleagues we have taught, or have taught with abroad, that may cause us to re-think some sessions we teach. As we are increasingly globally mobile, as staff and students, we can pool our contacts and increasing knowledge to develop policies that also demonstrate how our University has "learned".

Secondly, by allowing sufficient time for structured development of the curriculum and adaptation to online teaching, we were able to demonstrate our respect for the diverse ways in which our colleagues currently teach, support them in re-imagining how their modules might work for the target participants in an online distance learning environment, develop a shared team philosophy and knowledge, and apply this in a structured way to follow new university curriculum design principles. In reading this chapter, you will gain the following insights.

1. you will hear our response to the need to build an accessible curriculum around the transnational agenda in HE and learn what we each bring to this development;

2. we will share our approach to engaging with the GSMM programme team at Aston across a significant period of time, building a shared philosophy and aim, addressing anxieties and applying strong curriculum design principles. We explain how we were able to construct an online programme from existing campus-based modules, adapt these for the online environment, and simultaneously further develop the skills of these module leaders. Most importantly, this helps to cultivate a shared knowledge and understanding of what it means to teach online;

3. we suggest that there is much to be learned in terms of research and teaching from a potentially transformative "de-familiarisation" (Smith, 2009) that occurs in TNE projects. Robertson and Dale discuss an *"education ensemble"* (2015:150) to explore in the globalising of HE, and the multiple relationships that occur both with and within the societies we encounter. By taking a structured approach, we can simultaneously develop new courses *and* reflectively analyse our own professional development to yield new learning (Bartholomew, 2015) as we participate in TNE opportunities. This has implications for faculty, academic staff development teams, and indeed the learning and policy making of the university as a whole.

TNE and Globalisation theory

All too often the term "globalisation" is adopted and discussed in policy, strategy, and the media as if it were a *"thing in itself"* (O'Byrne, 2016:41). This can give the impression that it is a "condition of the world", and as such, a *"fact"* (O'Byrne, 2016:41). This reification of what is actually *"a process"* into being discussed as a *"fact"* can give the impression that globalisation is incontestable, which then closes down a necessary debate (O'Byrne, 2016:41). As we share details of the TNE initiatives we are involved in, we acknowledge that our activities take place within the broader ever-changing *processes* of internationalisation and globalisation. These are processes that may be perceived in different ways (both good and bad) by those who are stakeholders in them. Giddens, in discussing the globalisation of the world as a whole, interprets this as a *"stretching process"* where local happenings are shaped by events many miles away (Giddens, 1990:64). For Robertson (1992:8), globalisation involves *"compression"* and *"intensification of consciousness of the world as a whole"*. Rather than produce *"grand theories"*, O'Byrne (2016:41) suggests we might instead identify and interrogate aspects of the *"globalising process"* as it becomes applicable to specific areas of the social world. Therefore, here we move to discuss the changing market for education globally in the context of established theories on international marketing, notably:

+ the Uppsala Model which describes a sequential approach to internationalisation. As the organisation gains more experience of global trade, then increased resources are committed. This theory also introduces the concept of psychic distance (so many firms are attracted more to the US and Australia, for example, where a more British heritage exists;

+ the Transactional Cost Model, which presents the strategy of internationalisation as one based on minimised costs; so as global activities expand, asset investment can be allocated more efficiently from a cost perspective by more direct investment;

+ the Network Model, which describes relationships as being key. The basic assumption of this model is that individual organisations are dependent on resources controlled by other firms and, therefore, the development of networks through more relationships are key to a successful globalisation strategy.

Each of these models has been considered by academics as having different degrees of relevance in the globalised world of the 21st Century. With a more homogeneous world, for example, how relevant is the psychic distance component of the Uppsala Model? The International environment is also complex in terms of legal and regulatory factors and, therefore, cost cannot be the only consideration presented by the Transaction Cost Model. The development of relationships often also depends on individuals and, therefore, the Network Model presents a lack of predictability (Hollensen, 2015) as often relationships are too complex to be observable.

Our response to the need to build an accessible curriculum around the transnational agenda in HE

Internationalisation is multifaceted, with globally competing trends (de Wit et al., 2015). TNE intersects with many other agendas, such as a more economic and marketised approach towards education, seeking to attract international student fees, and the continuing professional development of established roles but also new ones to support global interaction, individual and institutional profiles, and strategic directions for research and teaching. There is also the need to increase people's digital capabilities as a part of individual learning and teaching literacies (Beetham et al., 2009) and to do so within quality frameworks and strong curriculum design principles (See Lamb *et al.*, this volume). Additionally, a call for meaningful student partnerships, human rights and development, diversity and equality, and due attention to the "lived" educational experiences of students and teachers requires that those developing colleagues to undertake TNE opportunities need to apply their experience in flexible ways.

In this section, we share the philosophy of the GSMM programme team, the market research undertaken, and the approach we applied in taking the development of the programme forward, but for now we emphasise the importance of a strategic focus on the learning and learners at the centre of each TNE project. *"We need to ask not so much "how global do we want to be?", but "what is it, educationally, that we are trying to produce?"* (Gilles, 2009:4–5).

In terms of context, the MSc Strategic Marketing Management (SMM) is a very well established programme and is one of the top 3 post-graduate programmes in the Business School. Of the students on this programme, 90% are international (and largely non-EU). The degree programme follows a simple model of 4 modules in Term 1, 4 modules in Term 2 and a 15,000 Dissertation module in Term 3. Core Modules are Marketing Management, Dissertation Research, Marketing Strategy and Market Research. Optional Modules are varied and include choices from other Academic Groups in the Business School.

Following a peak in 2006/7, the overall decline in overseas student numbers from 2012/13 began to have an impact at the programme level and the MSc SMM was not immune to this trend. This was followed by a 20% reduction in demand from the peak with a resultant plateauing of demand in 2014/15. The demand for this degree had been primarily the Asian market, specifically China, and in addition to the TNE trend, new Visa restrictions by the UK Government also resulted in a reduction in demand. In the context of theory, the international market for education can be considered as moving from a transactionally based model, one based on student recruitment, to a more network-based model valuing collaborative global relationships between institutions. The market was changing and the team realised a new approach was required.

Adjustments and innovations have been made to the programme (new options and a new title of "Strategic" to the name, for example, in 2014/15), and further changes are planned (the inclusion of specialisations for 2017 and new Entrepreneurship Module in 2017), but from 2013 the programme team quickly realised a need to retain the key strengths of the programme and broaden its appeal to a TNE student cohort.

The Marketing & Strategy Group consists of a mixture of experienced and newly qualified academics that are able to combine experience in the classroom with the latest in teaching techniques and methodologies. In the 2015 NSS, the Group scored 95% for student satisfaction and were ranked sixth in the Complete University Guide.

At the outset of planning a global iteration of SMM, the programme team felt strongly about three key factors.

1. Agreement on a philosophy for the programme. This was not the only Distance Learning programme within the School—the MBA had been offered as an on-line format since 2007. However, the team felt that if the new programme was to be successful a consistent feel and philosophy was required to run through the programme—not just a collection of on-line modules.

2. The team needed to take advice from colleagues with experience of curriculum design and module development of this type and were fortunate to have the support of CLIPP (Centre for Learning, Innovation and Professional Practice) in the provision of this development support.

3. Collaborating with the best business schools in the world. As TNE development continues and the "marketisation" of education increases, the quality of partnerships will increase in importance.

Taking these three key factors above in turn, we now explain our approach in moving from developing the philosophy to constructing the online programme, adapting existing campus-based modules for the online environment and simultaneously developing the skills of the module leaders. We believe taking the time to cultivate a shared knowledge and an understanding of both the programme aims and what it means to teach online is important.

Agreeing on a shared philosophy and aims for the GSMM programme

Firstly, our shared philosophy encompasses the following intentions for the GSMM programme:

+ fostering intellectual curiosity, conceptually challenging;

+ focusing on the practice of Strategic Marketing Management (in a global context), a practical curriculum with work-based assessment;

+ developing a global outlook (two compulsory immersion weeks in overseas partners), consumer insights, and multicultural teamwork;

+ flexibility of delivery — "blended" and, therefore, designed to be delivered with other classroom/non-classroom-based activities such as company visits.

Translated into programme aims, the intention is to provide students with:

+ the ability to demonstrate both critical understanding and application of core theory and knowledge in global strategic marketing management;

+ the competence and creativity to address contemporary and complex strategic marketing issues in a global context through flexible, adaptable, and innovative approaches based on sound analysis and to apply an in-depth and balanced understanding of global consumer insights;

+ the necessary skills in critical analysis in global strategic marketing management and evaluation of their own work and those of others;

+ an opportunity to interact and study with a range of students and to practice multiple management skills, including communication, independent action and multicultural/virtual teamwork;

+ the ability to undertake and utilise marketing analyses using appropriate business research methods and statistical skills to make marketing decisions;

+ an opportunity to work effectively as independent self-managed/ self-regulated learners, as well as part of a marketing management team, which will encourage   a positive attitude to continuing personal development and lifelong learning.

With the above in mind, market research was carried out via the Aston website in the summer of 2015. This indicated the on-line market for PG Business programmes had been growing since 2012/13, including demand from the UK. There were very few programmes with similar titles or modes of delivery. The research also confirmed the proposed pricing structure was valid for a programme of this type, including tuition in the two international residential programmes. This research highlighted the importance of research as part of the curriculum design process. Key results from the research of over 100 respondents confirmed that almost 40% would be interested in a programme of this type, in particular:

+ *"The global aspect, learning about business in companies beyond Europe."*

+ *"The range of topics covered in the programme."*

+ *"I am keen to widen my knowledge in global marketing and get more experience for better career prospects."*

+ *"The ease to work and pursue my education is highly beneficial. It also enables you to be more agile and flexible whilst pursuing the programme."*

+ *"Consumer Behaviour and Country Specific Consumer Insights and skills such as global team working skills and cultural awareness, Entrepreneurial Marketing, Digital Marketing, Marketing Channels & Strategic Sales Force Management and Marketing Consultancy are all great subjects to study as they form the basis for a successful career in Global Strategic Marketing Management together with the fact that the employee can study remotely without having to leave his current job position."*

+ *"This is interesting … key is the partner universities…. Letting people have access to those names on their resume would be valuable."*

Discussions were held with NTU Singapore and the University of Stellenbosch, Cape Town, on residential programmes. In the context of the

Uppsala Model of internationalisation, these institutions adopt similar programme styles and pedagogy of learning as the UK. This was an effective method of integrating global experiences for students from world leading, high profile institutions. In order to develop the programme further and integrate market research data, and in order to cascade the programme aims across the modules in an aligned approach, there were a number of key considerations for the programme team. These included taking a structured approach to:

+ give ourselves some time to do it—planned launch 18 months out;

+ get top management commitment;

+ allocate teaching resource early;

+ involve CLIPP colleagues and learning technology support staff.

Taking a structured approach through curriculum design principles

Allowing sufficient time is absolutely key if clear curriculum design principles are to be followed, including consultation with stakeholders. Aston University has some specific criteria underpinning new programme approval. This is discussed in more detail later, but an important aspect is that engagement with all relevant stakeholders has been non-tokenistic. This includes ensuring that assessment is carefully planned at the programme, and not just modular, level; thus, consultation with CLIPP colleagues was arranged to help facilitate such sessions.

Further requirements are that a widening participation agenda has been considered, that plans are in place for inclusive teaching that accommodates any disability. Student engagement in the evaluation and iteration of the programme should be built in and the needs of international students should be appropriately considered. Employability should play a part within the design of the programme, and support for student information literacy should be appropriately embedded.

Additionally, effective practice from within and outside the University informed design, including choices about learning technologies. Thus, in the sections below we explain how we took a structured approach, drawing on literature and the work of external bodies such as Joint Information

Systems Committee (Jisc) to meet university guidelines and also respect the diverse ways in which colleagues teach as well as their varied levels of digital skills.

It is good to be aware from the start too of a "hidden curriculum" that exists already across any campus-based provision and relates to the implicit attitudes of staff and the institutional norms, values and rituals (Pokorny & Warren, 2016). Therefore, whilst curriculum models, such as "constructive alignment" (Biggs, 1996) certainly assist us in programme design, it is important not to treat such models as a simple "recipe", as they need to be informed by teachers' professional judgements too in relation to how their students learn (Ornstein & Hunkins, 2009). The programme team, therefore, used existing processes within the University as a framework around which the new programme could be structured.

Individual meetings with faculty colleagues to re-imagine modules

One of the first steps in developing the new programme was to arrange a series of individual consultations with faculty members likely to teach the modules. Fourteen one-to-one 45-minute meetings were scheduled over three dates in March 2015 for CLIPP to meet with teaching staff to discuss their current modules and how these might be adapted to be taught in a blended approach. These conversations with colleagues were rich discussions that revealed people's teaching identity, enthusiasm and diverse teaching techniques, as well as more practical requests related to managerial challenges. What does become clear is that, like many programme teams, there is also much diversity in the experience people have had in designing online instruction and the variable digital capabilities of colleagues. Other challenges raised by staff were the issue of accounting for the hidden labour of office hours when advising students across time zones, workload models, and module administration (see Bartholomew *et al.*, this volume). In terms of recording material for students to watch on video, it was suggested that allowing around 5 hours of recording of online material to 1 hour of actual delivery would be necessary. The question of how often re-recording would be needed was resolved by the plan to record chunks of content that would not be dated or named and that might be more flexibly applied and reused.

Marking and staff capacity, skills development, and particular technologies that might support aims were all part of these engaged conversations. Some staff were already teaching online courses, for example, assigning groups that students self-organise on Facebook and facilitating them to report and present. Other staff had no experience of engaging learners online. They emphasised that staff and students need to be contactable in a personable approach and not simply become faceless. Therefore, exploring a range of ways to talk to students via technology, including ways they might talk to each other, was considered very important. There were innovative suggestions that staff could make their own YouTube channel to better broadcast their personality and as an engaging way to offer essay writing and career tips or discuss consumer behaviour.

The CLIPP team also discussed with staff ways that Kaltura (video upload facility), which is available in Blackboard (VLE Platform) for screen casting, could be used by students, e.g. as a tool for introducing each other. One colleague liked the idea that students could create ideas on their shopping experience in their cultural context. They thought they might video and navigate to a store, then upload their narrated video to a blog in Blackboard for comments. It was also suggested that sheets that tell students explicitly – *"this is how we do this"* would be helpful in this context. Some staff discussed mental challenges in getting their teaching philosophy across. They felt a staged approach would be necessary. It was thought by several members of staff that a greater consistency of tutor practice would need to be developed across the team in the online space. A generic structure with a shareable template and weekly reminders, e.g. on Mondays, an automatic reminder— *"do this…"*.

The programme team agreed the goal was a module set that would set the standard for online and blended teaching, including expectations, the need for consistency and for resources to be used in consistent ways (see Bartholomew *et al.*, this volume). Most staff looked forward to sharing their experience, ideas, pedagogy and practice (as a group) in the planning of the programme. For students, a generic document that details basic specifications of technology, browsers, and plug-ins they need in order to access materials was suggested. This would need to allow for the issue that in some countries students are not allowed a microphone or to access some websites or social media. An institutional policy for the application of social media in a teaching context is probably needed. In addition, student behaviour, as confirmed later by the market research comments, will vary considerably, and so flexible ways to access materials are needed. Some students listen whilst driving and, therefore, cannot type in to respond to tasks. Participation rates vary, e.g. some have not listened to the introduction by week 3 and some have not emailed or attended anything. Agreements on levels of resources and choices of books, as well as access levels from different countries to software and search engines, was discussed. Reminder posts on-line were also required by students.

In terms of the range of assessment, content front-loaded with a mid-term exam was considered, including broad questions that are not easy to Google. Open book exams in students' own location raised a possible cheating issue. Formative Blackboard quizzes were also thought to be helpful. In terms of the range of technology that staff expressed a wish to learn, this included running webinars in Collaborate. Here they requested a sheet to help them structure these sessions. Training was requested in Presenter software too. There is no scope here to discuss many other themes that arose, but it is clear that, as a first stage, these individual discussions of how people teach and what might need to be developed for a blended approach were really valuable in surfacing many questions to bring to the programme group meetings.

Programme group meetings to align the curriculum

A shared understanding of the institutional prerequisites and conditions needed to support the design of active and engaging digital learning environments for students has challenged UK universities over two decades (see Lamb et al., this volume). Integrating the many considerations above into a clear approach through curriculum design principles and quality frameworks offers a structured way forward. Choices of which learning technologies to adopt can be taken, based on how they support intended learning outcomes and programme aims. A curriculum planning workshop for the whole programme team was, therefore, arranged and included the newly appointed Programme Director. As well as enabling staff to come together as a group to develop their ideas, this meeting was intended to ensure that new curriculum guidelines adopted at Aston were observed by the team. These expectations are that normally:

- modules will not have more than four learning outcomes;

- modules will not have more than two items* of summative assessment (independent of the size of the module). * An "item" of assessment may have more than one "element" (such as might be the case with a portfolio) but the overall item will always return a single mark;

- assessment load per module will not exceed 2000 words per 10 credits;

- each module specification presented for review or approval should be accompanied by a summary assessment—briefing document, complete with associated outline assessment criteria;

- the inclusion of small (10 credit) modules within a programme will need to be specifically justified as a programme-level design decision at the point of approval/review.

The approach for the workshop included:

- discussion of shared programme philosophy/aims - to consider how these filter down to each person's module level aims;

- programme structure – the design of each module to help retain student engagement at a distance;

- shared ideas/techniques – for achieving the learning outcomes;

- a curriculum map – to identify gaps/duplications of learning outcomes, assessment types, and load;

- consistency of templates and reusable resources;

- ideas that may also inform campus techniques.

Later meetings covered the checking of the module specifications colleagues had produced and the paperwork that would be required for the university programme approval sub-committee.

Reflecting on learning through participation in TNE projects

With so many implications for universities, and indeed the whole sector, it is important for new global partnerships to also include capacity for reflexive research into what might be learned, shared and reapplied, both individually and collaboratively. At each stage of development of the new programme, the programme team members were encouraged to draw upon the value reflectively, analysing their own professional development, as a legitimate research activity that yields new learning (Bartholomew, 2015), as they participate in transnational education opportunities. We emphasise the importance of actively recognising the learning that takes place through participation in new international professional communities. Robertson & Dale (2015:150) refer to an *"education ensemble"* that might be explored in the globalising of HE. The concept of "ensemble" reflects crucial, multiple relationships, both with and within societies, that cannot be reduced to terms like "providers" alone, but need to acknowledge constituent parts, mechanisms, and processes as foreign universities operate within host countries, across borders, and via online course provision. The implications are not all observable but they have real effects (Robertson & Dale, 2015). Indeed, whilst establishing our own professional learning opportunities, it is valuable, at the same time, to recognise how universities as institutions might "learn" and write new thoughtful and critically reflexive policies accordingly (Hayes, 2016). Thus, transactional education teaching provision offers as much a development opportunity for the development staff themselves as it does for the intended student participants (see Lamb *et al.*, this volume).

Learning through de-familiarisation

Any university internationalisation strategy might be perceived as a detached document, with broad aims that mostly seem to sit outside of daily working practice on campus. However, a stronger institutional acknowledgement of the range of learning opportunities for staff from teaching international students at home and abroad could add a "living" cultural dimension to strategic objectives. So, we draw attention to the personal "de-familiarisation" processes we mentioned earlier and to related potentially transformative opportunities (Smith, 2009) that may cause us to re-think how we teach. In sharing a pedagogical practice that is familiar to us in diverse cultural locations or with international groups, we become aware of how learning and teaching are conceptualised in other cultures. Taking time to recognise *"the cultural situatedness of those principles"* (Trahar, 2007:12) that have become second nature to us enables us to encounter them afresh through the perspectives of another cultural context. This may cause us to stop and take the time to explore new literature recommended by participants or to re-visit a theory that has become overly familiar. It may lead us to question whether some ideas, such as "reflective practice", which are understood as unquestionably good in the UK, might need to be approached in another way in different parts of the world when teachers there are responding to different priorities, including poverty, corruption, and disease. Viewing models like the "Kolb cycle" and frameworks like the UKPSF through the lens of other cultures has the effect of "de-Westernising" these familiar teaching tools so that we look at them with fresh eyes.

Conclusion

At the outset through the launch of the MSc Global Strategic Marketing Management, the aim of the programme team was to make a positive contribution to the objectives of the Business School, building on the TNE agenda and the growth trend for on-line and distance learning programmes. From a theoretical perspective the trend towards TNE can be considered as a new phase in the global market for education as seen through the lens of the Uppsala Model. This growth is facilitated through networks and not simply through consideration of costs. As a stand-alone programme, the new degree would appeal to a growing breed of global student, one who is attracted to Aston and a Tripe Accredited School. The target student would be attracted to the flexible, online yet global approach but not requiring UK residency (with consequential visa requirements) and the opportunity cost of full-time study. However, the development of the new degree has also opened up an unintended consequence for capacity building in specific world markets where the development of TNE resources is limited. It is clear that China, Southern Africa, and parts of South America now have sophisticated teaching and learning resources. In the 2016 QS Global Rankings, for example, NTU Singapore is ranked 13th, Tsinghua University in China is ranked 25th (and 8th in Civil Engineering) and Hong Kong University of Science and Technology is ranked 28th. These institutions are leading organisations in global education and present very real competition to Western centres of learning, which have consolidated a position of dominance over the last 100 years. However, later developing countries still require the assistance of First World nations in capacity building in order to satisfy rapidly growing domestic demand for higher education. These countries include parts of ASEAN, Africa, and the Middle East. For educators in these countries, the provision of the GSMM package of on-line available resources can provide direct support to on-campus teaching and at the same time provide collaborative programmes that in some cases lead to the award of a UK degree. Some examples are as follows:

- collaboration with Muscat University Oman, utilising on-line material to teach BSc Accounting for Management;

- the National University of Laos and Chiang Mai University Thailand—supporting local faculty to deliver the MSc Global Strategic Marketing Management;

- collaboration with Danang University, Vietnam;

- online support for an MBA programme to a strategic partner in Lagos, Nigeria.

For these markets and institutions, the methodology of GSMM provides a teaching resource, not only to students, but also importantly to the faculty in facilitating on-campus tuition in a developing country. This longer-term capacity building also involves teaching and developing local faculty, with the longer-term capability this will build in these regions. In addition, through more localised delivery, these blended programmes provide the opportunity through articulation agreements for institutions to offer post-graduate study from a triple-accredited institution at an affordable cost.

About the Authors

Geoff Parkes is Senior Teaching Fellow, Head of the Marketing & Strategy Group and Associate Dean International at Aston Business School. He can be contacted at this e-mail: parkesgs@aston.ac.uk

Sarah Hayes is Senior Lecturer in the Centre for Learning Innovation and Professional Practice (CLIPP), Programme Director for the PGDip and Masters in Education, and Chair of the University's Learning Technology Management Committee. She can be contacted at this e-mail: s.hayes@aston.ac.uk

Bibliography

Altbach, P. G.; L. Reisberg & L. E. Rumbley (2009). *Trends in global higher education: Tracking an academic revolution.* Paris: UNESCO.

Bartholomew, P. (2015). Learning through auto-ethnographic case study research. In C. Guerin; P. Bartholomew & C. Nygaard (Eds.), *Learning to Research—Researching to Learn.* Oxfordshire: Libri Publishing Ltd., pp. 241–267.

Beetham, H.; L. McGill & A. Littlejohn (2009). *Thriving in the 21st Century: Learning Literacies in the Digital Age (LLIDA).* JISC project.

Biggs, J. (1996). Enhancing teaching through constructive alignment. *Higher Education,* Vol. 31, No. 3, pp. 347–364.

British Council (2013). The Future of the World's Mobile Students to 2024. British Council Education Intelligence, UK.

De Wit, H.; L. Deca & F. Hunter (2015). Internationalization of Higher Education—What Can Research Add to the Policy Debate? *The European Higher Education Area,* Vol. 3, No. 12. Springer International Publishing.

Giddens, A. (1990). *The Consequences of Modernity.* Cambridge. Polity.

Gilles, M. (2009). *Universities in a Global Context: How is Globalisation Affecting Higher Education?* House of Commons Seminar, Oxford: HEPI.

HEFCE (2014). *Global Demand for English Higher Education.* HEFCE, UK.

Lawton, W. & S. Jensen (2015). *An Early Warning System for TNE.* The Observatory on Borderless Higher Education, January 2015.

O'Byrne, D. J. (2016). *Human Rights in a Globalising World.* London: Palgrave.

Ornstein, A. C. & F. P. Hunkins (2009). *Curriculum—foundations, principles, and issues.* Boston: Allyn and Bacon.

Pokorny, H. & D. Warren (Eds.) (2016). *Enhancing Teaching Practice in Higher Education*. London: Sage.

Robertson, R. (1992). *Globalization: Social Theory and Global Culture (Vol. 16)*. London: Sage.

Robertson, S. L. (2010). *Globalising UK Higher Education*. Centre for Learning and Life Chances in Knowledge Economies and Societies.

Robertson, S. L. & R. Dale (2015). Towards a "critical cultural political economy" account of the globalising of education. *Globalisation, Societies and Education*, Vol. 13, No. 1, pp. 149–170.

Rumbley, L.; P. Altbach & L. Reisberg (2012). Internationalization within the Higher Education Context. *The SAGE Handbook of International Higher Education*. London: Sage, pp. 3–27.

Smith, K. (2009). Transnational Teaching Experiences: An under-explored territory for transformative professional development. *International Journal for Academic Development*, Vol. 14, No. 2, pp. 111–122.

World Economic Forum (1996). *Global Competitiveness Report*. World Economic Forum, Geneva.

WTO (1995). *General Agreement on Trade in Services*. World Trade Organization, Geneva.